Voices from the City

To Mette and Ane

HQ
1750.55
.Z9
B358
1987

Voices from the City
Women of Bangkok

Susanne Thorbek

Zed Books Ltd
London and New Jersey

Voices from the City: Women of Bangkok was first published by Zed Books Ltd., 57 Caledonian Road, London N1 9BU and 171 First Avenue, Atlantic Highlands, New Jersey 07716, USA in 1987.

Copyright © Zed Books Ltd, 1987

Cover design Andrew Corbett

Printed and bound in the United Kingdom at The Bath Press, Avon

All rights reserved

British Library Cataloguing in Publication Data

Thorbek, Susanne
  Voices from the city: women of Bangkok.
  1. Women—Thailand—Bangkok—
  Social conditions
  2. Bangkok (Thailand)—Social conditions
  I. Title
  305.4'2'09593   HQ1750.55.Z8B3

  ISBN 0-86232-463-7
  ISBN 0-86232-464-5 Pbk

Library of Congress Cataloging-in-Publication Data

Thorbek, Susanne.
  Voices from the city.

  Bibliography: p.
    1. Women—Thailand—Bangkok—Social conditions.
  2. Bangkok (Thailand)—Social conditions.   I. Title.
  HQ1750.55.Z9B358 1987   305.4'2'09593   87-13323
  ISBN 0-86232-463-7
  ISBN 0-86232-464-5 (pbk.)

Contents

PART 1: WOMEN AND URBANIZATION ... 1

1. **Migration** ... 3
   Introduction ... 3
   Migration ... 6
   To Bangkok from the north-east ... 11
   To Bangkok or to Chonburi? ... 16
   Where did the women come from? ... 20
   Women migrate ... 22

2. **The City** ... 24
   Slums ... 26
   Public investments ... 27
   The Work of the NHA ... 29
   Pressure on slums — land values and planning ... 31
   Private property ... 32
   Reactions against eviction ... 33
   Khlong Toey ... 34

3. **Slum Society** ... 38

PART 2: WOMEN'S WORK FOR INCOMES ... 47

4. **Women's Work for Wages** ... 49
   Wage work ... 52
   Unemployment ... 57
   Double work ... 58

5. **The Secondary Labour Market** ... 61
   Organization ... 65
   Resistance among the women ... 67

6. **Women Without Work** ... 72

7. **Prostitution** ... 79

8. **Urbanization and Women's Work** ... 87

PART 3: WOMEN AND THE FAMILY 95

9. **Caring for Husband and Children** 97
10. **Patterns of Settlement** 105
11. **Social Relations within Families** 110
    Men's control of incomes 110
    Men's control of labour and sexuality 112
    The household's importance for men 113
    The household's importance for women 114
    Conflicts about settlement 118
    Changes in family life 119
12. **Gender and Sex Conflicts** 122
13. **Slum Culture and Gender** 138
    Theravada Buddhism and folk beliefs in the slum 138
    Slum culture or working-class culture 143
    Slum culture — counter-culture 146
    The gender struggle in the slum 148
    Slum culture and changes in the family 150
    Women create slum culture 152
    Women as leaders 154
    The women's struggle and slum culture 155

Appendix 159
Bibliography 164

Tables
1.1 Population growth 6
1.2 Population development of greater Bangkok 8
1.3 Foreign direct investment 9
1.4 The mother's total income 13
1.5 Employed in-migrants and average amount of money sent home per sending 14
1.6 Women's occupations 20
3.1 Incomes of slum dwellers 42
3.2 Household incomes 43
5.1 Factory workers' incomes 63
6.1 Women's incomes 75
10.1 Family settlements 105
11.1 Use of incomes 111

Figures
1.1 Map 7
3.1 Diagram of research area 39
4.1 A sketch plan of Sii's house 140

Acknowledgements

I want to express my gratitude to the women in the slum area. Their help and generosity, their curiosity and open minds and their struggle for bits of happiness not only made this research possible, it made my residence in the slum one of the best experiences of my life.

The Duang Prateep Foundation, Miss Prateep and the staff at the school, and Somsuk Boonyabanghaa from the National Housing Authority willingly shared their knowledge and experiences of the slum.

Jeaw Sawamiwasd worked as interpreter, and I am grateful not only for her patient and clever work but also for her tenderness and consideration for me as well as the women we came to know in the area.

The grant for my fieldwork was donated by Forskningsrådet for udviklingsforskning and my fieldwork was supported by A. Rabibhadana then Director of the Thai Khadi Research Center, Thammasat University, Kiat Chirkul from the Department of Urban and Regional Planning, Chulalongkorn University, and V. Khongkhakul from the Department of Sociology and Anthropology, Chulalongkorn University. I want to thank these as well as many other persons and groups who showed much hospitality and willingly shared their knowledge with me.

In Denmark too, many friends and colleagues have discussed and criticized the work. I want especially to thank Ida Nicolaisen who supported me whenever I was in need.

Hans Ovesen has made the plans and drawings.

Marianne Lützen, Anette Hermund, Inga Sørensen and Vinni Steffensen from the Institute of Cultural Sociology have patiently rewritten the manuscript.

Part 1:
Women and Urbanization

1. Migration

Introduction

This is a case study of women's daily lives in a slum settlement in Bangkok. The case study is intended to elucidate an important aspect of the changes in conditions and reactions produced by urbanization.

My first reason for undertaking the study was curiosity. I had been studying Thailand and industry in South-East Asia for some time and I wanted very much to look at the question of how the women, main agents in the processes of urbanization, reacted. I thought too that the experiences and understanding of women's lives in very different conditions from that of Western women sets our own conditions into relief.

Most important, however, it seems to me that women in urban centres of South-East Asia are the potential agents for further social change. They make up a great part — in some zones the main part — of the working class created by foreign and local investment. They are driven from the countryside into slums in cities and these slums are their workplace where they serve their families. Both the physical conditions and the social relations in slums are of utmost importance to the women.

The changes in women's conditions as a result of the new industrialization drive have been studied, as have women's reactions to them. But to my knowledge such studies have not usually been concerned, both with the changes going on at the workplace and the changes in social relations within families. They have taken their point of departure from the workplace or the narratives and documentation local organizations (church groups, trade unionists, slum-upgrading staff) have provided. Inspiring and important as such sources and studies are, I have found it important to study the conditions and reactions of ordinary women, that is, not the most knowledgable or active, but the often passive, sometimes illiterate, women.

This study is thus of the actual material conditions and the social relations of women working for incomes and for their families, and also it is a study in working-class culture among women. I have thus accepted the proposition that sub-cultures exist which, to some extent differ from the mainstream understanding and I have studied the women's culture as evidenced in their interpretations of daily life. The dominant culture and the institutions transmitting this are not, however, systematically demonstrated here.

This small-scale, intensive study of some women in a slum settlement in Bangkok concentrates on analysing and describing women's daily lives and experiences and contributes to relevant theoretical discussions where my material provides a basis for this.

I chose 24 houses nearest to the one I rented in Khlong Toey slum in Bangkok; in these 24 houses lived 41 men, 45 women and 46 children under 17 years old, that is 132 persons. I used anthropological and soft sociological methods. I lived in the slum for six months and spent most of my time talking about everyday problems with the women living there: chatting, working or relaxing with them.

Through daily small talk I tried to understand which problems the women thought most important, which problems occupied them the most. I asked them to tell me more about these problems in talks when my interpreter was present, talks which often went on for several hours. On this basis I chose some of the women for taped interviews, where they told the same stories, although usually at greater length with more detail. Sometimes they added new experiences.

In addition to this I made a small survey, and this too was done in an unstructured way. Mostly through daily talk, I covered a list of questions with all the adult women in the area. (See Appendix).

I concentrated my efforts on the women in the area, and the role and behaviour of men are covered as the women described them. This focus on the women was for two main reasons. The first was practical: as a middle-aged woman myself it was easy for me to be accepted by the women. The first day they came to see me to wash my clothes and the house and commented and helped, we immediately found that we had common problems, from the water to the lives of our children. To talk with the women and develop close relationships with them following them to work, to temples or to a village up-country left hardly any time to talk to the men. Besides, this would have needed quite a bit of drinking and gambling and I am not very good at either of these!

Secondly, however, it seems to me that most studies on Thailand as well as many on slums and urbanization draw only or mainly on men, both as subjects and informants. Although it is, of course, preferable to study both sexes I thought it was time to set down the views and experiences of women.

To achieve close contact with the women, indeed to live in the slum without fear of robbery, I had to give an impression of poverty. I told the women that I was a schoolteacher, sent by my government to write a book for schoolchildren on women in Thailand, and that the government paid my ticket and 3,000 baht a month; my interpreter was presented as my Thai teacher. I had very few belongings, few and cheap clothes, no furniture. All that really impressed the women was a cover for the water-jars and an electric pan I had bought. Neither, after the first mistake, did I give any loans, but occasionally I did give small gifts of a few dried fishes, fruit and the like.

I think the women came to accept me in this role. Some expressed it directly: "You are poor like us. I can tell you." They confided in me about their husbands' misbehaviour, about gambling, the criminality their sons were involved in, torture in prisons and bribes. When the women thought somebody had told the police about gambling in a house nearby in the first month of my stay I was in no way suspected. I never told anybody else about the things the women told me.

In the process of getting acquainted with the women my interpreter was a great help. She was not only a good interpreter, she was also good at talking with the women and children in the area: kind, interested and concerned. Thus I think I succeeded in crossing the class lines. The problems which were most difficult were my own and my interpreter's reactions when we were told things considered immoral among the Thai and, to a degree, the Danish middle-class. This problem concerned issues such as abortion, fights and lack of solidarity between husband and wife and robbery and the heroin trade.

As can be seen in this study I have tried to avoid value judgments. Since I lived in a slum in Copenhagen while studying at the university I had a clear conception of many of the conflicts both with outside society and between the slum-dwellers themselves in such situations.

In the Buddhist culture of Thailand it seems that morality, lack of anger and conflict and "decent" norms for women's sexual behaviour are quite strong. In specific situations we sometimes reacted with fear or with a sense of moral distance towards some stories; but less so as we came to know the women and their problems.

My interpreter was of great value in interpreting Thai culture for me — explaining the content and forms of details in festivals, various routine matters, and the importance attached to certain details.

The authenticity of the material can of course be questioned, but there was no apparent difference between my part of the slum and the rest; and people who had been working in the slum either with the National Housing Authority (NHA) or the schools there were not aware of any differences. I chose the households I studied in such a way that they included people whom two different private schools had helped during the period of evictions nine years previously; but differences between the two parts were slight indeed.

The presentation in this book is rather unconventional. The methods I employed, and my intention of documenting daily problems and women's perceptions of and reactions to these, is reflected in the way the book is built up. Excerpts from the taped interviews, my own descriptions of the conditions in the slum and more general reflections and theoretical chapters or sections are interspersed throughout the book.

The book covers three main themes: urbanization (migration, the city and the slum); women's work for incomes (work for wages, self-employment and prostitution); and women's work for the family. In the last two sections I focus on the social relations in production and in the families, and analyse possible changes in these as well as women's reactions.

The taped interviews with the women were recorded and transcribed in Thai, and later translated into English by women graduates in English. I asked them to make the translation as close to the Thai language as possible, even if this meant very broken English. I later edited and rewrote the interviews in more comprehensible English; but still kept as close to the Thai language as possible.

I have found it impossible to translate the taped interviews into pidgin English or Harlem American, which would probably give the most truthful translation, and have instead tried to preserve as much as possible of the women's way of talking and Thai expressions. This style of translation may create an impression of non-fluency which is, of course, totally misleading. But I loved the way the women put things in their own language and have tried to keep as much of this impression as I could.

It is my hope that this work will be of interest to both the broader public — as I have

Urbanization

tried to give vivid descriptions and the women's own narratives — and to more specialist readers from the social sciences, especially people working with women and on urbanization and slums.

Weights and measures are as used in Thailand. The transcription of Thai words follows the Haas standard (Haas, 1980).

Names of Bangkok localities are as in the map of Bangkok.

Today cities all over the Third World are growing rapidly. If the existing trend continues at least half the population in Third World countries will live in multi-million populated cities by the year 2000. Most of these people will live in slums, many without income-earning jobs.

However, even living in the slums may seem attractive to peasants. As capitalist relations of production penetrate the agricultural areas peasants are forced from their land, either to more barren areas as subsistence croppers or to the city. The latest form of capitalist penetration, contract growing of cash-crops for the big agricultural firms, and the much higher rate of productivity in agricultural production ensuing in this type of organization, also contribute to the urban drift.

The growth of the urban population and the growth of slums makes it probable that social movements in the Third World will be urban-based rather than movements of peasants. This is already the case in some countries, especially in Latin America, but urban upheavals will probably be much more widespread in the future.

This prospect means that great importance must be attached to the migration process, its causes, and people's experience of migration, the growth of slums, governments' policies of eviction and upgrading of slums, and slum dwellers' own reactions to their problems.

Migration

Migration in Thailand has risen rapidly during the last 20–30 years. Before 1950 "regional shifts in population don't appear to have been important." (Ingram 1971, p. 55). But after the Second World War, and especially since the beginning of the 1960s, there has been a tremendous influx of people to Bangkok.

Bangkok is the most important city of Thailand. In 1972 Greater Bangkok was established as an administrative unit, with four *changwats* and four municipalities: Bangkok proper, Thonburi, Samut Prakan and Nonta Buri. In 1970 it enclosed 3,100 km^2 and had 3.7 million inhabitants. Today it probably has 5 million inhabitants.

The exact extent of migration is difficult to ascertain. Figures are often contradictory, and some people migrate without registering and live in slums in Bangkok without access to schools and so on.[1] In the revised Greater Bangkok Plan (1971) the following figures for population growth are given:

Table 1.1

Population growth (% annual)	1947–57	1957–67
Bangkok	7.1	5.2
Thonburi	6.6	6.6
Samut Prakan	6.7	7.0

(Quoted from Donner 1978, p. 793)

Migration

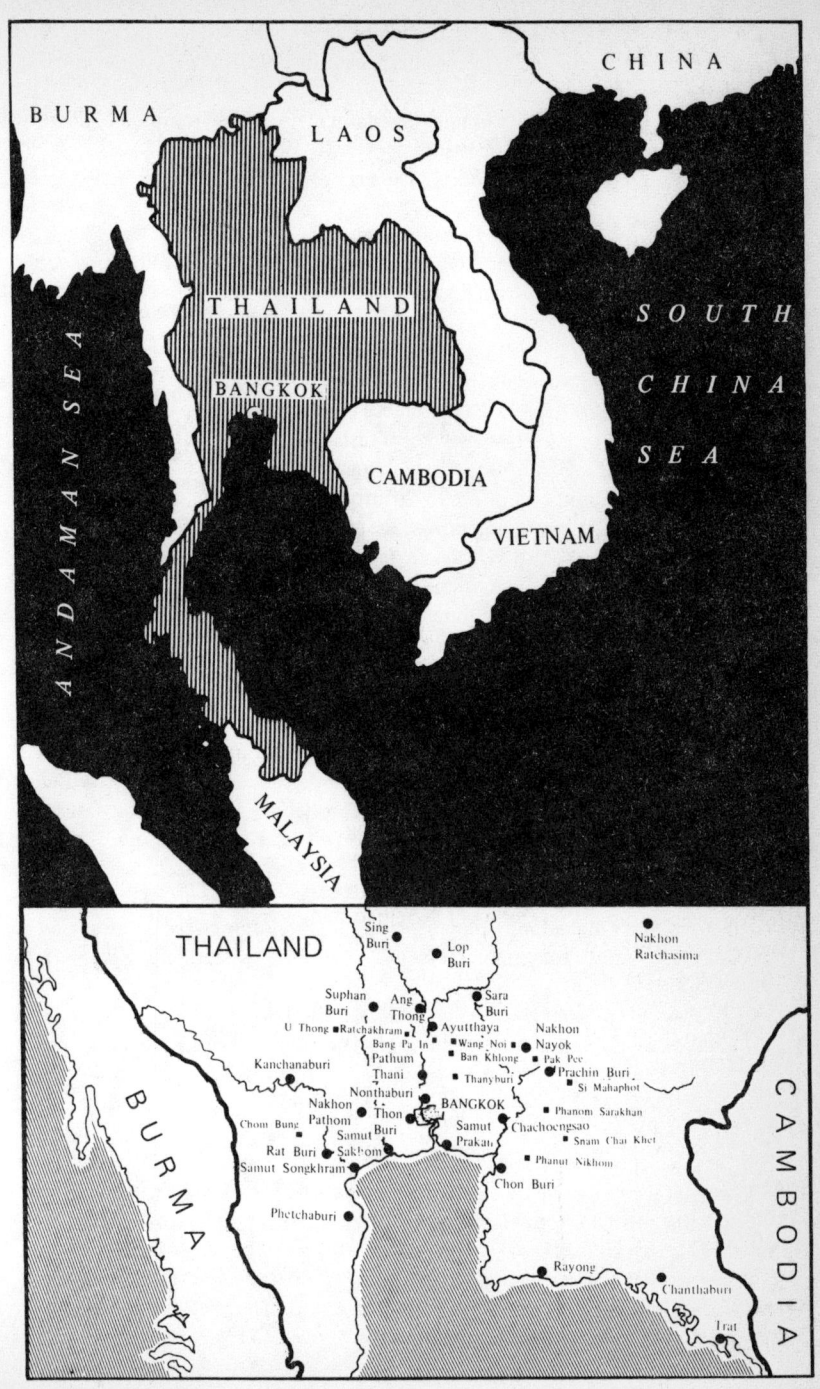

7

Urbanization

On the basis of the 1960 census it was estimated that a quarter of the population in Bangkok and Thonburi municipalities was born elsewhere (ILO 1965, quoted by Donner 1978, p. 793). Donner estimated on the basis of the 1970 census that 36% of the population in Greater Bangkok was born elsewhere. Former migrants made up 25% in Samut Prakan, 27% in Nonta Buri, 35% in Thonburi and 46% in Bangkok. Population growth in Greater Bangkok is shown in the following table:

Table 1.2
Population development of Greater Bangkok (1947–70)

Changwat	1947	1960	1970	Increase[a]
Bangkok	889,538	1,577,003	2,157,303	36.8
Thonburi	281,343	559,432	920,058	64.5
Nonta Buri	133,623	196,196	269,067	37.1
Samut Prakan	163,137	234,701	329,404	40.3
Greater Bangkok	*1,467,641*	*2,567,332*	*3,675,832*	*43.2*

[a] Increase % between the 1960 and the 1970 census.

Source: Donner, 1978.

Population growth has been high in Thailand. In the last 20 years the population has grown 2.7% annually. Thailand covers 513,520 km². In 1850 it had a population of approximately 5 million people. There was plenty of land while people were a scarce resource. Today approximately 45 million people live there.

Up until 1950 new land was cultivated mostly with rice, utilizing the old methods with next to no investment in irrigation or other aspects of agriculture. A Dutch adviser proposed an irrigation scheme for the central plain, the most fertile area, but the English financial adviser did not think it necessary to invest in agriculture (van der Heide, 1906). In the last twenty years the situation in the countryside has deteriorated quickly. New land is still developed but yields are lower. Public expenditure has gone primarily to military and administrative institutions, secondly to the development of an infrastructure and education. Only 6% of public expenditure has gone to agriculture (Turton 1978).

In these years the peasants have been indirectly taxed. Rice is a major export and a system of taxes, quotas and other regulations has been created which forces rice prices down on the home market. The rice premium has been much discussed and it has been estimated that peasants pay approximately 20% of their income in taxes (the urban population pay about 10%).

In the last 10 years, however, much less rice has been exported. This rice is grown on the central plain, mainly in areas where the government has invested in irrigation and it is possible to grow two crops a year. In most areas however, yields are low. The price of rice in Thailand is rather low too. This is due to several factors: government policy, oligopoly in trade, and competition from a few comparatively productive farmers whose land is situated near public irrigation. The government policy of forcing down rice prices on the internal market is motivated by the wish to keep wages low, both for employees of the state and workers. Low wages are of course attractive for foreign investment.

Poverty in the countryside is great and has grown worse over the years. The average (gross) yearly income ranges from 0–1,000 to 8–9,000 baht. The income left when investments in production have been deducted is hardly known. A study was made, however, by the Ministry of Agriculture (1975/6) and quoted by the Bangkok Bank. It states that, after deducting costs of production and rice consumed "our (average rice) farm household is left with a startling — and indeed pathetic net income for the year ... of baht 195.53" (quoted from Turton 1978, p. 109).

Migration follows a pattern. The provinces with high out-migration are either in the north-east, the poorest part of the country, with almost no investment in irrigation, or on the central plain, where agriculture is most influenced by capitalist forms of organization. The flow of migration is mainly to the premier city of Bangkok. But other provinces have high in-migration rates too: the most outlying provinces where there are still possibilities of finding new although usually infertile land, and some provinces with cash-crop possibilities such as tapioca, sugar-cane, or, in a few cases, corn.

Thai governments have pursued various policies, up until approximately 1960 import substitution was a major aim. In the same period firms were nationalized and public production initiated. Military leaders were pressed on to the boards of private firms in the name of "Thai-ification". Corruption was very widespread and many public firms were run without accounts and without surpluses (Riggs 1966, Skinner 1958).

From 1960 a policy of export-oriented industrialization was instituted. Laws were passed which gave foreign investment tax exemptions and the like; a Board of Investment was created to help foreign firms establish themselves, and former requirements to utilize Thai employees were lifted.

Foreign investment has grown quite rapidly although less so in recent years.

Table 1.3
Foreign direct investment (million baht)

Year	Value
1961–4	249.5
1965–9	926.5
1970	890.5
1971	808.4
1972	1,927.1
1973	1,604.9
1974	2,766.3
1975	1,744.8
1976	1,614.1
1977	2,163.8
1978	1,010.8
1979	1,047.7

Source: NESDB cited in Suthy Prasartset, *The Impact of Transnational Corporations on Economic Structure of Thailand*, Chulalongkorn University, 1980 (from Chiengkul 1982, p. 150).

The figures may be somewhat inflated, however, as some advantages for foreign investment would cease after five years, thus tempting investors to take profits out with the intention of later re-investment.

Both private and public investment are concentrated in Greater Bangkok. "A small and modern industrial base has been established in a highly concentrated pattern in and around Bangkok Metropolitan Area" (Pakkesem *et al.* 1978, p. 1). Between 1958 and 1978 the industrial areas in Bangkok have grown from 600 ha to 1,685 ha. In 1960 Lichtfield *et al.* (planning for the Bangkok municipality) projected 4,000 ha for industry in 1990; in the 1971 revision of the Greater Bangkok Plan the projection is 8,450 ha in 1990 (Donner 1978).

The main emphasis in the approaches of various Thai governments, following American and Asian Development Bank advice, has been a laissez-faire policy, promoting private enterprise, lifting restrictions on internal and foreign trade and investment, and in general letting agriculturalists fend for themselves. Foreign investment has been subsidized, as has the urban population generally through the rice policy. The peasants have grown still poorer because of this policy; one of the results of this is the high rate of migration to the city. The deteriorating situation in the countryside has produced a Communist-led guerrilla group under some Chinese influence. In urban areas, too, discontent has been rife and led to a student rebellion in 1973 and to much organizing and protest among peasants, workers and slum-dwellers in the three years with parliamentary government following the student upheaval. When the military took power again in 1976 the students fled to join the guerrillas. Now they have returned and the communist guerrillas seem to have been crushed, partly because of the loss of bases in Laos and Kampuchea following the Vietnamese conquest. Neither the Communist organizations nor the students, after they were outlawed, have worked in slum areas in Bangkok.

The extent of migration today is hard to estimate. If the trend from the 1960s is continuing migration will take three main directions: to outlying provinces where new but poorer land can be cultivated, to cash-crop producing areas, and to Bangkok. A continuation of the trend from the 1960s would mean that population growth in Bangkok is still roughly double the population growth in the country as a whole. In absolute figures this means 100,000–200,000 migrants to Greater Bangkok and natural population growth of another 100,000 persons.

One factor mitigating this trend is the relatively successful family planning drive in Thailand; it has been more successful in cities than in the countryside. This has brought the general rate of population growth down from 2.7% in 1970 to 2% in 1980. Whether the trend continues depends on the causes of and incentives to migration, i.e. on a combination of economic changes pushing peasants or other agriculturalists from the countryside and the pull to the city. For the would-be migrants these factors are probably interdependent since whether conditions push people away depends on the opportunities in the place they plan to go to. My own estimate, as well as the most frequently held view in Bangkok (expressed at a seminar "Cities" at AUA in Bangkok 1981 with American and Thai researchers), is that migration to Bangkok continues at at least the same rate as in the 1960s. One important reason is that new land is no longer available; the land frontier is closing (Feer, 1978).

In the following pages I will follow two women from Khlong Toey slum in Bangkok

Migration

back to their families in the countryside and discuss their reasons for migration. This will be followed by a more general picture of the migration of my sample of 24 women in the slum. On this basis I will discuss the economic reasons for migration. Lastly I will discuss how and why women migrate, giving an example of the process of going to the city.

My material is limited and where ever possible I compare it with other sources of information on migration to Bangkok. But the main point is not to get an average or generalized picture of women's migration but to see the women's experiences in the context of overall socio-economic changes.

To Bangkok from the north-east

Nŭu, a young woman, married with a daughter two-years-old, told the following story:

> At first father married mother, got children, got everything. Then my father drank alcohol and he did not stay with my mother. Father quarrelled with mother, they had five children. Grandmother [mother's mother] drove him out. [To his parents living just opposite]. She did not like when my father got drunk, he complained and cursed the children, hit the children. My older sister went to Bangkok, father was still alive, she had no *feen* [boy-friend or husband] yet.
>
> She got 150 baht a month, and she sent money to us, to feed her younger sisters. She did housework. She ate and stayed with the house-owner and send 100 baht a month. Now when I was 13, and my younger sisters and brothers were still small, my father died. We did not have money to study, so I left school. The teacher did not want me to leave, I got no paper with my picture from the school, no certificate. She did not want me to leave. We had no money. I pitied mother, pitied my sisters and brothers, pitied grandmother and grandfather. I went down to Bangkok for the first time in my life: with mind and heart I loved my mother, I had never left mother to go anywhere at all.
>
> When I came down to Bangkok they gave me 50 baht a month, I did all the housework, washed clothes, cooked rice, cooked food. They let me sleep downstairs. I was very afraid, I slept all alone, one person only. I was afraid, I did not dare to go to sleep. I cried and cried, every day, every day since I came to Bangkok.

Nŭu stayed two months in Bangkok working as a servant, then she returned to her village together with the father of a friend of hers (the friend was studying in Ramkamhaeng University of Bangkok). She stayed with her mother a year, where she worked in the ricefields. Then she went to Bangkok with her two elder sisters, and she worked in a weaving and hat-making factory.

> I made hats, I knitted wool. My older sisters, they were persons who could weave, they had a weaving machine, I was still small so they let me fold hats. I did not talk much, I was shy. Cée, the Chinese woman who was the owner of the factory, she pitied me. I had no money to eat rice, so I could eat and stay with her ... I was a

child. I worked long, long hours. I worked overtime. I got 300 baht a month. They let me do the work since . . . I woke up at seven o'clock then I rested and had morning rice, and then I did it again and again. I came to eat rice at five o'clock in the afternoon. When eating rice was finished I did it again until I was finished, until 1 or 2 in the morning, sometimes the whole night. But they did not give overtime [pay for overtime]. I lacked sleep, lacked to lie down. I liked to work there. My older sisters stayed together, so we had warm heart. I did the work on and on, but the work was not hard, I was comfortable, no one to fuss. Cée, she knew my heart. I was not a person to fuss to. I never did anything to spoil her. I folded hats, folded everything, I helped her.

Nŭu returned to her mother's village again after an unhappy love affair with the owner's son. Her mother also needed help in the paddy-fields. She stayed in the village for two years and here she met her husband-to-be, who came with a friend on a visit to the temple, and who made two more visits. They wrote letters to each other. He asked for Nŭu's hand in marriage from her mother and a conflict with the young men in the village was imminent but did not develop. Then,

At home it was dry and we did not have water to do the ricefield. I wanted to come to Bangkok to find money, to find something to eat. If I could work, then I could go and buy rice, buy something to eat that way.

I asked him [her *feen*] to find work for me, and he found work in a food shop. I sold food at Khlong Toey market. At that time I did not know it was the house of his older sister. But I was not allowed to go alone, only one person. My older sister she then came down to work in the same place. She did not have a *feen* yet. Mother knew that he had found the work, and I was not allowed to go alone. I went with my older sister.

Nŭu got married to her boy-friend later and his mother paid 200 baht so she could start working in a factory.

I visited her village with her elder sister Dam who sometimes stayed in Nŭu's house. We were going to fetch Nŭu's daughter, who had stayed with Nŭu's mother because Nŭu could not look after the child while working in the factory. But Nŭu missed her daughter a lot. Nŭu's mother was very sorry because she had to send the child to Bangkok with us.

Conditions in the village were shown to us by the mother, by Dam and by neighbours. Nŭu's mother owned 12 *rai* of paddy land where the water would stay after rain, and 6 *rai* of which only 3 were cultivated, higher up where the rain drained away sooner. They gave the harvest as about 30 *gasob* on the 12-*rai* lot and said they did not count the rest. (1 *gasob* they gave as approximately 75 kg. This amounts to 190 kg rice per *rai* on the best land.)

One of the mother's problems was lack of labour power to do the ploughing and harvesting. Dam would usually go back and help but they needed a stronger person. The mother had a son (dead), four daughters (all living in Bangkok) and two step-children (her brother's). They were 14–16-years-old and not very strong yet. She grew rice and had two buffaloes grazing with the rest of the village's buffaloes. She had had a pig and she had started to grow and weave silk that year.

Migration

The rice she grew was mainly for the family's own consumption; but this year she had sold 6 *gasob* for 1,500 baht. Her expenses for rice growing this year had been 120 baht for transportation of rice from field to miller and 480 baht for fertilizer and insecticide since she could not afford more. Help with ploughing had cost 800 baht including a mechanical plough and exchange labour. She said that she thought seeking guests were more expensive than agricultural labourers. Exchange labourers had to have food and drink and they were less careful with the work. Agricultural labourers got 30 baht a day and worked harder and better. Help with the harvesting cost 500 baht — three people for five days. They harvested five *rai*s and she, her step-daughter and Dam harvested the remaining seven.

This year she had sold the pig and seven piglets for 2,000 baht, but she had bought food for them too. She said that it had cost five baht a day. Food for pigs is the by-product the miller takes when milling rice. It consists of the brown *chan* around the rice and is the most nutritious part. But then the milling is free. She had sold one of her two buffaloes this year for 3,300 baht and had woven two pieces of silk which Dam had sold in Bangkok for 500 baht each. This year the mother had paid a debt to the local Co-operative — 4,000 baht — and her debt to her neighbours was rising. I did not ask about interest rates. According to the Ministry of Agriculture the average interest rate in the north-east on debt to neighbours was 80% per annum (1978/9). She estimated her income at approximately 3,000 baht and she had only one buffalo left now. "The only money I see is what my daughters send home," she said. There was a well for drinking water near the village but for rice growing she relied on rainwater only. She said that she had not had enough money to buy fertilizer and insecticide and there were worms in the upland field the previous year so the harvest was spoiled.

A budget for Nŭu and Dam's mother might look as follows. (But it should be remembered that all information was estimated and some was guessed at by Dam or the mother.)

Table 1.4
The mother's total income

Income		Expenses	
Rice sold	1,500 baht	Transport	120 baht
Pigs sold	2,000 baht	Fertilizer	480 baht
Buffalo	3,300 baht	Ploughing	800 baht
Silk sold	1,000 baht	Harvesting	500 baht
		Food for pigs	500 baht (at least)
		Debt to Co-op	4,000 baht
Total	7,800 baht		6,800 baht

Nŭu and Dam's mother seems to be a quite average peasant from this area. She owns 18 *rai* of paddy-land, 15 of which is under cultivation. In Si Sa Ked province 33.8% of the peasants own between 15 and 29.9 *rai* of land, 28.4% own less and 37.7% own more (Phipatseritham 1979, p. 20). The yield on the land seems quite low compared to the Thai average of 309 kg per *rai* (1978); but so are yields in the north-east generally (169 kg per *rai*).

Urbanization

The mother thought the situation had grown worse during her lifetime. The land planted with paddy was situated farther away so she needed cash for transport. The land was poor and so she needed fertilizer and insecticide which she could hardly afford. But she saw the worst problem as lack of labour. The exchange labour system was not working well. While we visited the village sowing was in progress.

She worked herself in the ricefield in the morning and went home at midday and did household chores while the two step-children and three other young people stayed; after 4 p.m. she worked at sowing again. They had lots of fun. She claimed the problem was because of the young, but it might be the break-up of social relations (and social control) in the village combined with the growing amount of wage-labour and general commercialization.

The mother did not like her daughters living in Bangkok. She needed their labour and she especially missed her grandchildren a lot and thought it was bad for them to stay in Bangkok with a rougher climate and cars. She appreciated Dam very much. Dam stayed in Bangkok where she made her own living, but she usually returned to the village to help with ploughing and harvesting. She also sent money home to her mother. So on the one hand the mother felt the lack of her daughters' help and missed them and their children. But on the other hand she was also dependent on their incomes and the money they sent home. The lack of food and money was the reason they had gone to Bangkok in the first place, as Nŭu explained.

The importance of remittances from children, especially daughters, in cities is also mentioned in a study of women working in massage parlours. Here up to one-third of current consumption was paid for by daughters' remittances (Pongpaichit 1982). In a survey from the central plain, where remittances are probably less important than in the poorest regions, remittances accounted for 28–30% of non-farm income (not counting income from non-farm employment). And a survey from rural areas in Thailand showed the following amounts sent home per month from employed migrants to Bangkok (unfortunately neither the gender of migrant nor the region to which the money was sent is stated).

Table 1.5
Employed in-migrants and average amount of money sent home per sending

Amount of money sent (baht)	Number of senders
less than 101	1,188
101 – 300	10,112
301 – 500	7,691
501 – 700	1,806
more than 700	3,640
unknown	184
Total	24,621
Total employed in-migrants 63,675	

Source: NSO. Survey of Population Migration 1979 (in Thai). (Chiengkul 1982, p. 147).

Phipatseritham points out that in agricultural provinces and regions quite a high proportion of income comes from non-farm sources. In the central region 40% of agriculturalists' incomes comes from non-agriculture. In the north-east this figure is even higher — 52% in 1976 (Phipatseritham 1979).

In the case of Nŭu and Dam's mother this income derives from her silk-weaving and the daughters' remittances. The rest of her income came from selling a buffalo and piglets; but this meant she would not have these sources of income the next year.

When such a high percentage of income stems from non-agricultural sources this is largely because rice prices are very low. The taxation on rice for export (rice premium, export quotas and the selling of cheap rice to the government) has been much discussed in Thailand. Chiengkul points out that the ten biggest exporters of rice (50.8% of export volume) are all on the committee which fixes rice premiums and are perfectly able to fix rice prices at the mill for most of Thailand (Chiengkul 1982). Usher (1965) pointed out that Thai peasants, through the rice premium and related regulations, were taxed by as much as 22% of their income (compared to about 10% for the non-farm sectors) and thus subsidized the urban population (from Ingram 1971, p. 259). But only peasants/farmers who produce for export are taxed and only 8% of rice grown in Thailand was exported in 1970 (20.9% in 1950), (Donner 1978, p. 88).

However, the premium (and related regulations) depress rice prices on the Thai market. This seems at least to be the conclusion of most authors.[2] And for most of the peasants who produce rice this means that their rice production gives them next to no money income. But the production of rice requires money inputs for various purposes and so farmers try to find income elsewhere. This is very difficult in many provinces and the peasants are thus very poor, dependent on children's (daughter's) remittances, looking for work and often going to Bangkok for this purpose.

Subsistence rice peasants like Nŭu's mother are embedded in a market economy. She exchanges milling for the nutritious brown *chan* of the rice which she later buys back as fodder for pigs. She sells a bit of the rice, piglets, cattle and silk. She buys inputs for rice farming and she has debts. But, most important, she provides labour power for Bangkok industry. Links between subsistence peasants and the market are indirect. The provision of labour power, trade and often debts are the links of most importance.

The poverty of the region is usually explained by the high pressure of population, the increasingly poorer land taken into cultivation and the lack of modernization. The region is, however, quite firmly linked to the modern sector; it provided most of Thailand's cattle in the 1950s and later many cash-crops such as *kenafe*, now tapioca and labour power. Yet the amount of surplus ploughed back into the peasant's work is small. Recently some dams have been built. One provides electricity not utilized for irrigation. Others supply plantations growing fruit for Bangkok. But to my knowledge none cater for the peasants' production.

In her village Nŭu's mother was in the middle range of land-owners. Her yields were probably in the middle range. She produced 190 kg per *rai*, the average for the region being 169. Yields have fallen during some periods, but have risen slightly in recent years.

The village specializes in silk-weaving. It is renowned in Thailand, some of the materials being extremely beautiful, and one piece was given to the Queen by the weaver. Polarization was visible in the village. Some families grew rice with wage-labour only, weaving silk full-time, with the men working in transport (car owners) or in government service or trade.

Migration from the village was common. Every family we talked to had to least one member living in Bangkok,, and some had one in Udorn too. Several women told us that their husbands went down to Bangkok to look for work several times a year, returning if they did not find anything. Some of the women were former migrants themselves. In Nŭu's family all the daughters had migrated to Bangkok. The son was dead, and the step-children were still young.

The economic situation of Nŭu's mother seemed very precarious. Nŭu migrated to Bangkok three times, each time to find food, earn money or help feed her brothers and sisters. It seemed as though an event like the father's death (although from her narrative he did not seem to be of much help) or lack of rain would tip the balance.

Other reasons for migration were important too, and in Nŭu's mind probably decisive. Nŭu's relations with her sisters was one of these. When she had to stay alone, sleeping downstairs and feeling lonely, she quickly returned, missing her mother and sisters too much.

She worked very hard at the hat-making factory too, according to her narrative. But the non-fussing of the Chinese owner and her sisters' company made her like the job a lot, even if she got tired and did not earn much. Her relationship with a young man was, however, the most important factor. The last time she migrated to Bangkok she had both her sister, her husband-to-be and work there.

In a sense, then, Nŭu was forced away from her village by the hardship of her family as subsistence peasants embedded in a money economy. She was drawn by the opportunities in the city too. After the first try she had the possibility of support from her sisters and her husband and his family; she had secured work and she was able to compare conditions and opportunities up-country and in Bangkok. Her main reasons for going and returning back were her relations to boy-friends, sisters and mother. The precarious economic balance of her mother's household was the ever-present background for her choices.

Back in the village her mother wanted her to return home. Nŭu's choice to do or not to do this was still dependent on her social relations. When her husband seemed to find a new girl-friend she left, but was stopped by him at the railway station. He promised better behaviour in the future and she returned to her home.

Her mother wanted Nŭu and her family back for several reasons. She missed her and her grandchild a lot. She also thought it would be a great help to have a man to do ploughing and work in the fields. But Nŭu's husband did not want to go and live in the village.

To Bangkok or to Chonburi?

Another case illustrates changes in the Thai countryside which involve not only the deterioration of the small peasants' situation but also the new kind of agriculture created by the policy of diversification and foreign investment in agribusiness. The case is an example of migration between the provinces.

Săm phaw is 44 years-old, mother of six children, grandmother of two. She has lived in Khlong Toey slum areas for more than 25 years.

She said about her move to Bangkok,

> My father died when I was small, small. I stayed with my mother at Khlong Darn, just here. [The southern periphery of Bangkok.] She sold the ricefield and went to buy a farm at Mount Boeng-saked, on the way to Rayong. She grows mango, uhm, and tapioca, coconut, sweetsop, *Hua-chai-tao*, many things and many fruits. She has a big place. Before, when we stayed at Khlong Darn, I helped my mother to till the ricefield. But at the time when I had children, had a husband, I had come to Bangkok already, mother she is so angry at me, she sells the ricefield and go and buy land elsewhere.
>
> Mother did not want me to marry. She had me as the only female, my younger sisters and brothers were still small. If I marry I cannot help my mother grow the rice, I cannot help with my sisters and brothers.
>
> Mother did not like my *feen*. She cursed, she said he was lazy, she said he was black and had pimples. He went to ask for my hand, but mother did not like him. So it happened that we ran away together, and I did not come home for three years.
>
> He said the ricefield was barren. He said I had never seen a long tail-boat, only a rowboat, paddle-boat, I had never seen a car.
>
> He told me, I should go and dress beautifully, and sit in his elder sister's house and sell things. There are cars, some coming, some going: in the morning when the sun rises, we can sleep until late.
>
> I thought it was difficult to stay in the ricefields, every morning you have to rise early. So he persuaded me to follow him to Bangkok.

Săm phaw's mother, whom I visited with Săm phaw's daughter (24-years-old) was 69-years-old. She told me that her husband had died when Săm phaw was 9-years-old and she was left with six children. She had some land at Khlong Darn, but had extreme difficulties in managing to work both for the children at home and in order to earn an income. They grew rice. To get money she traded from a boat, and then she had the housework. She had contemplated killing herself and the children several times, she said.

Săm phaw had to look after her brothers and sisters and since she was too young to do the work the mother had to clean and wash the house and the children at night. The mother owned two buffaloes and lent them to her neighbours. They would feed them and utilize them.

Eventually she remarried and moved with her new husband to a small town in Chonburi province. They had three children. When he died she was able to buy the land she now lived on, nine *rai* in a highland area, three hours by minibus from the nearest town, in Chon Buri province. But at that time she stayed in the town, rented some land, built her house, and worked the land as a tenant. Three years ago she had moved up to her new land. She had to go to court to be allowed to pull down the house and re-use materials for the new house up there, but she won the case. She had built the house herself and now lived with her youngest son of the second marriage, his wife and two-year-old son and grew tapioca. Săm phaw's younger sister stayed with her three children on another tapioca farm which she owned, an hour's walk from the mother.

She explained about the tapioca farming. One *rai* would give about 40 *hàab* tapioca (1 *hàab* = 70 kg). She had expenses for renting a tractor, labour for preparing the land, planting and hoeing — and in all 320 baht per *rai*. For harvesting (pulling) and transport she paid 12 baht per *hàab*. This amounted in expenses for growing and harvesting the tapioca to 20 baht per *hàab*. Her income would be between 22 and 55 baht per *hàab* of tapioca depending on when she was able to sell it to the local factory. To start growing tapioca she had got a loan from the driver who bought for the factory — 20,000 baht. She paid 300 baht a month on the loan although this was only interest (3% per month, 36% per year). She estimated her income to be 6,000 baht a year but out of this she had to buy her food (rice).

An approximate budget for Sămphaw's mother is given here. I think the information given to me was relatively precise. Other expenses and incomes are missing however; the budget is only for the tapioca growing. The tapioca used for export as animal fodder has a maturation period of 10–11 months, and only one harvest per year is thus possible.

1 *rai* produces 40 *hàab* = 7,800 kg.
Expenses per *rai*:
preparing the land . . . 320 baht
harvesting . . . 480 baht i.e. total expenses 800 baht per *rai* or 20 baht per *hàab*.

When she sold the tapioca she would get between 22 and 55 baht per *hàab* and thus earn an income of between 2 and 35 baht per *hàab*. On 9 *rai* of land, each giving 40 *hàab*, this would make a total of between 720 and 12,600 baht per year. Interest on her loan would amount to 3,600 baht per year. Thus her income would be between minus 2,880 baht and 9,000 baht per year.

Besides the tapioca she had two buffaloes and many kinds of fruit; but the prices on fruit were very low compared to Bangkok prices. Usually she did not sell the fruit although she rasped, pressed and dried mangoes before selling them in the market in the town nearby, three hours away by minibus. Sămphaw's younger sister grew tapioca here, but also owned land in Rayong province, where she grew sugar-cane.

They were both very dependent on the local factories as buyers of their products. Diversification was only possible the way Sămphaw's sister did it, by going to different provinces and by growing the crop a local factory would buy. If they grew anything else it would not be possible to sell it, they claimed.

Sămphaw's mother was heavily dependent on the factory both for this reason and because she was in debt. The debt could not be paid back on the low prices paid by the factory; she paid only interest and her chances of changing to other crops if prices fell were bad indeed. Both the women had had instruction from the factory on how to grow the crop.

Tapioca of this kind is grown only for export. Most of it is exported to the European Community, but this year import quotas have been cutting down on Thai tapioca exports. In the EEC it is used for animal fodder. Tapioca has taken on increased importance for Thailand in the last two decades. In 1960 tapioca earned 288 million baht in foreign currency, as against rice which brought home 2,570 baht. In 1980 tapioca was the second largest export crop, earning 14,887 million baht in foreign currency, whereas rice earned 19,508 million (Bank of Thailand, *Monthly Bulletin* January 1975 and October 1981, cited from Chiengkul 1982, p. 60).

Tapioca is the crop in Thailand where the difference between prices at the farm and export prices is greatest; the farm price in 1980 was 770 baht per ton, the export price 2,853 baht per ton (Chiengkul 1982, p. 61).[3] The farm price is close to the highest price Sămphaw's mother told us about, equivalent to 54 baht per *hàab*.

Sămphaw's mother is a modern farmer. She is directly connected to the factory, having received a loan and instruction from it. She has invested quite a bit in the business and up to now the market for tapioca has been very good. But this modern farmer, growing a new successful crop and following advice from the factory is as badly off as the traditional rice peasant from the North-east. She has a higher cash income after deducting expenses, but she has to buy her food. She worked all day from 4 a.m. to 7 p.m. and she had no chance of paying back her debt and could only just manage to keep feeding herself and producing tapioca. She was heavily dependent on the local factory with no chance of switching to any other kind of production.

In a way she was worse off than the north-eastern peasant since she did not live in a village. There was a long way to walk to neighbours and transport to town was expensive and time consuming. In Nŭu's mother's village there were many neighbours and plenty of talk and help between them. Besides this Sămphaw's mother's work involved great risks.

Sămphaw's family is an example of migration to an area with cash-crop possibilities. Rice growing in their place of origin was economically unviable and the situation was made even worse by the death of the husband. After seven years of struggling with the rice farming without a husband, the family broke up. Sămphaw went with her boy-friend to Bangkok and the rest of the family went to Chon Buri.

Agribusiness penetration of agricultural production has been much researched in Latin America but only very recently in South-East Asia. A report from the Asian Development Bank (ADB) concludes,

> There is a general consensus in the literature that the rural poverty problem has worsened considerably in the ADB region in the past decade ... It has thus become obvious that absolute economic growth can be accompanied by a relative impoverishment of certain strata ... (Asian Development Bank: Rural Asia: Challenge and opportunity 1978, quoted from Hawes 1983).

An International Labour Office (ILO) study comes to a similar conclusion on the basis of case studies in East and South-East Asia.

> The most outstanding fact to be noted is the worsening distribution of income and the declining real income of the rural poor at least in a number of cases ... Indeed the evidence from the case-studies points to an even stronger conclusion. In each case a significant portion of low income households experienced an absolute decline in real income. (ILO: Poverty and landlessness in rural Asia. Geneva, quoted from Hawes 1983 p. 21, 22).

In the last 20 years modernization of Thai agriculture, and the growing agribusiness

Urbanization

activity combined with population growth, has resulted in 30% of the agricultural population being rural workers without land of their own (*Far Eastern Economic Review*, 1978). Thailand has had a good overall economic growth rate — 7% in 1981 — but at the same time the distribution of income has worsened. Even farmers directly connected to agribusiness have high debts and take high risks.

In Sămphaw's family, too, migration was heavily dependent on personal relations; Sămphaw wanted to escape from the hard work in agriculture with her boy-friend while the rest of the family moved to Chon Buri with the mother's new husband. The social network means that decisions about where to go can be made with knowledge of alternatives. Sămphaw's younger sister who ended up growing tapioca in Chon Buri and sugar-cane in Rayong province, went to stay with Sămphaw for a month before she made the decision to stay in Chon Buri; visits to the mother were made once a year.

Where did the women come from?

In my 24 houses 33 families lived (a family being defined as at least one parent and one child). Of the women, 24 were migrants and only 3 of these had lived for less than ten years in Bangkok; most of them had lived in the slum areas for most of the time. They did not think their families were exceptionally poor. Like Nŭu and Sămphaw they would talk about the fruit, the plentiful space, the water nearby. And they probably did not come from especially poor families.

I asked for the occupation of each woman herself and her parents and got the answers shown in the table.

Table 1.6
Women's occupations

	Parents	*Woman*
Rice, subsistence	6	6
Agricultural labour (rice)	3	3
Wage-labour, other	2	5
Still a child	—	3
Trade	1	2
Tapioca	1	—
Fruit (orchard)	2	—
Other	—	2
No information	5	3

These answers are surprising as none of the women or their families grew rice for sale. Some might sell a bit of rice now and then but their main purpose in growing rice was for the family's own consumption.

The high degree of wage-labour is surprising too. Eight of the women worked for wages and the figure is understated since some of the husbands were wage-labourers:

the husbands of the two traders were a janitor and a policeman respectively, and one of the "others" was married to a man working in construction for the Americans at Sattaheep. While 11 of the 24 migrating families thus lived on wages mainly, only five of the parents to the migrating women did this.

The information about the occupations of the women and their parents is from the time of their migration, mostly twenty years ago. It seems that money economy and wage-labour were widespread even at that time, and that the modernization of the agricultural areas contributed to the drift to the city. This finding is supported by the information about which provinces the women came from.

Thirteen of the women came from the central region, and of these, nine came from provinces along with the highest out-migration from Thailand. Some of these were located close to Bangkok and with high rates of tenant farming: in Ayutthaya, Samut Prakan, Pathum Thani and Nakhon Nayok more than 60% of agriculturalists are tenant farmers. (Nakhon Nayok and Ayutthaya provinces offer farmers extremely small incomes and Ratchaburi and Nakhon Nayok provinces have very small holdings.)

Of the 13 women from the central region 11 came from provinces with serious problems for agriculturalists and from provinces where the influence from Bangkok and modernization of agriculture is most widespread.

Eight of the women came from the North-east. They came from Si Sa Ked, Buri Ram and Surin, provinces with extremely small lots compared to the north-eastern standard. Three women came from Buri Ram, Surin and Korat which have high and increasing rates of tenancy. The north-eastern region is the poorest in Thailand. Population growth has nevertheless been high for many years, peasants without access to land moving to provinces, where the soil is poorer but available. The north-eastern region has, however, supplied Thailand with most of its cattle, several cash-crops and labour for Bangkokian industry. In the 1950s a very rich trading company concentrated on the north-eastern region (Skinner 1958). Interest rates on debts are high compared to other provinces (Rozenthal 1970) and the links to the modern sector generally quite strong. The provinces my eight women came from are those with rising rates of tenancy and one of them —Korat — has both high out-migration rates and modern agriculture (fruit, tapioca). Two of the women came from the northern region, one of them from Phitsanulok province, which also has especially high rates of tenant farming.

Nineteen of the 24 women came from provinces with serious problems for agriculturalists and of the remaining five, three had parents who moved around from province to province. (The information on migration is from Vichit Vadekan *et al.* 1976 and the information on conditions in agriculture is taken from Phipatseritham 1979.)

My women came from provinces with great problems arising from the modernization of agriculture. Some of these provinces have irrigation schemes (Korat, Pathum Thani, Samut Prakan) and high or rising tenancy in agriculture; others have extremely small plot sizes and low incomes compared to regional standards.

It seems that modernization has a different impact in different provinces. In some provinces where irrigation schemes or easy access to the market in Bangkok makes profits higher, former peasants lose their land and wage-labour and tenancy increase. In some provinces the increase in productivity is lower, but in these the population pressure on land is high and plot sizes are decreasing. So far, it seems that the introduction of cash-crops has not pushed peasants to the city but attracted new in-migrants, as in Chonburi.

Women migrate

Women and men migrate to Greater Bangkok in roughly equal numbers (Vichit Vadekan et al. 1976). But the explanations given are not the same. Women stress family matters while men mostly give economic reasons (Chamratrithirong et al. 1979, p. 22).

This was the case with the 24 women too. They would start out with the family and only after much more talking would they mention the economic conditions. This can be seen in Nǔu's and Sǎmphaw's stories. Both talk about a boy-friend as well as their family of origin. For Nǔu her main motive is to help her family; but her relationship to boy-friends plays a role too in deciding where to go and where to stay. In Sǎmphaw's story her relationship with her mother and boy-friend are important; but so are the work in the ricefield and the possibilities of exciting experiences in Bangkok. This can be seen as an expression of the way in which economic and family matters are interrelated for women. They work in the public sphere trying to earn money and they work in the family and they do not usually distinguish between them in the same way as men seem to.

All the women except three asserted that they were helping their family when they went to Bangkok. Some helped like Nǔu by earning their own living, some sent home money too. Others went to help with work in shops or houses belonging to their families. A few were married already and went with husband and children to find work. Even three women who came to Bangkok at the ages of 10, 13 and 13 helped, one by working in her elder brother's household, one by working in her mother's sister's household and later by earning a wage in a factory, and one by working on construction sites.

The three exceptions were Sǎmphaw, who actually wanted to get away from the responsibility for brothers and sisters and the hard work, Kàj who did not have a family and had earned her own living from an early age, and a woman who came to escape from an arranged marriage.

The women did not express dependence on their families (either of origin or the new), but talked about their contributions and responsibilities. In a way this was also the case with Sǎmphaw, who did not want to continue her contribution but did not deny its reasonableness.

The women were especially concerned about their mothers but also about younger sisters and brothers. In the process of migration kin were very important to the women. Most had come to Bangkok when they were young (18 of the 24 were less than 20-years-old) and only one of these could read.

One of the women came alone (she was 14); the rest came with maternal aunt or sister (8), with a boy-friend/husband (2), with parents (3), with friends and usually a broker (3), and with a brother (1). When the women came to Bangkok nearly all had relatives, mostly a maternal aunt or sisters or friends, in the city. I will give one example.

Kàj was born in a knife-making village in Ayutthaya province. Her mother died when she was three-years-old, her father when she was nine. As far back as she can remember she has worked in knife-making, working 12 hours a day polishing knife-handles for very low pay; but then she lived in the house of the owner of the shop. She made her own rice in the morning and often got a bit of fish or shrimps from neighbours and friends. At times she worked as a temple "boy", collecting food for the monks, and she had a very good relationship with the oldest monk in the temple. She was strong, she was not afraid of anybody and would defend herself if necessary, she said.

She talked about going to Bangkok.

> I had two sisters, with different fathers [her stepmother's daughters from a first marriage]. They came to stay in Bangkok. Then they came up here to fetch me. When they first came I did not go with them, I did not want to go. They stayed for a long time here, too long a time, they suffered a lot. It was hard work, they had to work at night too [producing knives].
>
> I was 16-years-old. Later I went to Bangkok to stay with them in their house, where they made dresses. I stayed with them for one year and four months.
>
> Early in the morning I would make rice, clean the house serve the food. Then I would go and take a look at this and that. How did they make the dress? How did they cut? They explained it to me, and I learned a lot. Later I made brassieres. I got five baht for each. I stayed there for one year and four months.
>
> Then I stayed with my sister. She was pregnant. She could not do the work, she could not fetch water. I stayed here in Khlong Toey in Block 1. But at that time the port had not built much. There was no customs house.

She met her husband-to-be in the sister's house and got married at the age of 19; later she got a divorce and married again.

I have chosen her because she considered herself an orphan and had worked very hard for little pay since she was a small child. But she had sisters in Bangkok and her links to them were of primary importance for her migration; she lived with them until her marriage. This was very typical for the women. Most of them lived with sisters or mother's sisters in Bangkok in the beginning and nearly all of them had friends or relatives. The networks were of the utmost importance in finding a place to stay and to work.

Links up-country were usually maintained. Many of the women would go backwards and forwards in the first few years after migration and most of the women still visited parents or relatives up-country at least once a year, or received visits from them. These networks also meant that women might come and visit Bangkok and explore possibilities there before eventually making a move.

2. The City

Bangkok is *the* city of Thailand, 32 times bigger than the next biggest town Chieng Mai and housing 56% of the nation's urban population (Romm 1970, p. 7). The physical features and structure of a city reflect the material production and the social structure of society. Bangkok is a typical modern industrial city. The structure is diffuse. In the centre old buildings dominate the scene reflecting the national history as much as the dominance of the state in Thailand today. The centre mostly consists of old temples and palaces and modern administrative or military buildings and two universities.

Industry is spread throughout most of Bangkok mixed with residential areas. In recent years industry has mainly been situated along the communication routes primarily to the south and east of Bangkok. The working class live around factories and wherever there is free space. The most spectacular modern buildings are the high-rise buildings such as banks, hotels, foreign embassies, missions and the offices of international agencies. Several sub-centres exist with shopping, banks, entertainment. Characteristically, one of the more important is the area where the foreign communities originally developed (Silom Road, New Road). The physical structure thus reflects the overwhelming role of the state and of Western and international agencies, the dominance in the economic field of financial institutions, tourism and haphazard unplanned economic development.

Bangkok was created in 1782, when King Chakri decided to move the capital of Thailand (then Siam) from Thonburi, where it had been located since 1767, to the other side of the river. At this time the social structure in Thai society could best be characterized by the concept of the Asiatic mode of production. The peasants produced mainly for their own consumption; there was very little trade and the surplus which was produced went to the local nobles/princes or to the king and his dependants in Bangkok. It was delivered in the form of corvee labour, products of special kinds or, in a few cases, in money. It was a one-way flow from countryside to the city and the only returns were the kingdom and the temples themselves and their cultural value. People were classed as commoners or slaves and within a wide range of nobles and princes by so-called *sakdhina* points (this also involved disposition of graded amounts of land) (see Thorbek 1977 and Elliot 1978).

The king had in principle total power over his subjects. A few years before the French Revolution in Europe the king had physical structures reflecting this kind of society built in Bangkok.

Before the capital was built, a few fishing villages and a small Chinese trading post were located at the river bank. The king's temples and palaces, palaces for nobles and princes, and a harem, a small secluded city-within-the-city, were enclosed by a wall. Those within lived in great isolation. The king had total authority and everyone had to prostrate themselves before him; commoners were not allowed even to see him. But in reality he had great difficulties in maintaining his position and was suspicious of every contact between his subordinates (Bowring 1977, Pallegoix 1854). The harem served a political as well as sexual and prestige function. The women were hostages, picked from the women loved by nobles and princes in provinces up-country, as one way of ensuring the king's control. Outside the wall around the king's palaces was the ricefield and here lived the servants, slaves, artisans (slaves mostly) and traders. The city was surrounded by the river Chaophraya to the north, west and south. To the east a wall and a canal, Khlong Ong Ann, were built.

Pallagoix described this city in 1854.

> There is not a single carriage in the capital, everyone travels by boat. The river and canals are almost the only busy roads. Only rarely in the middle of the city and in bazaars or markets do you find streets paved with large bricks (Donner 1978, p. 786).

Houses were built on stilts and of wood and bamboo. In 1855, however, King Mongkut was forced to open the country to the west, first to the English. He had to abolish the king's monopoly on foreign trade and allow foreigners to trade directly with the inhabitants, to abolish taxes on trade in the country and on export and import, and to allow foreigners to live in the country — not under the Thai laws, but under their own laws administered by the Consul, who also had to be permitted in Bangkok.

King Mongkut expanded the area of the city. He built a new canal in a concentric circle around the old, Khlong Pradung Krung Kasem; he built a new road, the New Road leading from the centre, to the area where foreigners had settled and he built a new canal which is now one of the main streets in Bangkok, connecting the centre with the Port Khlong Toey.

Bangkok grew. Some migrants must have come to the city, whatever historical sources tell. Villages originally located near the city were incorporated; among these were villages whose inhabitants were Mons, Vietnamese and the like. These were people whose ancestors had been war booty and were kept as slaves, but who lived in their separate villages.

Many Chinese immigrated too, before 1900 probably 15,000 a year. In the 1920s 70–140,000 arrived at Khlong Toey Port a year (but this included returning visitors) (Ingram 1971 p. 2, note 15). Around 1950 roughly half the population in Bangkok were ethnic Chinese (Seidenfaden, Book I, 1967, p. 124).

The Chinese worked as wage-labourers or businessmen — they were not allowed to own land. The Thais were taxed when travelling, the Chinese were not. In the 1930s Thompson complained that the Thais were not willing to work as wage-labourers and thus prices on labour rose (Thompson 1967).

Thais migrating to Bangkok have probably done so in connection with the expansion of the military, the educational system and the administrative system.

Urbanization

After the Second World War Thais have had to learn to work for wages and migration has risen — the expansion of the city has been a major problem. At the moment Thais probably migrate to Bangkok at the rate of 100,000–200,000 a year. It is quite possible that the number is higher. Thus unemployment, slums and fear of protest either in overt social form as social movements or in the unconscious, individual form of criminal behaviour are on the increase.

Slums

The growth of the population has resulted in the growth of slums and squatter settlements. The exact locations in the central parts of the city are known, as the NHA takes aerial photographs and pinpoints possible slum areas on the basis of the closeness of buildings. Later it makes surveys in order to confirm the social and economic conditions in these areas.

New migrants probably begin by living with friends and relatives in slums or other buildings as the migrants in my area did. Some new migrants then go to the outskirts of the city to areas where industry is located. Whether it is still possible to buy land cheaply enough in such areas or whether buildings are put up without renting the land is unknown to me. Such areas might be less densely populated than the centrally placed parts of Bangkok-Thonburi and slums in these.

The concept of slum is a vague one and any account of the number of slums will depend on the definition used. Lichtfield *et al.* wrote in 1960 about the Municipalities of Thonburi and Bangkok,

> An analysis of the information gathered in the course of our land use survey in 2501 [1958] indicates that there are approximately 740,000 persons within what is termed condensed or blighted housing, areas which should be eliminated (Lichtfield *et al.* 1960, p. 84).

According to this study the area with condensed and blighted housing comprises 34.2% of the Bangkok municipal area and includes most of the inner city, especially the part now called Chinatown.

In a United Nations definition a slum is described as

> a building, group of buildings or an area characterised by overcrowding, deterioration, insanitary conditions or absence of facilities and amenities which, because of these conditions or any of them, endanger the health, safety and morals of its inhabitants or the community (cited from Vichit Vadekan 1976, p. 110).

Utilizing this definition the Municipality of Bangkok found in 1970 that there were only 150,000 people living in slum areas (Vichit Vadekan 1976, p. 116).

The National Housing Authority has on the basis of aerial photographs made surveys of slums in Bangkok. Like the AIT (Asian Institute of Technology) they distinguish between squatter settlements and slum settlements — squatter settlements being an area where people build houses or huts without any agreement with the owner of the land and slums being areas where people have some sort of agreement with the landowner, verbal or written, for a shorter duration. People living in overcrowded, unsanitary houses built of new or secondhand materials having a long-term agreement with a house- or landowner are *not* considered slum-dwellers according to this definition.

The NHA estimate in 1980 was 300 slums or squatter settlements with approximately 480,000 inhabitants in Bangkok-Thonburi. In 1981 a new estimate found 410 slums with 516,600 inhabitants. Neither survey counted mini-settlements with less than 80 houses.

In a study for the AIT, Wang Shieh-Yu found that the total number of slum-dwellers and squatters in Bangkok-Thonburi municipality could be estimated at 865,000 people. He assumed that these mostly belonged to the lowest 40% of income earners. The rest of these lived as follows: 150,000 were in public housing; 234,000 were rural commuters, 126,000 were employees living in employers' houses and barracks and 440,000 owned their own houses.

Of the 40% of families earning the lowest income up to half lived in slums and squatter settlements (Shieh-Yu, 1979). The slums are diffusely spread throughout the city leaving unused pieces of land, even in central Bangkok; and industrial areas notwithstanding, industry is spread out in a haphazard and unplanned manner between residential and shopping areas.

Approximately half of the low-income population in Bangkok lives in slums characterized by lack of secure tenure of land, overcrowding, houses built from sub-standard materials and in generally bad physical condition. Most of the houses are built on stilts to avoid flooding; there has been no drainage and filling in of land. In some areas surrounding communities fill up their land and pump out water, the water often being drained off to the slum area nearby. Sewage systems may exist in the form of septic tanks, but not as pipe systems. There is usually no garbage collection. Drinking water is seldom communally installed, although individual dwellers may have a connection to the municipality's system or a private well and pump. Electricity is usually installed.

These problems are however not peculiar to slum-dwellers.

Public investments

The problems with flooding and water are common to most people in Bangkok; they are the result of the geographical situation. Bangkok is situated on a swamp just beside the River Chao Phraya.

> The natural ground elevations in the urban area are between 1.00 and 2.00 m above mean sea level. Stage records on the Chao Phraya river at Bangkok for the period 1940–57 show a maximum stage at 2.29 m above mean sea level. Stages above 2.00 m have been recorded often during a sixteen year period, the mean annual height is greater than 2.00 m above mean sea level (Lichtfield *et al.* 1960, p. 2).

The problems are increasing, since Bangkok is sinking towards and below sea level. Donner explains:

Two interacting factors are responsible for this: firstly the increasing weight of buildings due to a growing population and the introduction of multi-storey buildings of heavy construction and, secondly, the increasing amount of groundwater which is actually pumped out of the ground to satisfy the increasing demand for water in the capital (1978, p. 771).

These quasi-natural conditions cannot but create problems. In the Lichtfield plan it was proposed to build two canals reaching from the north of Bangkok down south to the Gulf of Thailand.[1] These canals have never been built but have now, 20 years later, been proposed again: but local landowners (of the land planned for the canals) have protested strongly.

Nor has the municipality invested much in filling-in, drainage, sewage or drinking water. These investments or services are in most of Bangkok–Thonburi taken care of by private landowners, if at all. So drinking water, for instance, will go to the persons/areas with the strongest pumps. Most of Bangkok–Thonburi is flooded, including the roads, in October, when rain is heavy and when tidal water comes up from the sea. So those sewage systems which exist function for only part of the year.

A multi-million city has grown up with next to no investment in the control of water; most investment has gone into the building of roads and highways. Even in this field little has been done about public transport, which is time consuming and of generally bad quality. People who can afford to, buy cars, thus creating traffic problems.

Neither government nor municipalities have much money for investment. This is partly a result of inadequate taxing of those in the upper-income brackets and of the land. The lack of taxes on land is the more surprising since the prices of urban land are comparatively high. An IBRD (International Bank for Reconstruction and Development) mission gave the prices as 200 dollars per acre in peripheral land and 200,000 dollars per acre in business areas near the city centre. It has been estimated that the price of land represents 60% of the cost of housing in Bangkok, as against 20–35% in cities in other countries (Romm 1970).

There are no laws on zoning in Bangkok–Thonburi, industries and residential and other areas are mixed, with very few recreational amenities. Industry, however, seems to expand mainly to the south along the river and industrial zones have been created in recent years in Prapadææng and Samut Prakan. In the revision of the Lichtfield plan from 1971 it is hoped that zoning can be accomplished by 1990 (Government of Thailand 1971, in Thai, quoted in Donner 1978).

Neither government nor municipalities have invested much in the infrastructure apart from facilities for private cars in Bangkok. Nor have they had an active housing policy. Up to the mid 1950s land in then peripheral areas was divided and sometimes subdivided by the owners, mostly farmers or peasants, and sold. Small lot houses and larger ones began to proliferate. From the mid 1950s land developers went into the business. They bought land from the former peasants and owners. Sometimes they developed it by filling-in, draining, providing a water supply and access roads. Sometimes they just subdivided and sold the land. The land developers could usually create some form of long-term credit for the buyers.

The prices of land increased during this period 8–12 times (Durand-Lasserve 1980).

At the beginning of the 1970s the economic recession had its repercussions on the housing market and from this time on land developing gave way in importance to the new housing industry. The firms involved in this were often former land developers, who went into building, or new firms (from construction, finance or other lines of business). Credit was provided by private banks as well as the new Government Housing Bank (Durand-Lasserve 1982).

In 1972 the National Housing Authority was created; for some years its main purpose was in building more or less for the poor. In 1973 the objective was set at 20,000–24,000 units per year and a government subsidy of approximately 60% was expected. This however, never materialized (Durand-Lasserve 1980).

The Slum Upgrading Office was created in 1977 within the NHA. The focus of the organisation shifted to the upgrading of existing slums and perhaps resettlement in site and service schemes instead of building new flats (until then mostly in high rise buildings). Durand-Lasserve thinks that the government's interest in the housing situation of the poor, beginning in 1972 and growing between 1973 and 1976, should be understood as a bid for political support, especially by the liberal government which was not supported by most of the military.

The lack of investment in the infrastructure, especially in the control of water, the lack of zoning and taxing, and the laissez-faire attitude of government and municipalities towards the housing market have resulted in bad physical conditions in vast areas of Greater Bangkok; this situation creates problems for slum dwellers as well as for people who have bought a small plot of land or a relatively cheap house. (Samrong is one example of such an area. This was a place in which many people in Khlong Toey were especially interested). A decree from 1972 requested land developers to develop land before selling; but it has never been enforced. Slum and squatter settlements, however, have problems with lack of secure tenure of the land over and above the physical problems.

The Work of the NHA

The NHA has since 1977 worked much more with slum upgrading than rehousing. The upgrading of 53 slums has affected 14,480 families. This has cost the government 36,300,000 baht and about 85,000,000 baht has been paid by the World Bank in the form of loans (Slum Upgrading Office 1980).

The NHA faces many problems, the worst probably being the difficulties involved in securing tenure of the land for slum-dwellers. Some slums are situated on government agencies' land. With these the NHA started by buying the land and afterwards sold it on hire-purchase terms to the dwellers. This, however, met with legal problems and now the NHA is trying to lease the land for long-term periods (Rabibhadana *et al* 1981/1982). On private land the NHA has tried to reach an agreement with landowners involving long-term leasing, no increase in rent for five years and no change of land use for ten years after upgrading. But by 1981 only a few landowners had agreed to have their land upgraded on these conditions.

New laws have now been passed. In principle it is possible for the NHA to expropriate land or request the landowner to upgrade, if the land is declared a slum area. If the owner does not comply with the request the NHA can ask builders to do the work and charge the owner for the costs. These laws have not been utilized so far; it is not likely that they will be in the future. The landowners are usually politically influential as individuals and as a group, and the NHA is politically sensitive both as an institution and because its leadership is elected.

With the increase in land values it gets harder for the NHA to work without expropriation of land. The possibility of buying land from owners has been contemplated, but experience has shown that prices rise quickly when it is known that the NHA is interested in buying. So the NHA is often forced to buy at above market price (Thai Real Estate Association and NHA personnel, verbal communication, January 1982).

The team from Thammasat University evaluating the NHA has warned against trying to force landowners, by legal means, since it is doubtful whether the state and political institutions can or will support such measures. Schlomo Angel from the AIT has proposed land-sharing. This would involve dwellers in slums moving closer together in the existing area, thus making part of it available to commercial or other development. The profit from development could then finance the building of new, more orderly and more densely populated houses for the slum-dwellers, in so far as agreement with the landowner can be reached (Angel 1982).

A third proposal has come from R.S. DeVoy and C. Readrungreong. They propose creating a land bank involving government buying of peripheral or other cheap land for future use. In the meantime the land could be utilized to earn the bank a profit and finance further buying or development, building or upgrading (DeVoy *et al.* 1982). The NHA has contemplated upgrading without security of land tenure and without guarantees against increasing rents and changes in types of land use.

Site and service schemes have so far been over-successful. Situated with due regard for employment opportunities and transport, such schemes could perhaps help to inhibit the development of new slums. So far, however, the standard of the infrastructure has been much better than usual in Bangkok, and accommodation in at least one scheme has been much sought by middle-class families, but not by slum-dwellers or other poor families (NHA, August 1980).

The objective conditions for slum upgrading are thus difficult. Internally, the Slum Upgrading Office has had problems too. There has been a bias towards physical upgrading and little has been done about social and economic upgrading or even organizing the slum-dwellers. Physical upgrading has been carried out in at least one area where the physical conditions are much better than in normal working-class areas. Slum upgrading has been carried out without consideration for, or effective measures against, social side effects in the slum area, resulting in rising prices for houses (or rooms) rented out or sold. Physical upgrading without the organization or involvement of the inhabitants has led to the deterioration of the physical structures created. In some cases upgrading has been carried out without coordination with other public agencies. This has resulted, for instance, in garbage being collected, but not removed.

The Thammasat University team has proposed reforms. In order to promote inter-disciplinary work and increase the emphasis on social and economic upgrading, the organization of the office has been discussed and changes instituted; now upgrading is planned and done by inter-disciplinary teams and the work is evaluated by leaders with more varied backgrounds. At the moment the team are working and consulting on criteria for evaluating social and economic upgrading following research done on the actual strong and weak points of work in different slums.

Social and economic upgrading have different implications for different people. In some cases they seem to imply effective organization in the slums. In others it is claimed that changes in the economic and social situation of slum-dwellers ought to be made and programmes for education, loans and the selling of cheap goods have been worked out.

Social and economic upgrading seem to function best if backed up by considerable research both on the social structure in the area in question and the problems the dwellers actually face. The physical aspects need not always be the most pressing problem. And since the slums differ from area to area, and different groups of people have different problems in the same slum area, a good deal of work is necessary to make social and economic upgrading successful.

Pressure on slums — land values and planning

In years to come problems with slum and squatter settlements will probably increase. At the same time slum-dwellers in Bangkok are under increasing pressure to move out, especially in the more centrally placed slums. This pressure stems from increases in land value and better planning. The higher organizational power in the state institutions makes changes in the utilization of public, and to a certain extent private land more feasible (Baross 1982).

In recent years 129 slums with approximately 37,530 families have been or are under eviction in Bangkok (Boonyabangha 1982). Most of these slums are situated in central Bangkok and the risk of eviction is greatest on government land, especially on land belonging to the biggest landowner in Thailand, the Crown Property Bureau. This institution is legally entitled to utilize its land commercially; it has not so far done so to any great extent and it now owns many slums. The Crown Property Bureau does not allow the NHA to upgrade on its land, nor has it been willing to accept arrangements which secure tenure of land for the dwellers, nor to accept responsibility for these. Of the 37,000 families under eviction or threatened with eviction 24,000 families came from government land and 13,000 from private land.

Among the causes given for eviction the most frequent is the wish to utilize the land for commercial or other development such as shop premises, warehouses or tennis courts; about 28% of families were evicted or threatened with eviction with this explanation. This reason was used slightly more by private landowners than by government agencies. Of the families under eviction 27% were given unclear and non-specific reasons. These were slum-dwellers on disputed land and land claimed by the Crown Property Bureau.

The third reason given was that construction of roads was about to start. About 22% of families under eviction were evicted for this reason; it was mainly given by private landowners.

Lastly about 13% of evicted families were evicted to make room for government

Urbanization

buildings, schools, offices, mostly from government land; 10% of evicted families were evicted to make space for residential buildings, roughly half from government and half from privately-owned land (Boonyabangha 1982).

As can be seen, more than a third of the inhabitants were evicted or threatened with eviction to make space for more profitable investments in commercial buildings or in residential buildings for higher income groups. This was the case both on government agencies' land and on private land. Another third were being evicted to make room for government buildings and roads, on both private and government sites. In the last case the reasons given for eviction were unclear. This was especially the case on the Crown Property Bureau's land. Thus an increased possibility of utilizing land more profitably, and the better possibilities for control with public land, are the main reasons for eviction.

Private property

The concept of private property, a precondition for land values and planning, is legally clearly defined. In Thailand, however, this concept is rather new.

The first law requesting landowners to register their land was enacted in the reign of King Chulalongkorn (1868–1919). At this time people were allowed to settle on unclaimed land and cultivate it (up to 25 *rai*). For the first three years they were exempt from taxes and corvée (labour). Ingram reported that in 1970 7,500,000 *rai* were owned by persons and agencies with a full title-deed. About 40,000,000 *rai* had persons living on them who did not have any registration or paper entitlement to the land at all; 13,700,000 *rai* were registered (*Nor Sor* or *Baj Chong*) but those living there did not have a full title-deed. This means that only 12% of the land was legally fully owned by the people who claimed it (Ingram 1971, p. 266).

At the beginning of the 1950s a law was enacted stating that only a full title-deed conferred ownership of land. This naturally created much discussion and many struggles about land ownership. In Bangkok Akhin Rabibhadana reports that as late as the 1960s land ownership was disputed in the slum area he studied, the Vietnamese temples village at White Bridge, between the temple and the Crown Property Bureau. "The ownership of the land was until October 1970 uncertain" (Rabibhadana 1980, p. 10).

Private property and commercialization are also beginning to affect the slums. Of my 24 houses, two were simply given to or lent to relatives, two were rented out and five were sold, although the prices hardly covered the price of the building materials.

The traditional idea that unused land can be used and then claimed is, however, still alive. One of the women in my houses said for instance that people here had civilized the land. Before they moved in, it was wild. High grass grew, there were snakes and often flooding. They had built on it and developed it; there was very little flooding now and it was safe and usable, and now the Port Authority claimed it for its own purposes.

This idea is often found together with social awareness. It is felt that people who have lived on land for years and utilized it have a right to stay and develop it further. The feeling is especially strong since many of these people are poor and do not have many, if any, alternatives. Legally the ownership could have been theirs if they had known, and the legal ownership is in some cases doubtful.

Reactions against eviction

Evictions have often been met with protest from the slum-dwellers. In many cases people from the area in question have organized themselves, negotiated and refused to move out. In a very few cases, there have been physical struggles. So far, people have mostly been forced out.

In a few cases evictions have been rather rough. In one (1982) people were put in vans and driven to a field outside Bangkok. They sat there crying, with no water, no shelter or shade, no materials for houses available and no transport. One of my women had experienced a rough eviction. She had three children and was pregnant. Her husband had just left her. Other people pulled down their houses, but she could not do the physical work and stayed alone in the area. The Port Authority installed a machine which pumped out mud and everything got dirty. At nights men came to her house and she was very scared, thinking about what could happen to herself and her eight-year-old daughter. She then ran to a Vietnamese temple nearby and a man from there came to help her. Eventually some high school students helped her, and she moved to the place where she now lives. But still she could not build her house alone and for some time she stayed underneath the house of a neighbour. She felt very bad about this situation, sleeping near dogs and getting ash, ice and water in the face or on the head when people upstairs threw it down through the floor.

Other people in the area confirmed the story about the eviction. They had all lived on the heaps of materials from their old houses, not knowing where to go or what to do. They were not organized, and explained that each family was called to court individually and each family tried to find a solution individually. When the police came they would run away. Eventually Father Meyer negotiated a solution with the Port Authority so that people could live in the new place (where they were now) and organized some high school students to help. The women were very grateful and said that the students, even if they were white (light-skinned) would go and help carry materials at midday in the sun while Father Meyer organized food for everyone.

In another case, the Rama IV slum eviction, people organized themselves. The Rama IV slum was just opposite the Khlong Toey market and had about 4,000 inhabitants. The slum had a long history. In the mid-1960s several fires broke out in the slum at the same time. Arson was suspected, all the more so as people whose houses had burnt down were not allowed to build new ones. This was the case with a school catering for 1,000 children, and with people who had paid rent or a guarantee sum. The area was first inhabited 80 years ago, and for many years it was cultivated as orchards. But as the city grew a factory was sited nearby and the place took on residential and small business (repair, small production) functions. After the fires the area deteriorated. People were not allowed to build proper houses so they made huts and shacks for temporary use.

The land belonged to the Crown Property Bureau, but had recently been leased to a development company. The inhabitants pointed out several irregularities between these two agencies and raised charges of corruption in the Crown Property Bureau. They mostly thought that it was the petty officials who were cheating, as they still had great respect for the Royal Family. In 1981 they gave the slum a new name, calling it the "heaven of the princess". The charge of corruption was never investigated and the Saha Krungtheep Pattana Company still leases the land (much more cheaply than the slum-dwellers were able to).

In 1978 the slum-dwellers organized a cooperative unit called Khlong Toey Community Development Credit Union Cooperative Ltd. This organization proposed a plan for the development of the area. It proposed using part of the area for residential units and part for business purposes including shops. Every effort would be made to uphold the cooperative idea. The cooperative would own the land and lease it to tenants, business and shops. The leader of the community organization was a woman who worked as a doctor and had a clinic in the slum where she lived. The organization was democratically organized, with elected leaders and a monthly meeting open to all dwellers in the slum where problems were discussed.

The organization stressed that people had been living in the area for 80 years and had developed it by their own efforts. This process had been set back by the fires and the deterioration of the area had begun; but still the inhabitants organized their community, cleaned it and collected garbage. The area ought to be for all the inhabitants and some of the profits from businesses and shops ought to go to the community.

The slum organization in Rama IV conducted negotiations with the Crown Property Bureau and the Development Company trying to work out a concrete solution. They proposed to let the Saha Krungtheep Pattana Company utilize some of the land (the part most suitable for shops along the Rama IV road) and to keep the rest for the dwellers.

The negotiations, however, led to nothing. The dwellers were not willing to give up the cooperative idea. The Saha Company took them to court individually and they were told to move out. At the same time the company tried to make individual agreements with some of the more wealthy dwellers, promising that they could stay if they wanted to. At the moment the slum still exists in the same place and the inhabitants continue to organize and protest against the eviction.

Khlong Toey

In 1982 some of the people in Khlong Toey slum were also evicted. Khlong Toey is the port of Thailand. It was established in 1937; it was in that year that the bar, which made it difficult or, for greater ships, impossible to reach the harbour, was first dredged. Today Khlong Toey is the main port of Thailand and is especially important to the import trade. On the land belonging to the port a large slum has grown up in the last 20–30 years. Until 1981 it was considered the biggest in Bangkok; but in the 1981 aerial survey it was established that there was an even bigger slum in Thonburi. The inhabitants in the latter, however, have not yet been counted.

The Port Authority of Thailand and a mission from the World Bank (in a report dated 15 October 1980) have planned for the expansion of Khlong Toey port. It is also proposed to expand the port at Sattahip, a former naval base, to a container port.

Since one of the bottlenecks at Khlong Toey port is caused by the volume of goods and the lack of warehouse space, one of the main proposals involves the expansion of warehouses. They will mostly be leased to foreign businesses and are expected to yield good returns. The decisions to expand Sattahip to a container port and to expand Khlong Toey port are highly dependent on the investments made so far. The problem with both harbours is that they have to be dredged constantly and still cannot take the biggest ships. Another deep sea port is needed. At Khlong Toey the problem has been aggravated by the building of the Yanhee dam north of Bangkok, which has slackened the current of the river, and thus created more silt (Donner 1978).

Heavy investments have been made or are planned in traffic connections. Roads, highways and rail connections are being, or will be, built. Behind the existing slum at Khlong Toey free space is available which could be utilized both for habitation and the expansion of warehouses. The problem is, however, that the area is rather swampy. At one point the water is six metres deep (Somsook Boonyabanghaa, verbal communication). Originally the Port Authority planned to fill in this area, but at the moment it considers this too expensive.

The Port Authority therefore served notice in May 1982 on 1,000 families in parts of Khlong Toey slum (among them my 24 houses) and they had to move. All the women in my houses who had lived there for more than three years had been evicted before, some of them several times. Most came, however, from two areas nearby — either from the checking point or from inside the wall near the rails. At the last eviction (1973) they had been helped — some by students from universities and Prateep School, which were situated in the area — others by high-school students and the Father Meyers School. The former group lived in what was called the new village. They had straight walkways and originally the same amount of space for each house (15 square wa) 1 wa = 2 metres. The other group lived in what was called the old village. They did not have straight walkways and the houses were built wherever people felt like putting them.

The schools still worked among the people; in this area mostly the Prateep School. They had elected village leaders, two or three from each walkway. These village leaders elected a board and a committee was set up consisting of well-known and well-intentioned people, the chairman being a former prime minister. Through the village leaders connections with politicians from at least four different political parties were established.

Through the NHA negotiations had been going on with the Port before the notice was served. A survey was conducted jointly by the Port, the NHA and the police. Six men went from house to house and asked how many persons lived in the house, their occupations and their incomes. Negotiations with the Port Authority and NHA led to the offer of alternatives: they could either go to the flats the Port had built in seven-storey houses, or they could move to the area behind the existing slum and build new houses there. The NHA had not been able to secure tenure of land: it was leased for one year only. The NHA said that they were willing to invest in walkways, sewage (septic tanks) and a water supply. The NHA also contemplated buying secondhand materials for new houses and selling this cheaply to the people.

The reactions among women in the 24 houses are important as they shed some light

Urbanization

on the options available to people in this situation. None of the women were actively taking part in meetings or organizing. But some of them knew exactly how negotiations were going and who was supporting them. Others did not even believe eviction was coming before the notice arrived. The refusal to believe in eviction was quite widespread, and people carried on repairing, building or painting houses until just before the notice arrived. "The Port have talked about eviction every year, they won't do it."

Faced with the notice of eviction distress was widespread. Wood and corrugated iron for new houses was estimated to cost 30,000 baht or more and few people thought it was possible to utilize materials from their old houses. Lack of secure tenure of the land was much discussed, and the women were well aware that they could be forced to move again at any time.

The choice of a flat in the high-rise building was seriously contemplated by only a few women. They knew it was not expensive — 300 baht monthly, including water and electricity was the usual estimate. Running water was very much appreciated. And the women knew quite well that they could go and live in the flat for a few years and then, if they wanted, sell the right to rent it and move to a house elsewhere. The main reason given by the women for not wanting a flat was the size. They consisted only of one or two bedrooms and a small kitchen and this was thought to be too little room for a family.

The number of persons in my 24 houses was as follows:

houses	14	4	3	2	1
with persons	3–4	5–7	8–10	11–13	15

The average was 5.5 persons per house

The next reason was the heat in the high-rise buildings. The existing houses, made of wood, all had spaces which were open so that the wind could blow, and at the same time they were in the shade. It was said that the flats were incredibly warm. No one thought of air-conditioning as an economic possibility.

People who did not have a relatively secure income did not think about going to a flat at all. Other reasons were commonly mentioned. Children could fall and might die. If fire broke out they would be helpless. The flats were situated nearby, that is, near the Port, where most of the men worked. Nobody mentioned the lack of opportunities to sell things at or near the house. Nobody mentioned being cut off from neighbours and friends; but this would happen in any case since the new plots at the back of the existing slum would be distributed by lot. This was appreciated, and so was the orderly placing of houses.

Only two young women wanted to rent a flat. They both had husbands earning a small but steady wage, owned their own houses in the slum and were thus eligible for one.

Overcrowding in the new flats is very evident. Even though the slums are overcrowded too, there is much more free space outside the house, and this is put to good use. In the new flats this is not so. The heat in the new flats is intense. They are built of concrete and one-sided and without air-conditioning it gets very hot. In the slum-houses, on the other hand, the wind blows and it is often possible to find outdoor space, often under the house, with shade. In the physical sense the houses in Khlong Toey slum were as good or better than most cheap housing.

3. Slum Society

The slum at Khlong Toey harbour is the biggest in Bangkok. The first houses were built about 25 years ago. Many new ones have appeared since then and they are still being built at night, under cover of darkness. The first houses were pulled down long ago; people have moved to new sites in the area every time the harbour has expanded.

I lived in a house I had rented for six months and selected the 24 houses nearest mine for an intensive study. To get into my area you had to walk from Checking Point (the entrance to the harbour) down a gravel road pitted with large holes. To the right lay the slum houses and huts; on the left the Port Authority had built a three-metre high wall. At the top were four rows of barbed wire which the slum-dwellers use to hang newly washed plastic to dry on. The wall affords little shade from the burning sun. The strip of shade is between a half and one metre wide in the day-time hours; even if you walk close to the wall your head is still exposed to the sun. Women going to the market often carry gaily coloured parasols.

The houses are varied: some are good, built of teak, raised on stilts above the muddy ground; others are just small huts thrown together with odd bits of wood and sacking. There are large puddles and small ponds along the road, and tall, coarse grass is growing between them. Rubbish lies everywhere, mostly paper and plastic and sometimes a pile of scrap metal which the Port Authority or one of the factories in the harbour area have thrown out.

People, mostly women and children, are standing or sitting in the ponds washing plastic. On the gravel roads people are walking in and out of the slum, and a little further down the road a herd of the nearby slaughterhouse's cows are grazing. It looks as if they are eating the rubbish. Later you turn in on to a wooden walkway. It is raised half a metre off the ground. A good, solid, well kept walkway leads up to my house. It was built the last time people were forced to move, nine years ago, by students from Thammasat, the slum women say; by the NHA, say the staff of the NHA.

There is also a short cut. Here the walkways are just built from single planks; several are broken, and in some places the supports have collapsed. When you go along the walkways it is like going through people's living-rooms. Most of the houses are open out towards the walkways and groups of women, with an occasional man and many children, sit talking.

In some places there are small stalls or shops. Here, a group of women sit folding paper bags: there, they are polishing bunches of sticks by rolling the bunch over the wooden floor with their feet. Under one of the houses, which are built on stilts, a man

Slum Society

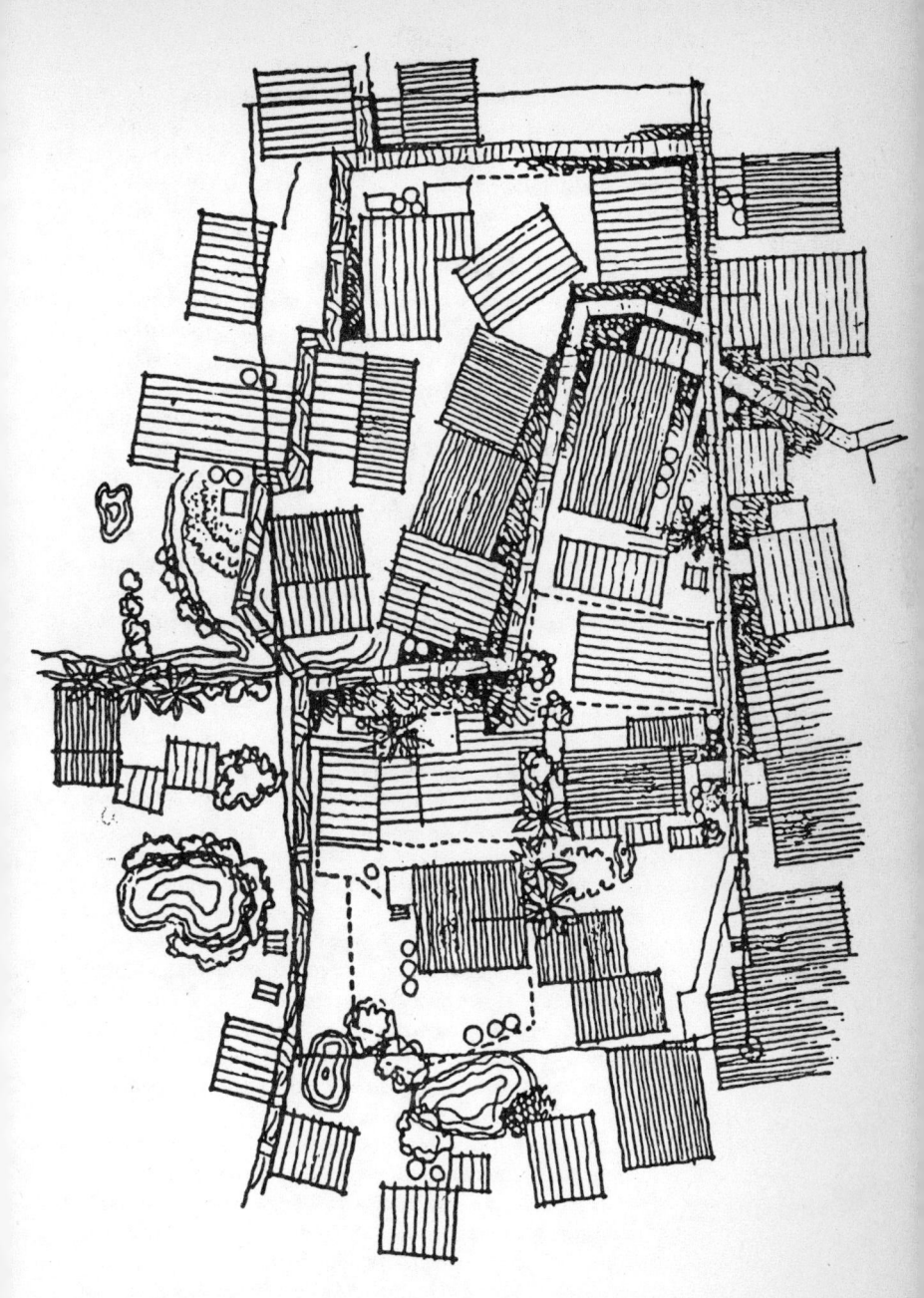

Diagram of Research Area showing disposition of dwellings

Urbanization

is lying in a hammock with a small group of children around him.

Four or five roosters strut around under the house pecking at the ground; a little further down the footpath you can see a small group of ducks walking in the mud. A rat scuttles past my feet and there are a lot of dogs that growl and bark when you pass their house. Several of them are incredibly mangy, and wild, emaciated cats are skulking in the corners. Later I discovered that mice live in the roofs and swarms of insects infest the houses. The worst nuisance is the mosquitoes that come out towards evening.

The daily rhythm of the slum is relaxed for those who do not have to go to work. At about six people wake up, the women tidy things away, prepare and serve rice and wash the children. At about seven the men begin to leave the slum to go to work, an hour later the children go to school. The women get started on the cleaning of the house and the washing, and at about ten they begin on the other chores. At about two they often go to market, and the afternoon is spent preparing food; sometimes they wash more clothes for payment. The water lorry comes in the afternoon too, and women and their grown-up children run back and forth with yokes and buckets to fill the big water pitchers (*tùms*) that stand by the houses.

Then those men who have found work today come home, bath and change clothes, often to a loin-cloth; they eat, and in the evening men and women sit together in groups and talk. Some drink Thai whisky, others gamble, but that goes on inside the houses, hidden. Many watch television — especially if there is a Thai boxing match or a Chinese action thriller or science fiction film on.

On some evenings there is theatre — Likee — in one of the open spaces, on others loudspeakers bellow out advertisements for a bus trip to a temple in the provinces — a *tham bun* trip — all over the slum. The noise is almost always deafening. If nothing special is going on, people play music on tape recorders or record players, and the sounds from the various kinds of entertainment contend to drown one another out. At about ten the slum falls quiet.

The first impression of the slum is of an immense vitality and zest, an intense feeling of fellowship. There can sometimes be arguments so loud that they almost drown out the noise of television and music; but in general there is great friendliness, a lot of joking and laughter and cheerfulness.

The rhythm of the day is not so inflexible that it cannot be easily interrupted. A woman can go off to the country if her husband accepts it, while a neighbour or daughter looks after her home. Men who have not found work during the day sit and talk to the women. Children, youths and grown-ups mix with one another without major problems arising. The loneliness of European working-class wives is unknown here; everyone talks to lots of other people every day.

Our stricter, Western sense of the rhythm of time and the separation and institutionalization of age groups is here as yet no more than a cloud on the horizon, it seems. The first impression of the slum — as a place with vitality, where importance is attached to love and friendship, with much tenderness and respect within families — remains and is strengthened as I get to know the women better.

They tell me in great detail about falling in love, about children who are good, live at home and help to find food and about longstanding friendships between women who have lived near one another. But it emerges that this zest for life, this longing for love and friendship, often has to flourish against a harsh background.

The sense in insecurity in the slum is great. Only a few (five) families have access to a welfare fund, and sickness and accidents can hit anyone and be a great burden. Within six months five men had been badly hurt in traffic accidents which not only required money for doctors and treatment but also prevented them for working for at least a month. One woman, whose husband had died the previous year, and who received aid from the Port Authority welfare fund, still had to pay 1,000 baht a month on a loan she had taken out to pay for the funeral. And that was up-country where the rice was much cheaper than here, she explained.

Most people lived together with or very near close relatives: middle-aged parents with grown-up, often married children and the parents' own parents. Economically speaking, this lifestyle was a necessity. Old people were completely dependent on their children, and for the young the income a couple earned was often far too small to run a home independently.

For the young prospects for the future were insecure. A young man with no particular education could look forward only to the same wage for the rest of his life, and it was harder for a young woman: she could only anticipate fewer opportunities to earn her own living later. The feeling of insecurity was aggravated by the police. The most widespread of the illegal activities was gambling. There were many forms — the one where most money was lost was dice. Both men and women played, while men could lose two or three thousand baht in an evening women had far less money in their hands: their losses were more in the region of two or three hundred.

The loss was one thing; worse was the frequent harassment by the police. A couple of times a month, they would find a group of gamblers, confiscate the pool and the bets and take about 100 baht from each player in bribes. Now and then a man would be taken down to the station and then it would be still more expensive to get him out again.

But many of the activities of the slum were prohibited: share-games, loaning against interest, home distilling, prostitution, abortion, theft and the sale of heroin. No one could feel safe.[1] People were without legal rights in the face of the police and prisons. A bribe could turn a court decision, heroin was planted on suspects, torture was used in interrogations. If a man confessed, the sentence would be halved, and when a man had once been imprisoned regular payments to the prison staff were demanded: to get him a slightly better cell, to have him moved to another prison or indeed to prevent him being moved; for food, Thai whisky and cigarettes for the man and the staff.

Incomes in the slum varied widely from family to family or from individual to individual. It is always difficult to get precise information about incomes. In most countries people answer as they would answer the tax inspector. In the slum there was an extra element of doubt as to how large the incomes actually were, or how often the building workers, for example, had work. But there was also the fact that most people had a strong interest in declaring the lowest possible incomes. This was especially true for surveys made by the NHA and other aid-granting institutions, as the aid granted would depend on how poor people were. Consequently most people declare their regular monthly income and forget overtime money, tea-money and the incomes of other members of the family.[2]

I checked my information by asking different people in the same family, by

Urbanization

comparing different people's incomes for the same work, and by observing how often people were at work. My data are not especially precise, but are roughly correct. They are much higher than the ones given in other studies. In a survey the NHA found an average income of 1,500 baht a month per household two years ago.

In my 25 houses the incomes were as follows:

Table 3.1
Incomes of Slum-dwellers

Baht per month	Men Occupation/No.	Women Occupation/No.
Under 1,000:	Plastic washers/1 Unemployed/4	Odd jobs/5 Household tasks/4 None/16
1–2,000	Teachers/1 Typists/1	Factory workers/1 Building/4 Household tasks/1 Sewing outwork/1 Plastic washers/1
2–3,000	Carriers/9 Loaders/1 Chauffeurs/1	Loader/1
3–6,000	Taxi drivers/2 Skilled workers/3 Regular port workers/4 Building/3 Lorry owner/driver/1 Singer/1 Diamond polisher/1	Potters/1 Restaurant workers/1 Money lenders/2
More than 6,000	Regular dock work/3 Hǔa nâa/1 Night taxi driver/1	None
	Students/2 Elderly/invalids/3	Students/3 Elderly/invalids/2

Slum Society

More indicative of daily life conditions than personal incomes are household incomes taken in relation to household size. In my slum houses they were as follows:

Table 3.2
Household incomes

Baht per person per month	Number of households	Number of persons
under 500	5	20
500–1,000	5	26
1,000–1,500	9	51
1,500–2,000	5	21
over 2,000	3	14

The differences in incomes and living circumstances in my slum area were very great indeed. In the richest family there lived a man who had begun as a carrier at the harbour over twenty years before, but who now worked as a crane driver and chauffeur. His income was about 15,000 baht a month. His wife was one of the best potters in Thailand, employed at a ministry with a salary of 5,600 a month. The man's mother, three of his and his wife's children (two of them at university), two children the man had with a minor wife (mistress), and his late brother's daughter all lived in the house.

They had a large house with almost all consumer goods —gramophone, fridge, freezer, television and a motor-cycle. They had their own well and almost always had water, a roof without holes in it, panes of glass in the windows, tables, chairs and beautifully carved wooden beds. The wife very much wanted a washing machine.

They had bought land in Bangkok but so far no infrastructure — roads, water —had been built in the area. They had land in the provinces, although it was only on *nor sor*, which they rented out to tenant farmers who grew tapioca. But they had great problems collecting the rent for the land.

The wife complained about the man's minor wives. He was constantly finding new ones and had eight to ten in the slum, she said. One of the minor wives had a good job, though, and the husband had presented this mistress with a car. Their relationship was extremely bad. The wife was angry about his minor wives both because they wounded her dignity and because they were expensive. She felt that her husband ought to pay more into the home than direct expenses and that they ought to manage the profits together.

The poorest woman in the slum lived in completely different circumstances. She had come alone to Bangkok as a fourteen-year-old and had ended up as a prostitute at the harbour. She had been grossly exploited by a pimp while she was young. Now she lived in a little hut with an adoptive son and a man who was badly addicted to heroin. He was a porter at the harbour but rarely worked; he did not think she should feed the little boy she had taken in and he often beat her.

She had no regular income, but got free rice at the Prateep School. She often talked or worked a little with a couple of the other families who lived nearby and she survived on the odd meal she could share with them. She starved. What she could get in the way

Urbanization

of small and irregular income she spent on the boy.

For many of the women in the slum the household income as a whole meant very little. Their and their children's daily life was at least as dependent on the distribution of the incomes within the families. It was difficult to get a breakdown of expenses: the women seldom knew what the money was being used for. Large amounts went on men's personal expenses. Gambling used up a lot of the money. Most men drank hard while gambling, and this certainly did not reduce the losses. When their reserves had been used up they would borrow money: the ringleader of the gamblers in the gambling house in my area lent it out at 30% interest per week. Men would often therefore borrow money elsewhere afterwards to pay their gambling debts, and even if the interest was lower when borrowing from a relative, at the harbour or from a pawnbroker, it was still very high. And then there were of course the bribes to the police.

Other expenses were incurred by the men in connection with minor wives. In most cases the minor wives were women of the wife's own age who had children. But this state of affairs made men's expenses greater, not less, especially if the husband was the father of the minor wife's child/children. Visits to restaurants, going on the town with friends and buying motorcycles were more male expenses which ate into the family budget.

The general attitude was that incomes were personal. The one who had worked for the money also had the right to dispose of it. One woman expressed it by saying, "I won't steal money out of the house. He has to give it to me."

The idea that wages and incomes were personal property was, however, modified by two opposite tendencies.

Most women would expect a husband to give his wife a reasonable regular amount for the household expenses: for a family of 6–10 persons, about 100 baht a day, less if the wife had an independent income. The wife's income was expected to be used for household expenses. Some husbands did give a regular amount of this sort, others did not. In several cases the husband gave his wife money for the household expenses, only to demand it back again.

The notion that incomes were personal was, however, not only modified by the tendency to think that a husband ought to give his wife money for the home, but also by an opposite tendency that the man had a right to any surplus.

If a woman gambled and won she would ask everyone not to tell her husband — even in a family where all the incomes were pooled together and were managed by the wife. In some families the husband confiscated the wife's own income if he needed money and she had some; in others he borrowed it from her.

Grown-up children who earned money were also expected to contribute to the household expenses. Sons, like husbands, gave what they thought they could afford, while daughters who did not have their own homes to run generally reckoned on giving a regular amount every month/week. Norms were, however, not fixed. Everything depended on relative earnings and the expenses people had. But all unmarried daughters in the slum contributed a regular sum to their mothers when they had work.

The poverty in the slum was thus a matter of insecurity, problematic prospects for the future and, as far as the women and children were concerned, the distribution of incomes within the family/household.

Almost all the women stated that they were poor. "Look at me. I'm still living in conditions like this after twenty years in Bangkok."

The slum women felt themselves to be poor, and for the most part felt themselves to be in opposition to the rich, to the society around them. One young woman explained to me at an early point during my stay.

> In Thailand, the way things are is that rich people despise the poor. Here in the slum I can tell people about it, here we can chat about it. We're all poor, you're poor too. But I couldn't say it to her . . . I'm poor, and she'd have said I was rude, I had to be polite. Rich people despise the poor here. Is it like that in your country too?

People in the slum (with a few exceptions) spoke a dialect which in pronunciation, vocabulary and grammatical structure deviated from standard Thai. Some expressions would cause a well educated middle-class Thai to turn pale.

The feeling of being poor and the solidarity between poor people was especially marked when people came face to face with public institutions such as eviction orders from the Port Authority and the police.

The schools in the area had tried to organize themselves to deal with the threat of eviction; in my group of houses it was the Prateep School which did this. None of the women took part in the meetings; but some were very well informed about the course of the negotiations, having heard about it from neighbours. There was a widespread idea that it was important to help one another, to organize.

Some women thought that the Port Authority wanted people moved out so that its leaders could make extra incomes (tea-money) by letting the land out as storage space and warehouses to foreign firms; one woman pointed out that the poor people of the slum had good political allies, support in society outside (a former prime minister was the leader of the school's committee).

Solidarity was strong when faced with the police. No one denounced anyone or said anything about who had done burglaries, who was a pick-pocket, who was selling heroin. People covered up for one another and gamblers were warned, if possible, when the police came into the area, by messengers from other parts of the slum.

A reaction from a young woman meeting a pick-pocket who works the market where she usually goes is typical: "Have a good look at this face. Look at this face and remember. It has no money on it. Remember that."

When a man was taken by the police the women often showed a great deal of solidarity. A wife could, for example, borrow at high interest to get her husband out of gaol and work hard afterwards to pay the interest back. Another woman sold all her possessions and borrowed as much as she could to go on visits to the prison, to get money for bribes so that her husband's conditions could be improved, to prevent him being moved further away.

In the slum women exchanged information: you could hear who had been tortured, who went where; and they helped one another with details about the journeys, about prison conditions, gave the addresses of relatives a woman could spend the night with if necessary. In most cases a couple of women would go off together to visit a man in prison or to negotiate about informal contributions to police or prison officers.

Urbanization

The daily life of the slum was intense. It was a place with a lot of rowing and conflicts, a place where people did not talk politely to one another. Comparing it with Western conditions, it must be said that, given the population density and the almost total lack of private life, the conflicts and rows were relatively limited. But compared with other Thai communities it was probably true that the intensity and level of conflict were high.[3]

Most people, however, expressed the wish for a happy and pleasant life — *sanùg, sabaaj*: merry and pleasing. Much emphasis was placed on good relations with other people and a lot of friendliness and helpfulness was evident. People in the slum set no great store by hard work. They wanted money, but it was not a virtue to be thrifty, industrious and ambitious.[4]

The exceptions were a Christian Thai woman and a Vietnamese. The Christian woman had been converted three years before, and since then her daily life had taken a new course. She and her husband had stopped gambling and drinking and he was still trying to give up smoking. She thought they had had a much better life since then, and she had put on weight. The Vietnamese woman was proud of the fact that she worked so hard, never wasted time with chat and empty talk. She lived relatively isolated from her neighbours and made her most important social contacts within the Catholic Church.

The Thais on the other hand preferred a fun-filled, pleasant life, good friends and love. One young woman encapsulated this typical Thai attitude in a joke: "The Chinese are clever at saving, the Laotians at working and the Thais are clever at eating and drinking."

Part 2:
Women's Work for Incomes

4. Women's Work for Wages

Introduction

In the slum women's work was above all insecure. A lot of paid work was done intermittently, depending on the economic situation, the amount of housework and the demands of children and the need for help from other family members. Women worked for the family: took care of children, made food and washed clothes, and in many cases they also had paid work. Some of this work was visible, as it took place in the slum and attracted attention. Much of it was not immediately evident; it was hard to talk to some women, as they left early in the morning and came home late. When they were at home they were busy with the housework. Others lived elsewhere: with the family they did domestic work for, or the family they worked for at the market; some slept in the sleeping quarters at the factory, others at building sites.

Let me introduce the women who worked in the slum by taking a walk through my area. Without going further than my own house you can hear a small child crying. This is Nŭu's daughter, who is being taken care of today by Nŭu's sister Dam while Nŭu is working at the factory. The little girl is used to a much less rough type of social interaction than that which reigns in the slum and the other little girls are teasing her because she doesn't wear trousers under her frock. In the house just opposite mine two young women, Pùu and Pân, are sitting on the steps talking and embroidering a white pattern on brown woollen blouses. They are sitting here so that they can keep an eye on the empty house; the woman of the house isn't at home, and the eldest daughter is teaching at the school.

To the right of my house some very charming wild flowers are growing among the grass. Behind this lie three houses that are locked up and closed out towards the walkway. They are guarded by the rich man's eight dogs, which growl and bark at anyone who approaches. One of the houses belongs to the rich man. His wife, Cĭaw, is at work, the children are at school or university; the smallest is at the kindergarten. Only his old mother is in the house. Another house is the singer's. He is asleep after a night's work and his new sister-in-law, Nípapheen, is tiptoeing around so as not to disturb him. In the next room live the singer's sister and her husband. She is several months pregnant and is working at the building site like her husband. The third house belongs to the Vietnamese woman. You can hear how she is sitting sewing on her machine, but the house is completely closed off.

I go on to the left, and at the first corner is Sii's house. She is sitting on the platform outside the house roasting bananas, which she sells. On the broad step leading up to

49

the platform sit two neighbours, also in their fifties, talking. Sǐi has three grandchildren whom she always takes care of, and her daughter Tǐm's three small children are crawling around her and playing. Tǐm is at the building site.

One of the neighbouring women is taking care of her grand-daughter while the daughters are at work, one at the harbour, one in service. She reproaches Sǐi for not attending to the little ones properly, and shows me her own grand-daughter with pride.

The other neighbour has no small children to look after. She lives just beside her son and her daughter-in-law, Bun; but Bun prefers to ask another neighbour to look after the children when she is at work. Mother-in-law has plenty of things on her own plate anyway. She has borrowed 2,000 from the pawnbroker and to pay the interest she goes to the rubbish dump to find plastic, which she then washes and sells. This is dirty, ill-smelling and despised work, finding plastic, and today she simply doesn't have the energy.

I turn down along the back of her house, past Sǐi's spirit-house and the tamarind tree. Here is Bun's house, but she is not at home. On the other side of the walkway, however, are Àat and Praanii, 16- and 18-years-old respectively. They live with their father and a little sister. The mother has moved away, but has a house nearby. Today Praanii is looking after her brother's two small children. They both take anything in the way of small jobs that comes along: washing clothes, cleaning; but it doesn't amount to much. Their older sister lives at the factory where she works.

Round the corner to the left lies a large house occupied by two families. Under the house there is quite a large empty space in the shade and beside it there is a little pond. Here the heat is reasonable.

The Christian woman lives here and she is chopping up firewood. Cíab lives across the way, but is sitting with her little adoptive son sorting bits of plastic, keeping the white pieces separate. It is hopeless work. In the pond sit Bàd and her husband washing plastic; an old lady, the mother-in-law, waves to us from her platform. The daughter-in-law is nine months gone, but still works at the building site.

Kàj comes, walking along the walkway. She is my next-door neighbour and has been to market and bought a bucket full of ice lollies. She has a fridge, and wants to get her son to sell them when he comes home from school. To the right is Chalǔaj's house. A lot of women are sitting here: Chalǔaj's mother, who is shouting, talking and gesticulating: Chalǔaj's daughter, Túg, her son is the same age as her younger brother, and they are playing with Bun's son who is the same age. For Bun is sitting here today too, with another of the neighbouring women, Ùbon, whose daughter is at school.

Chalǔaj lends out money, and today she has made Thai iced coffee; I buy a little plastic bag and attempt to work out the profit. But she doesn't sell soda pop and Cola any more: it doesn't pay, as no one brings the bottles back.

Khǐaw's mother is lying in the shade outside her house asleep: Khǐaw is at a building site.

Beside this Khǐad has made a little restaurant. She has a table and a couple of chairs and a shade made of blue plastic. Her youngest daughter, Sǐi's daughter-in-law, helps her shell prawns while she herself chops vegetables. The elder daughter stands watching and the three small children crawl around between them.

At the table Bunryang sits and stares out at nothing in particular. She is desperate, tired of looking after children and the house, tired of a husband with many minor wives, and pregnant with a fourth child.

Her neighbour is busier. She too lends out money, but today she is washing a big pile of clothing for a teacher at the school. "Can't you see it's much better than going into town to work?" she asks. "Just think about the buses, they're terrible in this heat."

A bit further on the walkway opens out on to a better one. A young disabled man sits here, with beautiful wavy hair, making a game with dice, pictures and squares. Sămphaw and Lee are playing a little, while the next-door neighbour, Kèe looks on.

She is in an advanced state of pregnancy and is comparing prices and treatment at different hospitals. Her youngest, adoptive son is with his grandmother in Korat; her youngest daughter is at home. She has just popped in to the hairdresser nearby. Kèe owns that house too, but lends it out to her sister. The sister lives in Nonta Buri, but works in Bangkok doing accounts for a transnational company; she is unmarried and has a couple of tiny hairdressers' shops like this one. The young girl who is to work in it will live in Nŭu's house. Nŭu's husband is Kèe's brother. Sămphaw's two grown-up sons, a daughter of 18 and the eldest daughter, Tíg's children are also watching the game.

The impression you get from the slum — that women work at something that provides an income in or near the house — is strong, but it is misleading. A census at the beginning of May showed that women have the following jobs:

Wage labour	14
Other work for industry	2
Extended household activities	4
Extended household activities off and on	5
Students	3
Old and sick	2
No income-earning work	16

The conditions for these women's work for an income are among the best in the Third World. Industry has recently moved to South-East Asia — especially industry eager to employ young women (see Elson and Pearson, 1980). Thailand is one of those countries to which industry has moved. Local investment and striving for industrialization have both contributed to the high growth of GNP. Both foreign and the national capital employs young women. In industrial plants in Greater Bangkok slightly more than half the workforce are women (Sarkar 1974).

The people in my slum houses were not among the poorest; they were quite well off compared to new migrants and workers without stable jobs. Economically speaking the objective conditions for women's work for an income were good compared to most other countries in the Third World as well as to some sections of the working-class in Bangkok.

Culturally speaking, too, women in Thailand are relatively well off. Traditionally they have participated in the work producing rice and other necessities and as late as in 1968 Myrdal found they made up nearly half the workforce — 80% of all women participated in production, the highest figure in the world (Myrdal, 1968).

In Thailand it is considered proper for women to work in production. Thitsa (1980) relates this finding to the concepts in Theravada Buddhism of women as more material and less spiritual human beings than men. As material beings women ought to join in production; this is reinforced by their access to education. The first laws on public education from 1933 proclaim equal access for boys and girls. This education is secular while the education in the temples organized by the order of monks, the Sangha, can only be obtained for boys. (See Tambiah 1976 who stresses that this education is a useful road to social mobility among poor boys, especially from the north-east.)

Women's position in villages up-country was subordinate to men's; women were the hindlegs of the elephant, as the saying goes. Still there was equal inheritance for boys and girls and the spirits connected with birth and death, marriage and family life were inherited through women and the location of new couples was matrilocal. The female line of descent was the nucleus around which the household was built and towards which men were responsible (J.M. Potter 1977, S.H. Potter 1977, Turton 1972).

Wage work

Among my women two married young women Nŭu and Tíg had factory work; so did two unmarried young women: one, Phen, was only 14-years-old, the other Meew was 20-years-old and living in the factory dormitory. Most of the women had had one or more jobs in a factory formerly. The following description of the conditions of work in industry is built on tape interviews with Nŭu and Tíg and on the accounts of other women of their former jobs.

One of the women, Nŭu, earned the minimum wage about 1,600 baht a month; she worked for a transnational concern which registered in the labour department in May. Phen worked at the same factory. Registration meant that the workers' real names were used. Previously, the factory had given them new names so that no two workers were called by the same name. This ought to have meant that the factory required identity cards from the workers. These are not issued until a person is 17 and this means that the factory then does not use child labour. However, this was not the case at this factory, which continued to employ children; nor did the workers get their expected two uniforms a year. Overtime was cut while the rate of the work was forced up, and extra days off became almost an impossibility. Nŭu told me about it.

> If I go, then I am afraid of being fired from work, afraid they will fire me.
> Like my friend the other day. She will leave to marry, and she was still not allowed. So she resigned.
> Her *feen* is drafted soldier, they love each other like this, they will marry each other, they make appointment to say it straight.
> Now Rúnii she so ask the boss, but he don't let her go, don't give her sign, don't allow her to leave.
> We must say we have business really. We have to lie to our chief. She did not want us to go anywhere, she will be cursed.

The other adult woman Tíg, sewed jeans. She earned 800 a month and thought it was too little, but reckoned on learning to sew and thus becoming qualified. Other women had previously had work at a factory. Most had worked for about half of the minimum wage. The working hours were eight hours a day, six days a week.

Maternity leave, insurance schemes for industrial accidents or other forms of social security were unknown among the women who worked or had worked in factories. The only insurance scheme they had experienced went the other way: on being employed at the transnational factory the women paid 200 baht as insurance against their possible destruction of a machine. The money was paid back after a six months' trial period, and even then in instalments. Nǔu explained.

> Oh, the time at the shrimp factory! That mother [mother-in-law] guaranteed 200 baht. The factory call it guarantee money: a guarantee for getting a job. When we work and get through six, six months like this, then they pay the guarantee money back.
>
> If we work and don't make it through the six months, then they take it away.
>
> I worked, but I didn't manage six months, so they kept it.

None of the women had worked in factories where the machines themselves set the working rhythm (such as assembly lines). The pace of work therefore had to be kept up in other ways. All the women did some form of piecework, and then there was the work leaders' (*hùa nâa*), the directors' or the directors' wives' or daughters' supervision of the work.

Tíg told me,

> The owner of the factory had a big mouth. His wife ... his wife and the eldest sister were the same ... bad, too much ...
>
> They ordered us to sit spinning the thread, right? They would sit looking on from their air-conditioned room. So they sat looking and we worked, spinning the thread like this, sitting face to face.
>
> There's wood in the middle, and we sat opposite each other. We weren't even allowed to talk to each other. For example, this other woman, she didn't know, so she asked me which direction to spin, to the right or left?
>
> I told her to go to the right, just like this. Right away the wife is there of course: Have you come here to chat with each other or have you come to work?

The women felt the supervision of their work to be both humiliating and frightening. Nǔu reserved her anger for the director, not for her *hǔa nâa*. She said,

> He is the owner of the factory, he is a big manager. When he comes they say: watch out yourself. We cannot talk to each other ... I must notice everytime when I work, I must look at the window ... I must watch out, he will emerge, when will he emerge, sometimes when I work he go and hide, he has many places to hide, sometimes at this window, and then at that side.
>
> Now I work, I usually will look at this window every time.
>
> He likes to wear glasses, he stand and stare at people. It is mostly the boss. When she [the *hǔa nâa*] see the boss she then tell that: there your father comes already.

Women's Work for Incomes

> The *hǔa nâa* who control us is a woman, her heart is cool, is kind, she does not scold the subordinates. But the boss, he call her to curse, he says that she don't control the subordinates well.

At most factories conversation between the workers during working hours was forbidden, even for giving instructions to other workers. This was also true during waiting time.

At some factories the work was very specialized, and for this or other reasons the women had to spend long periods waiting for their work. As it was piecework this waiting time was unpaid and in most factories conversation was also forbidden at these times. In some of them a director's wife, monitoring the workers from her air-conditioned room, would stop the women's conversation by criticizing them through a loudspeaker, so everyone could hear it.

At Nǔu's factory the management punished infringements with pay-cuts. "If we make something wrong they cut. If we do not make it clean they cut the money again [the octopus]."

At Nǔu's factory the workers helped one another during waiting time.

> We go in and help each other, and he see it, then everyone, the whole table was cut five baht each, five baht. Oh they come and ask: help that section OK? In the morning time if the section who arrange the cuttlefish [put it into refrigerator] do not have work, we then go in to help inside first, we were cut five baht each and then one baht each too, that makes six baht.

At most companies there was overtime at intervals. At one of them there had been a long waiting period and overtime on the same day. The women were usually informed about overtime on the same day and thus had no opportunity to arrange to have their children looked after. Overtime was obligatory and often the women were not told how long it would last. It was paid at the same rate as ordinary work.

The women's anger was often first and foremost directed towards their *hǔa nâa*. The latter would criticize the women's work, which they found unfair.

Tíg said, "She's employed me to do the work and so I do my best to help her." The women felt that they were doing their best and expected to be treated with a reasonable amount of respect. They found it intolerable to have to bear being criticized and spoken to rudely.

It was worst, of course, in the cases where a *hǔa nâa* broke an agreement: paid a lower wage than had been promised, forced a woman to work overtime despite a standing agreement that she could not do so on that particular day of the week. On the other hand, the women who liked their work had a *hǔa nâa* who treated them reasonably, spoke properly to them and kept agreements. In some cases these workers had a special relationship with their *hǔa nâa*: went to parties with her, or went on the town with her and other workers.

The atmosphere of the workplace was of great importance to the women. At a factory which made fireworks there was sometimes waiting time without work. So the manager of the factory suggested to the workers that they should go and see a Likee play, or organized things so they could all eat together. The workers found their workplace pleasant and worked overtime at other periods where there was a lot of

Women's Work for Wages

work without protesting.

Several women had begun working in factories at the age of ten, and some had been a sort of mascot for the other workers. They enjoyed that a lot: but in most cases it was hard for the children. Tíg said,

> A Chinese man, he set up an ice-cream factory, right? Then he looked for child labour. At that time I was a child. I'd never worked then, I didn't know . . . Then Cée [a Chinese woman] asked around. She came to a house belonging to my neighbour. That house also had a daughter, and I was a friend of that house. Cée said: Bring this friend to work, too — to be friends.
>
> Then she asked if I wanted to go. I said yes. At first they only gave me five baht . . . from 5 in the morning until 8 in the evening.

Some factories had dormitories for the workers. In one case there was a long room where a plastic mattress was rolled out along the length of the floor. Women from different shifts slept on the mattress, and there were great problems with working properly and getting up in time because they couldn't sleep while the others were talking, eating or relaxing. Tíg told me,

> I walked, and reached the factory at 7 a.m. — I walked absent-mindedly.
>
> A friend was sitting there. He said: Hi, Tíg! You're so late today! I used to see you coming at six o'clock, yet today you haven't reached the factory yet.
>
> Then I said: Today I'm bored, I don't feel like working, tonight I want to sleep. I'm sleepy. I played cards because I couldn't sleep. In the early evening, at 7 o'clock, there are lots of people, they're noisy. Some people hadn't slept, some had slept already.
>
> It's a dormitory — long, long like this, and they've only put down one plastic mattress for us to sleep on.

The women's factory work was paid at far below the minimum wage. The workers who got the minimum had worked for several years at the same factory. Sometimes they were also given special responsibility, although none of the women in my houses were or had ever been *hǔa nâas*.

The employers are interested in a stable workforce and are willing to pay more to keep women. The transnational firm where a couple of the women (Phen and Nǔu) from the slum worked thus paid the minimum wage only to those workers who had paid a guarantee sum on first being employed and had worked for the firm for several years. Newly employed workers got a much lower wage. But the women were only in rare cases able to work continuously. Young, still unmarried, girls could do this; but for the married women it was almost impossible.

Their daily work with the family meant that they took extra days off every now and then: when the washing had piled up and there were no clean clothes for the men and children to wear, when they had a headache or stomach pains. A weekly day off was nowhere near enough for them to manage their everyday workload.

The children also meant frequent interruptions. A child could become ill, and the mother would have to go to the clinic with it, or the grandmother might not be able to manage to take care of it while it was ill. Childbirth and pregnancies were hard to manage at the same time as work. Husbands would often complain that the home wasn't functioning, that the child/children were crying, that they were getting worse food than usual.

The legislation which does exist in Thailand on the special protection of women — time off with pay for childbirth and so on — has no practical effect. Even the firm that was registered with the Labour Department did not stop using child labour, did not pay the minimum wage to workers, did not set up a welfare fund, and failed to give the workers two uniforms a year.

For the women, the most important aspect of work in factories — the crucial point which decided whether they stayed at a workplace or left it — was that they were treated as human beings, that their dignity was not hurt. They complained most about a job or left it because a *hǔa nâa* or director's wife had treated them rudely, been suspicious of them, criticized them or had broken agreements. The workplaces women liked were workplaces where they were reasonably treated — where they could relax together while they were waiting for work, and where the *hǔa nâa* spoke properly to them.

Women also worked at loading and unloading at the harbour. In my houses one woman worked at the harbour unloading gravel. Four women worked at building sites. The woman who worked at the harbour lived with her husband and a little daughter together with her mother and a sister. The mother looked after the child and the housework, and the couple had steady work and each earned about 2,000 baht a month.

The four women who worked in construction had work for from two or three weeks in the month on average. Their wages varied a little, but were between 50 and 75 baht per day (men on building sites were paid double this, between 100 and 150).

Working hours were as with factory work — in principle 48 hours a week; in practice there was great variation. As with factory work there was no form of insurance schemes, maternity leave or similar benefits. The danger of industrial accidents must have been considerably greater on the building sites. Many workers slept at their place of work, and there were often small children present at the workplaces with their mothers.

One of the four women, Khǐaw, was only 17 and it was her first experience of paid work. She was completely worn out when she came home — rested, slept and felt miserable when she was at home.

Another of the women, Tǐm, had three children. She had had many years' experience and was strong. At first she worked because her husband didn't give her money for the family, then because he moved out. Her mother Sǐi looked after the children, but couldn't see to the household work, given her own large household and her work of production and selling at the house. On a day when Tǐm had overtime, she had to fetch water after midnight.

The other two women were both pregnant. They worked in construction in the eight and ninth months of their pregnancy respectively (they both gave birth by Cæsarean operation). Other women had previously had work on building sites. One woman had hammered rust off the ships in the harbour. She still did it, although very rarely. She had contracted bad lungs, she said, from breathing in the rust particles in the holds (there was no safety equipment).

Unemployment

According to official statistics unemployment in Thailand is low — in Bangkok about 3–4% (Department of Labour 1978, p. 19). For the women in the slum it was significantly higher. Among the women in the slum, some (especially young women without a husband and children) said that they wanted work; others (especially married women with children) said that they didn't: they had plenty of work looking after the family.

Statements like these are difficult to evaluate; more characteristic was a readiness on the part of both groups to take whatever work became available. An example was Bun, married and a mother of three, who said that she didn't want work, that she had enough with the family. Anyway, she had had several factory jobs before she got married, it was too boring in the long run. But when she was offered a chance to cook food, sell things and wash dishes at a little booth in the market, she took the job at once, had her children looked after by her friend Chalŭaj and was away for at least twelve hours a day.

Tíg is 26, a mother of two, and has had at least 12 years experience of various types of wage-earning work. Pùu, her younger sister, is 24; she has had 10 years of schooling and no husband (at home). She lives with her parents. Tíg lives just across from her, and her mother, Sămphaw can look after the children (but not the rest of the housework).

Both of them ask around among friends and acquaintances about job possibilities, and Pùu reads advertisements and notices at factories offering jobs. She finds a notice at a textile factory nearby, and when it turns out that her father knows a *hŭa nâa* there he invites the (male) *hŭa nâa* and his friends to dinner. They eat and drink together one evening and Pùu is promised that she will hear from them. When she hears, shortly afterwards, that they have taken on other young women, she looks for something else.

The YWCA is looking for two women in the kitchen, and she and Tíg go out there and get the job. It is a half-day job, and it turns out that there is unpaid overtime every day, working on days off (folding and ironing napkins) and that the first week's work is an unpaid probation period. They give up on this job.

I then recommend Pùu to a small hotel where I lived for my first week in Bangkok. Here she has to work for 12 hours a day for 800 baht a month and pay her own board. She must also preferably live in. She does not take this job.

Then they both got work at the transnational firm where Phen and Nŭu also work. They have to clean squids as piecework. After the first week, when the wages are to be paid, it emerges that they will not as promised, get about half of the minimum wage, but a quarter.

> For that you're got to stand with your hands in water all day. I was scared they would rot away. And when you get home you stink like a dead dog.

They both give up on this job.

They search again, and Tíg who has worked before making fishing-nets, is employed making jeans for 800 baht a month. Pùu is not taken on. She has seen a notice from a clock factory, and hopes to get work there soon. But she has problems with her eyes: they hurt in the afternoon from too much light, but she hopes to get the job anyway.

This very active job-hunting on the part of two young, relatively well-qualified women went on for the best part of a month with these results. When they had begun to look for work, they had explained that they considered a monthly income of 1,000 baht the lowest they could accept. They didn't even manage to get that much.

The high unemployment is an influential factor in making sure that women tolerate the miserable conditions. Nǔu was very aware of this.

> They want to fire us, they want new people in. Some of those who come to apply they accept, so who will have to leave? Now those who want to stop work will be cut off. Those who do something wrong, they're cut, then.

At some workplaces women worked side by side with children — the competition for work was stiff.

Double work

Women had great difficulties in managing their double burden of work. Nǔu took an extra day off every now and then and used it to go to market and buy vegetables, fish or shrimps which she would then sit and work with. At one time she took several days off when her daughter was ill. At this time the daughter was living with her mother in Si Sa Ked. Nǔu's two sisters paid for her ticket there and back and she went up to see the child and took her to a doctor. She had to borrow the expenses for the doctor and medicine, and of course the factory docked her wages more than was justified.

> I went to visit my child ... because my daughter was not well, she did not eat rice for four days. Didn't eat rice, ate nothing ... and then she had fever, had jaundice. When I went to visit my child, I had money for the cost of transport, I had 400 baht. My older sister paid for the ticket. My older sister, Phîi Cîj. And the other one, the dressmaker, pitied me too. She paid for the journey back.
>
> My child was staying with mother. We went to see the doctor and so she got better.
>
> Then they cut out 240 baht [from the wage at the factory]. I spent money. I had a debt: 90 baht. My feen had no money, he gave his money for the motor-bike.

Tíg told me about her various workplaces. She had left work many times. When her mother (Sǎmphaw) became ill and went to the hospital she asked Tíg to come home and look after the household for her father and the sons.

> I had to quit again. Mother was not well; she had a stomach operation. When I first quit I lost my heart because I had to quit my work. I lost my heart, lost my heart ... My mother said that if I didn't quit, who would look after my brother? Who would cook rice? So I had to quit this job.
>
> When I got up in the morning I had to take rice to mother at the hospital.

She broke off her work when she got married, but took it up again when her husband was called up for military service. She broke it off when she gave birth to her son, and later when she became pregnant again. She broke it off again when her

brothers teased the little daughter and made her cry while Tíg was away.
She described breaking off her work at the time of the second pregnancy like this.

> My husband, he asked: What's happening? I said: I'm afraid I've got the morning sickness: when I see something I want to vomit.
> That day I wanted to go to work again. In the morning, Tùm [her son] was crying, and my husband carried the baby, so he could come with us, too. He said: Tíg, go back home . . . you don't have to work.
> Take the baby home again.
> I wanted to go to work, but he said: Go back go back.

She wanted to work, but she couldn't. "I fainted and fell over many times. I'd got the morning sickness."

While I lived in the slum Tíg looked for and found work again. She was pregnant for the third time: she had forgotten to have her Depo Provera injection.

The women had a difficult time because they were labouring under the double burden of work. It was hard going from day to day, when the washing piled up, and the husband complained about the food, and they had to find ways of having the children looked after. It was difficult, too, when there were births and pregnancies.

The women who worked for wages did various types of work. In the month of May two worked in domestic service, two at the market, two in factories, one in the harbour (loading), four in construction and three in other jobs (teacher, typist, potter). Payments in the different types of work differed. The potter who was highly qualified earned 5,600 baht a month, the teacher, the typist, those working in construction and the harbour, and those on the minimum wage earned about 1,600–1,700 baht a month and the rest in domestic service, on the market, in factories, but not on minimum wage earned about 800–1,000 baht a month or less.

The wages in domestic work and on the market were roughly the same as the wages in factories. The two exceptions were a young girl who earned only 250 baht a month and a woman who had worked in the French Embassy and had earned 2,500 baht a month. But for most of the women the payment for a month's work was about 700–800 in domestic work, factory work, or in a small stall on the market.

For women working in construction the payment depended mainly on the amount of work. This meant that women working in construction would sometimes try to build up a special relationship with one of the men recruiting labour, thus securing relatively stable employment.

The working hours were in principle a six-day week but women in domestic service usually had to be available 24 hours a day, the year around. An example is the woman who had worked for the French Embassy. She went to church on Sunday afternoon and for two hours on Wednesdays. She gave up the well-paid job because a new ambassador did not accept that she should go to church on Wednesdays too.

None of the women had any kind of special qualifications except the potter. Qualifications in Thailand are mostly acquired while people are at work. After some years a man can become a painter, a carpenter or a mechanic and get better paid and more stable jobs, if he has done the right kind of work long enough to get special qualifications.

The potter had learnt her trade in this way too, originally cleaning up in a workplace for pottery in a ministry. Now she is one of the best-qualified potters in Thailand, teaching potters from all over the country. Her qualifications taken into account, the wage was not that high. The teacher who worked at the same school for 10 years did not get more than the minimum wage, just like a typist who typed English letters.

None of the women got any insurance or social security or protection under the labour laws. None had any fringe-benefits. The women who had children to take care of had in most cases their mothers to look after the children while they were at work. Those who worked in domestic service left their children with a husband, a husband's mother or their own mother. The cook in the French Embassy could only with difficulty remember how many children she had. They were grown up now and had lived with their father up-country while she worked for the embassy (for twenty years).

Compared to the work of men in my slum women had much worse jobs. The payment was lower, the conditions of work worse, no women except the potter had any qualifications learned at the workplace and no women had access to welfare funds and the like.

5. The Secondary Labour Market

It has often been assumed that the harsh conditions of women in the Third World are caused by their lack of integration into the development process, into the modern sector, into capitalist relations of production. The women in my houses in the slum who had wage-labour were, however, quite firmly integrated into capitalist relations of production; but they were integrated into a secondary labour market.

A segmented labour market exists in all countries where industrial production goes on. This has been defined as follows.

> The primary market offers jobs which pose several of the following traits: high wages, good working conditions, employment stability and job security, equity and due process in the administration of work rules and chances of advancement . . . The secondary market has jobs which, relative to those in the primary sector, are decidedly less attractive. They tend to involve low wages, poor working conditions, considerable variability in employment, harsh and often arbitrary discipline and little opportunity to advance (Reich *et al.* 1973).

For all the women in my houses who had wage labour, except the potter, several of these traits characterized their jobs: the pay was poor compared to the men's as well as compared to the minimum wage; working conditions were very poor, most of the women changed jobs often and those who did not did not learn new skills or get such acknowledgment and they did not advance to higher positions. The discipline was indeed arbitrary and often gave rise to conflicts in which the women felt helpless.

In later years the movement of capital of Third World countries, and especially to South-East Asia, has become widespread. Much of it is going to Free Trade Zones, Export-producing Zones, and the like and more than a hundred such zones have been created in 55 countries. Besides, many Third World countries have, like Thailand, passed laws designed to attract foreign capital. Export-oriented industrialization is strongly advocated by international agencies such as the World Bank and the IMF (International Monetary Fund) and the main incentives for foreign investment are the absence of taxation and restrictions on investment and trade, of restrictions such as price control and rationing at the internal market and first and foremost a surplus of cheap labour, usually young and female.

The importance of the cheap, patient and clever female labourers is often enough stressed by local politicians, by directors of zones as well as by directors of firms which move production to South-East Asia. The point of utilizing women in production is that their wages are low while the productivity is comparable with productivity in USA, Germany or Japan. In fact the ratio between output and wages is approximately ten times higher in South-East Asia than in USA (AMPO 1977).

Not surprisingly, female workers make up 70–90% of the workforce in the Free Trade Zones in Mexico, Malaysia and South Korea for which figures are available (Thorbek, October 1982). In Thailand women make up slightly more than 50% of the industrial workforce in Greater Bangkok.

Capitalist firms, both local and transnational exploit the Asian woman's nimble fingers, patience and dexterity. This however, hardly explains why women's labour is especially cheap. Several economic arguments have been put forward; but most of these beg the question and are based on doubtful empirical grounds.

One of the more vulgar arguments is women's lack of physical strength. But considering the kind of physical work women often do, and considering the technology utilized in much work which makes physical strength inessential, this argument hardly applies. More convincing economic arguments for the great differences in wages in Third World countries in general have been summarized by Roberts (1978). He points out the close interconnections between the large-scale and the small-scale sectors of the urban economy, and the higher wages for permanent workers in the large-scale sector of the urban economy. The differences tend to increase in periods of economic expansion.

The main explanations for the higher wages of the permanent workforce in the large-scale sector compared to those of the temporary workers in both sectors and those of workers in the small-scale sector are a) the higher capital intensity in the large-scale sector, which makes higher wages less disadvantageous for capital invested here; b) the much higher productivity, which means that the rate of exploitation (ratio between output and wages) can be the same or higher in this sector despite higher wages; c) the interest among employers in a stable, responsible and loyal workforce; and lastly d) the much better possibilities for organization among workers in the large-scale sector and the resultant possibility of trade union control of the recruitment of workers and of mobility, if any, among them.

These explanations, however, hardly account for the wage differentials between men and women in my slum houses. It is difficult to compare wages between the genders, of course, since men and women mostly do different kinds of work. We can, however, compare men working in warehouses in the port area, where they did not work more with machinery than the women, and women in the transnational company which had registered with the Labour Department. (The result would be similar if workers from the port area who worked as carpenters or painters were taken as an example but the differences would be much greater if dock-workers were taken as the basis for comparison)

The only occupations where men and women did the same work were construction and loading. One couple worked with loading for the same wages but in construction the men had at least double the pay of women. If they did not have any special responsibility men would earn 100–150 baht a day, but two or three men in my houses worked as *hŭa nâas* and at least some of the others had higher earnings. Women earned 50–75 baht a day.

Although the factors mentioned by Roberts may contribute to the wage differentials, other factors have to be taken into account since women also earn much less than men in comparable jobs where capital intensity, stability of the workers, and the size of the workplace are roughly the same. But first of all the problem arises of why women are not employed in the types of jobs or the sectors which give the high remuneration. Even when the wage differentials are accepted as the point of departure, why do women end up in lower-paying jobs?

Table 5.1

Factory workers' incomes (baht per month)

	Men	Women
Regular	5–6,000	1,600–2,000
Temporary workers	2–3,000	400–1,000

It is at times claimed that women are used in branches of industry which work on an especially tight budget where competition is keen, while men are employed in bigger, expanding industries. This is however a doubtful proposition. Braverman has pointed out that in the USA "in all the most rapidly expanding sectors of the working class women make up the majority of workers" (Braverman 1974, p. 385). In South-East Asia the electronics industry is a case in point. It is very profitable — the growth of the US market for the industry as a whole is just over double the average of all industry in the USA, and in certain sections even higher (Hancock 1980). In the last ten years the expansion of the industry has gone overseas — the growth in workers employed has been nearly a quarter of a million, all of these employed overseas, so that approximately half the workforce now work in the USA (Green 1980) and half in South-East Asia and Mexico.

Even if the industry seems very healthy in terms of profits (although most unhealthy in terms of the worker's health (Occupational Safety and Health Administration in USA)) competition is keen and technical development rapid, so a new product can hardly be expected to last more than a couple of years (Hancock 1980). This is a major incentive to use living labour in the form of Asian women rather than technologizing the work process.

Women are not employed, it seems, by especially weak and non-competitive industries but on the contrary in those which expand the most. The kinds of industries women in my houses worked in — service, manufacturing and construction — are quite typically women's occupations, along with commerce. (More men than women work in construction, however (Raviwongse 1980, p. 13)). All these trades have a rising share in GNP (Donner 1978, p. 67–8).

As an explanation for women's working in the secondary labour market the argument that the trades where women work is smaller and more competitive than those where men work is hardly justifiable on empirical grounds. Besides it still begs the question of why women should be employed in these trades.

More to the point is the argument that women's qualifications are generally lower than men's. It has been claimed that this was the case in Europe and USA at the time of industrialization and that it is still the case in most countries and especially in the Third World. In the USA and in Western Europe men might have had better qualifications for some types of work handling machines when industrialization got underway. Hartman (1976) thinks that men's skills, acquired in former times when they worked as craftsmen, may have given them some qualifications which women did not usually possess, since women worked mainly as helpers and did not go through apprenticeships.

In Thailand explanations invoking inherited skills are very doubtful. Before the European penetration most craftsmen were slaves, the skills and the status of slaves were inherited in families. Their work was not much valued on account of their low social status and there existed nothing akin to the European crafts in the cities (Bowring 1957). In my houses I found one example of such inherited skills: the potter's father had made simple pots for daily use, she said, but she had loved to play with clay all through her childhood and had probably a form of inherited skill which made her learning process in the ministry much easier.

But since the handling of machinery is hardly something inherited from former times, and since craftsmen were few, had low status and hardly worked in occupations comparable to those in modern factories, such gender-specific inheritance of skills seems highly unlikely.

All the men in my houses had learned their special skills at the workplace. The exceptions were that some had driver's licences — five worked as drivers or chauffeurs. But aside from this, the dock workers, who had the really high incomes, the workers in factories in the port area and the construction workers had learned whatever they might have had of skills at the workplace. Apprenticeship is not an institutionalized phenomenon in Thailand (nor is it in most Third World countries) and no men in my houses had had vocational training.

Among the women, one had some further education — the typist. The potter learned her skills at the workplace and the teacher had only her own ten years at school. Some other unemployed young women had gone to school for ten years too and had high marks from school.

But even if it can be claimed that men have better qualifications for the higher paid jobs this does not seem to explain the inequalities between sexes. The question must be posed: why do women not learn the new skills or do not have their special qualifications acknowledged?

It seems hard to explain women's bad conditions and payment on the labour market from sheer economic reasons. Hartman has seen women's conditions as an effect of the interplay between capitalism and patriarchy, with each of these systems having its own dynamic and often reinforcing each other.

She defines patriarchy as a set of social relations based on men's control of women's labour, especially the labour of maintaining and producing human beings. Women are thus not only suppressed by the capitalist mode of production but also by men who have a material interest in the control of women's labour. They create a solidarity between themselves to maintain (or develop) control of resources, not only in the form of women's labour but also access to jobs (Hartman 1981).

In the last part of this chapter I will look more closely at men and women organizing at work, in order to show how the placement of women on a secondary labour market is maintained.

Organization

Legislation in Thailand stipulates equal payment for equal work (Young Yoon 1979) and gives special protection to women. Women (and children) are not allowed to work in hazardous jobs, such as cleaning machines in motion, nor in building jobs over ten metres above the ground, nor with circular saws. Women may not fabricate or transport explosives or highly inflammable material or work under ground level. Women under 18-years of age, who are married, are not allowed to work in bars or massage parlours. Women who have worked for at least 180 days at a workplace are entitled to 60 days' paid maternity leave (Raviwongse 1978, pp. 15-16).

From the point of view of the women in my slum houses this legislation is meaningless, since it has no practical effect on their work. Whether it is still utilized by the police or administrators in public agencies to extort bribes from companies which do not observe the laws, as Riggs described the process in 1966, is unknown to me; it may, however, have another effect on women's work by excluding them from some kinds of better paid work (such as driving lorries transporting petrol). This has been the case with similar legislation in Western Europe and the USA (Hartman 1976), as it seems to be so in Vietnam today (see Molander 1978).

Organization among workers is of major importance in ensuring observation of legislation on the labour market as well as payment and conditions of work. Trade Unions in Thailand have only for short periods of the workers' movement (as they are in some European countries). During the short periods where workers have actively organized themselves, women have done so as much and as successfully as men. The first strikes in Thailand happened shortly after the 1932 revolution among rickshaw coolies, workers in rice-mills, railway workers and dyers. The dyers were women and were the only group who won their dispute (Thompson 1967).

After the Second World War unions were organized. The most important union had connections with the Free Thai movement, but this union (CLU) was soon outlawed and other unions were created by the government. The government-sponsored unions were denied membership of the ICFTU (Thorbek 1973) because of the government's control of the unions and the unions' acceptance of laws prohibiting strikes until the local police had tried negotiations.

When the government was liberalized in 1956 (because the dictator was looking for new alliances among the liberals) unions were temporarily active again but they were very soon disciplined by the new dictator, Sarit. It was only in the period from 1973-7 that parliamentary rule was re-introduced and unions emerged again, along with labour unrest. In this period women workers both participated in strikes and demonstrations and organized themselves. Since the coup of October 1976, unions have once again been disciplined. Smooth and pleasant relations between unions and employers both exist and are expected in Thailand (Mabry 1979).

Women working in big textile companies are organized, and a survey recorded 25 textile unions (Raviwongse 1978, p. 19). Among the members 80% were women, among the presidents of the unions two were women, and among the staff in the unions 20% were women. I was interested in women's unionization and asked all the women who had worked at the harbour, in construction or in factories whether they were or had been in trade unions. It was a question I persisted in asking, in spite of many problems in being understood; these talks about unions were an interesting learning process for me.

At the start I found that the women were very uninformed on the issue of trade unions and organization at the workplaces. It was only as time went by and I got to know local conditions better that I realized the context in which the women saw the union question. This was their concrete experience of the trade union at the harbour, of which their husbands were members — or a more general knowledge of how trade unions in Thailand function.

The first problem was that the women quite simply did not understand what the word union meant. There are trade unions in Thailand: but only about 2% of workers are organized, and of these over half work in the public sector (*Investor*, 1982). My interpreter explained to me that the word union had an official ring to it in Thai, and in point of fact the four big labour amalgamations in Thailand work in close cooperation with the state and the police and the secret police are represented in their top positions (Brunn 1982).

Some women answered by explaining how the workforce is recruited and organized.

> No, we don't have any union. When a foreign ship comes into harbour and wants workers to hammer rust off, they go to the Port. The Port goes to a *thâw kèe* and he goes to *hǔa nâa*.

The background for this response is that the union the women know — the dock workers' — has as one of its most important everyday functions the job of providing new workers. Employment at the harbour thus depends on good connections with one or more of the leading unionists and the possession of an amount of money acceptable to him and on having cultivated his acquaintance for a period of time.

The woman's response, which at first surprised me by being so far from what I had expected, in fact showed excellent understanding of how the local union functioned. The women who understood the question better answered by saying, "No, no welfare at all", or, "No, it hasn't registered with the Labour Department" and then telling me about the expected advantages for the workers, if the firm registered. Unfortunately the most palpable change for Nǔu was the escalation of the pace of the work and stricter monitoring of absences. Finally, some women answered by saying that they had no union as they worked at a small concern.

Unions in Thailand are in fact organized branch by branch *and* regionally and those who work for small concerns have no chance to organize within the official system. For the women of the slum the unions were irrelevant. They felt them — rightly, I think — to be official bodies, whose only practical importance was that they recruited new workers instead of the firm itself, at any rate, they were felt to be something which only men at large workplaces, with strong leaders, could have.

Whatever the Thai trade unions' role in forwarding the interests of workers might be (and they seem to work mostly for fringe-benefits for workers employed, not for the betterment of workers as a class either in economic terms or in terms of civil rights) it seems that the effects for women in the slum were that they were kept out of the more remunerative jobs in the harbour by the unions' recruitment policy.

The women did not have any concept of unions as something not closely connected to the government or even as something relevant to themselves. Women did, however, react to the payment, the conditions and especially the disciplining at workplaces. Their possibilities of resistance were small indeed given the keen competition both between themselves and between women and children for jobs, and the lack of support from any groupings or organizations. I will give some examples of the kinds of protest which the women told me about.

Resistance among the women

It gave the women strength that they always looked for jobs together, either with a sister, a friend or a neighbour. It was not always the case that they both got a job; but they had someone to discuss conditions with and just the presence of a sister or a friend at an interview with an employer or *hǔa nâa* felt good.

In some cases a woman got a job and could help a friend later. Young women found the very thought of a workplace with many people, where they didn't know anyone, unpleasant. It was crucial for them to have someone with whom they could share experiences. Nǔu told me about a former job where she had worked for a meagre wage with a lot of unpaid overtime. But a combination of the facts that the owner did not criticize her or scold her and that her two sisters worked at the same company meant that she liked the job.

Tíg complained when things did not work. When her husband-to-be asked a friend to introduce him to Tíg the friend said, according to her, "I don't like her . . . this woman . . . she has a big mouth, she cannot find any boy-friend, she curses a lot, she plays cards."

Tíg explained about her cursing him.

> He went to repair the machine when the machine was out of action. He was a mechanic. So I called on him to come. He opened it up, but he didn't put lubricating oil in, and when he opened it it made a noise, a very loud noise.
> I was excited, I said:
> To employ you is to lose money: you don't do anything, you always hide and sleep.
> Then, working at night, those mechanics often looked at the machine. But he hid so he could sleep. Then I didn't know where to find him: when I found him, I beat him.
> Then he said: oh, why is this machine always out of action? Then we were quarrelling, but he was not serious. He liked my friend too.

Tĭm and Khĭaw were involved in a case where a *hǔa nâa* in the building trade would not pay their wages when the work was done. Khĭaw, who was experiencing this for the first time, returned home, and her mother went for three weeks in a row to the *hǔa nâa* (who lived more than an hour by public transport from the slum) before she got the wages.

Tǐm, on the other hand, sat down outside his house. She waited there all night; she wanted her wages, and she got them in the morning.

The most common reaction among the women, when things went wrong, was to give in notice and leave the job, for example when faced with compulsory extra work or broken agreements with a *hǔa nâa*.

Pùu and Tíg, however, tried to organize a collective bargaining situation. They got jobs cleaning squids. In the transnational company they were offered a piecework rate of three baht per kilo of cleaned squid bodies (which gave a wage of about half the minimum wage), but when payday came they got only half of this. Their reaction was to discuss the affair with the other new employees, 20 workers in all. They agreed what to do and went to the *hǔa nâa*. Tíg told me,

> The workers asked this: May we ask for three baht? When we started to work, why did you say you would give us three baht? And when we have done the work already, when everything is finished, when it is time to get the money, why are you giving us only six satang, only six satang?
>
> We said this, but Phîi Daa said she wouldn't give to us. Then she said: Hey, those that want to work, go and work: those that don't, go back home.

Eight of the twenty workers went home, and Tíg and Pùu said that the others were only children who were on their summer holiday. Some had run away from home to work. They had nowhere to go.

Tíg was furious at this forewoman. "Daa" is a nickname, it is the name of an insect, a water-bug, and is used for pimps, Tíg told me,

> The boss, Daa — a woman — this Phîi Daa, she said to me: You must get it clean. If it isn't clean, I'll have you wash it again.
>
> The liar! I did get it clean! I thought that she had employed me, so I had to do my best for her. If I had known she would give me what she did, I'd have sliced them all up. It's true, I'd have sliced them all.

Of all the women, Tíg was the one with the longest experience of factory work: with interruptions, she had worked in different factories for twelve years. She was the only one of the women who had experienced a strike attempt, characteristically enough before the October 1976 coup, under parliamentary rule. Tíg said,

> There was a leader of the strike, a man. He was working in the repairs section and then he came to ask everyone to strike. He wanted us to strike. To strike for higher wages and for money for clothes, clothes which he called form [uniform]. Then we talked about this all over the factory, but the talk had not reached the ears of the *thâw kèe* yet, it had not reached the ears of the masters. Then there was a woman, a woman from Isan [the North-east, mainly Laotian speaking region]. She had just arrived, looking for work. She went to ask the boss, the *thâw kèe* man.
>
> The leader of the strike had come to her too, to ask her to join in the strike.

Then this woman did not know the word strike and so she went to ask about the meaning of the word, she went to ask the *thâw kèe* man: What is the meaning of the word strike?
That man asked her: Who is going to strike?
This Isan woman then pointed to the man who persuaded us to strike.
The *thâw kèe* man then asked her: When are you going to strike?
So she told him: This next morning (tomorrow). The leader of the strike was going to distribute a paper, a strike paper. He was going to distribute it to the workers when they arrived at the factory. He would wait in front of the *soi* [small road] until all the workers were coming in to work. They had already typed the paper. They had written: In this factory there is no nothing: no welfare, no nothing. The workers have worked for 5–6 years and the payment has not been raised. In one year it has been raised 10 baht, that is all, and it took a long time before they raised it.
There were many sections, and both men and women, involved.
Then the *thâw kèe* told his subordinates to come at about 8 o'clock in the morning, to come and meet here . . . Inside there were more than 300 people . . . every section . . . come to meet in the middle of the lawn. They told us to stand there and listen. I also went there to stand and listen with them, too. Then the manager, he brought this man who had persuaded us to strike, brought him out in front of all the employees . . . he was exposing him to shame . . . the *thâw kèe* of the factory, right . . . then they came to call for us but no one knew . . . just meet in front of this lawn, something more than 300 people . . . stood listening to him.
Then he cursed: You know this?
This man is no good. He said this: he persuaded all of you to strike right? . . . if you all leave the factory, where will you work?
Like this, he said it, said: The company doesn't want this man . . .
But the workers sympathized with him, sympathized with the man who was dismissed. He was good. Afterwards, then we sat cursing the woman who knew nothing: You stupid son of a bitch!
She said she didn't know, she said this.
We said: You didn't know? Then why did you have to ask *him*?

The women of the slum were not compliant workers, if this is taken to mean that they accepted their conditions without protest. It is possible that the young women acted compliantly, humbly and politely in front of employers, directors, directors' wives and daughters and perhaps *hǔa nâas*. It is probably true in many cases. But it is quite certain that this was not an expression of acceptance of the miserable conditions. At home in the slum they told me about injustice, broken agreements and bad treatment. They felt that they were good at their work, did their best to do right by the person who had employed them, and felt that they also had a right to treatment as human beings.
Women from the slum reacted against their miserable conditions. The difficulties in organizing can be seen from Tìg's experiences. The high unemployment and the competition with children for jobs in one case forced down the wage to a quarter of

the minimum wage and the attempt at collective bargaining was spoiled by the children's acceptance of this payment. In the other case the strike was prematurely revealed by the woman who did not know the word strike and asked the wrong person. Since women's organizing gets no support from trade unions or groups it can hardly compete with men's trade unions, which are tacitly supported by government.

When it comes to access to work, and especially work which gives a reasonable wage, men's traditions and their organization into informal groups are of considerable importance. Traditionally, Thai society has been structured to a high degree, round patron–client relationships (Rabibhadana 1969). In villages upcountry most organizing is done by men — that is, in work such as building dykes or in school and temple committees, it is men who are elected village leaders. Thus Thai society has long traditions for men's organizing themselves, bargaining for power or economic gain in all layers of society.

The tradition where a man — a patron — builds up a group of dependants, a group of clients, and where other men know the necessity of joining a patron to achieve some sort of benefit, still works in everyday life. The *thâw kèe–hǔa nâa* organization is an example of such a system, and most recruiting of labour in construction, and to some extent at the harbour, is done in this way. How far the system permeates the trade union recruitment of permanent workers for the harbour I do not know. The principle is that a company which wants work done, for instance wants to get a ship cleaned or a house or motorway built, asks a *thâw kèe* to deliver a specified quantity of labour. The *thâw kèe* asks his *hǔa nâas* each to deliver smaller quantities, and these *hǔa nâas* may go on to others, who go on to others until one of the small *hǔa nâas* in the slum promises to supply, for instance, ten labourers.

The main necessity for a man wanting work is, then, to have as good personal relationships with other workers and superiors as possible. A man will not usually apply for a job, but will wait for an offer. To seek out work for oneself means a drop in prestige and a prejudice against a man's qualifications. In such cases the payment will often be lower (see Rabibhadana 1980 for a similar account). Qualifications and wages are thus determined by a person's ability to avoid showing that a job is needed. Whether this is so, is evaluated by the next-highest worker/*hǔa nâa* in the system. A *hǔa nâa* and his workers will also often constitute a convivial group by drinking and going out together.

This system had extremely bad consequences for the women. No one knew how large a part of the wage sum a *hǔa nâa* took for himself. A *hǔa nâa* in my houses, when I asked him about his income, answered as he sat and drank with seven of his workers, "I earn so much that I don't want to say." Another said, "We're all poor; we do the same work. We share alike."

In some cases problems can arise, as in Khǐaw's and Tǐm's case, where they could not get the money they had earned from the *hǔa nâa*. These problems may arise for men too. But for women this way of evaluating qualifications and the price and quantity of work is disastrous. Women do not get any qualifications acknowledged, and no women in mixed workplaces were *hǔa nâas*.

Men's informal groups and organization tend to devalue women's work both in terms of qualifications and in terms of payment. The informal interaction of men between a small patron — the *hǔa nâa* — and his group of dependants, is beyond the reach of women, who do not join in the same pastimes and cannot indulge in drinking and talking at night time without destroying their reputations as women or provoking their husbands' or father's jealousy.

The chances for women to break through this system were seen in terms of a woman establishing a special relationship with a man of importance at the workplace. Such an especially good relationship could be, but need not necessarily be, based on a sexual relationship. If a woman found a protector, as he was called, she could get more work, she would often get relatively easy work, and she would be paid a higher wage. She would, practically speaking, have no opportunity to compete on an equal basis with the men, because it was men who assessed work and qualifications. Her only chance of finding a stable and reasonably paid job would be to establish special connections with a protector.

Women in Thailand work for wages. They are sought out by industry, especially while they are young, and there is no prejudice against women working for wages or incomes. Still, they are much worse paid than men, a fact which is only partly explained by pure economics.

Part of the explanation is the common interest shared by most men and capitalist enterprises in favouring men on the labour market. Capital wants to exploit the possibility of very cheap labour by employing women; men themselves want to get as high earnings as possible. Women protest about their bad conditions, but it seems that men both have a better basis for organization in their traditional roles and tacit support from government as far as trade union organizing is concerned. They have succeeded in monopolizing the most remunerative jobs and in upvaluing their own and devaluing women's qualifications and access to work through informal organization.

Behind the conditions for women on the labour market lies a belief shared by capitalist enterprises, the state and men who are workers, a belief that the family and the work of maintaining and creating human beings are the responsibility of women. Women working for wages thus have a double burden of work: catering for men and the children at home, and working for wages. This double burden creates extreme difficulties for women, and society in the East and the West adds insult to injury by treating women much worse than men, when they work for wages, because they have to serve the men at home too.

6. Women without Work

About half the women in the slum houses did not have a job. Some of these did something to earn an income: two washed plastic, two earned money by producing and selling food, and two by loaning out money for interest. But most did little or nothing to earn money.

Those who did not work for an income were in most cases women whose husbands earned a good wage and gave them money for the necessities of the family. But some of them were among the poorest in my slum houses, such as, Cíab, who was starving and too weak to work, or Khǐaw's mother, who was very tired and depressed, and two other women (Bunryang and Nípapheen) who were very depressed and had lost all hope of changes in the future. The two who washed plastic were in great need and did not have other resources. Bàd was one of the two women who found and washed plastic.

She was a minor wife and even though the husband stayed in her hut most of the time, he did not give her money. In actual fact, he earned very little. He sometimes helped her to wash plastic, sometimes looked after their child (seven-years-old) and often he read newspapers and books (the only person outside the school I saw reading a book).

Bàd thus had to earn money for herself and her family. In the beginning she found and washed plastic. This was dirty and unpleasant work. She went to the rubbish dump in Samrong and here she found plastic. This was the worst part of the work — it was ill-smelling, hot, and despised. She did this for four days a week. Afterwards she washed the plastic, and this was much more pleasant. The water was cool; several women, children and a few men worked near each other.

The plastic was then sold to a Chinese for about seven baht a kilo. Bàd claimed she earned 30–35 baht a day if she worked hard. Her husband earned much less, since he was not good at finding the plastic. The plastic is brought to the small factory owned by the Chinese. Here it is processed into small black pieces with heat and chemical baths, and then sold to a factory which produces sandals which sell for 10 baht at the market.

Bàd had to earn money — but she did not go on with washing plastic if other opportunities arose. In May she got a job at the market selling food for a woman and she worked there for a month. She then earned 1,000 baht but working hours were longer. When the job finished she returned to washing plastic, hoping something better would turn up.

Among the women who did not have a job four were self-employed. They were all middle-aged and married, and three of them lived together with, or near, grown-up children and grandchildren. Two produced and sold food. One — Sǐi — took care of her grandchildren all the time and also had a large family to care for (a husband and one to three sons). She made sweets (rice-scones) and roasted bananas, and if she had some money she bought finished sweets at the market and sold them in the slum. She both produced and sold her commodities seated on her platform (but went to market very early), and the smaller children could play around her or under the house. She earned 30 baht a day, she said. Besides this, part of what she produced was eaten by her children and grandchildren.

Khìad established a small restaurant. She invested much more than Sǐi, she had a piece of plastic for a shade, a table, a bench and two stools to sit on, a bench for the hot plates, plenty of pots and pans and a table for displaying her food. She worked very hard, at least 12 hours a day (a grown-up daughter helped to look after the household). She earned more than 100 baht a day, she said, plus the food for her (big) family.

Two other women earned an income by lending out money. One, Chalǔaj, had a big family, and her grown-up children and a son-in-law gave their earnings to her — getting board and lodgings in return and bargaining for money for beer and entertainment. The other had a husband who earned quite a lot. She only had one grown-up brother of the husband living with her as a dependant and she had some savings in a bank from former times.

Chalǔaj lent money to friends free of interest, to others she lent money against a surety (a TV, a ring) at 10% interest, without a surety for 20% *a week*. Chalǔaj's profit was pooled with the many other small incomes in her family, while Deeng's was mostly saved for future expenditure.

Besides these four women, many others worked at income-earning activities at more scattered intervals. Such activities were washing clothes (laundry), washing and finding plastic, folding paperbacks and selling these to shops, making mobiles from plastic straws, running lotteries, buying ice-cream or soft drinks at the market and selling them in the slum (only women who had a fridge), making Thai iced coffee and selling it in small plastic bags, repairing or doing embroidery for neighbours or embroidering blouses and knitting socks for factories.

These were all income-earning activities which went on in my 24 houses, although very intermittently. In other parts of the slum there were small shops, charcoal-burning and the making of small sticks to be used to hold banana leaves together around cakes and the like.

The competition between different women was keen, and the incomes were low and unstable unless much money and work were invested in the business. An example is Sǎmphaw's folding of paper packs. She brought a big heap of old papers and sat for a day sorting them and gluing the smaller pieces together. In the evening she produced a small table approximately 30 centimetres above the ground where she could sit on the floor stretching her legs under the table while working.

For ten days she sat folding the paper into packs and gluing them, and then sold them all to a shop, getting 150 baht for them.

She worked fairly continuously for ten days and only earned 15 baht a day. She did not find it worthwhile and stopped it. The reason she had started the work was her debt. She had drawn a pot in the loan game at high interest and had to get the money to pay it back. Shortly after, however, she and her husband won a small prize in the official lottery, and they could pay both her interest and get their TV home from the pawnshop. So she did not go on with this work.

Folding paper packs or washing plastic was the kind of activity women turned to when they were in real and often acute need of money. Besides Bàd another woman found and washed plastic. The reason she started this work was a debt at 20% interest per week. To get the money for the interest she started washing plastic, and at the same time she sent a letter to her daughter who lived in Singapore, asking her son-in-law for help. Similarly, Tìm did laundering for a few days when it was raining and the work on building sites was stopped because of the weather.

Other kinds of activities gave such a small remuneration that the women did not think of them as work at all. These were forms of outwork: embroidering blouses and knitting socks, work which the Prateep Foundation obtained and distributed in the slum. The embroidery of one blouse was paid at the same rate of five baht and only the most skilled woman could by continuous work make nearly two in one day. This was not considered a reasonable income and she and other young women only did it now and then while they sat chatting together. But even when Pùu was in the worst distress she did not think of embroidering as a worthwhile income-generating thing to do.

More remunerative was the lottery, which three middle-aged women in my houses ran now and then. They found high quality fruit at the market or produced something really tasty. Then they folded pieces of paper and put numbers from 1 to 50 on and sold these for five baht each. The prize would be shown before selling the lots and afterwards a small child drew the winner. In this way a woman could earn approximately 150 baht in a few hours. But competition was keen, of course, and it could only be done at long intervals.

Most of these activities were normal household chores which were extended to the market sphere and done for money. Some were done as help to friends and neighbours and paid or not depending on the relationship. A few depended on patience and learned dexterity (e.g. folding paper packs). Since the qualifications of the women did not differ much, and since everybody wanted to seize opportunities for earning some money, competition in the slum was keen. Only those who could invest something, work hard and continuously and had a social network could earn a reasonable income.

The social network was important since it was usually friends or acquaintances who bought things. In the case of the lottery and other food production the reputation of the woman in question meant a lot for the business. For the moneylenders their security for getting back the loan (if lent without surety) was their knowledge of the borrowers' reliability, and their ability to influence opinion about the borrower in the slum.

In my houses those who worked continuously as self-employed women were all middle-aged. Young women would explain that they could not run a lottery, or they could not sell something because they were shy. It seems that the social network built up through the years and the greater self-confidence among rather older women was of importance. In other parts of the slum younger women worked in small shops and the like, as did some men. In most cases, however, they were part of a family business: the whole family worked together or the mother and daughter worked together or perhaps the mother and son. In my houses family labour was not exploited. A son, a daughter, more rarely a husband might help the mother in the business, but the help was casual: it could not be expected or counted upon.

Since women's capacity to work is heavily influenced by their responsibility for children, it is often assumed that they work for wages when young before marriage, and after marriage and having children change to one or another kind of extended household activity, at least while the children are below school age. (Tilly 1978 and Scott 1978 have shown this to be the case for women in England and France in the period of industrialization.)

This was however not the case for the women living in my 24 houses. If we divide them into young women without children, young mothers with children and middle-aged women, they had the income-earning work shown in this table.

Table 6.1
Women's incomes

Age/Children	Waged	Self-employed	Washing plastic	No income-earning work
Over 17/None	5	0	0	3
Over 17 under 35/ small children or pregnant	7	0	1	9
Over 35/None	2	4	1	6

As can be seen, young women had wage-earning work if they could find it. Young mothers had either wage-earning work or no income-earning work at all (one washing plastic, alternating with wage-earning work) and middle-aged women were mostly self-employed if they had to earn money. The women who did a bit to earn something at long intervals (lottery, folding and so on) were mostly middle-aged too.

It is sometimes assumed that subsistence production goes on in the slums. This was not the case in my houses. A young girl had ducks. She had bought some eggs and heard the picking inside the shells, so decided to feed them up. She did not know what to do with the ducks and considered them pets. The eggs were not collected: probably the rats ate them. Another woman raised roosters, but that was for cock-fighting. Outside my area a man kept pigs and some others kept cows, but all the animals, if not pets or wild, were raised for sale.

Similarly a few trees grew and tamarinds were of course taken and eaten, mostly by children. Some women had potted plants whose leaves could be eaten as spices. But this kind of activity was not widespread, in fact a European housewife will generally practise more subsistence production than the people in the slum did.

The links between women in the slum and their families up-country were maintained, but they were not exploited commercially. When a woman visited family up-country, gifts would often be given, and the woman would bring rice, fruits or vegetables back to the slum. These were not sold, but either consumed by the family or given as gifts to friends in the area.

Nor did the women from the slum usually make use of this opportunity to buy cheap fruit and sell it in the city. In one case two women went up-country to buy cheap mangoes in the season, but these were not sold but given as gifts to friends. Only in one case did a woman sell things from up-country. This was Dam, who, with a friend from the village, brought a vanload of ducks which were sold to a merchant at the Chinese New Year, and who sold silk in Bangkok, woven in her village (at the same price as in the village).

Thus some women were self-employed (food and money-lending) and, if they had investments to make, were able to work continuously, and were a part of social networks or had some standing in the area, earning incomes comparable to those from wage-labour. Usually they would feed their family on their products and incomes, and whatever remained was in principle their own money.

Other women worked indirectly for industry (washing plastic, embroidery) and the plastic washers could earn incomes comparable to wage-workers; but the work was despised and was only done by women in great distress. The other kinds of indirect work for industry were so badly paid nobody considered them income-earning work. Lastly, some women earned a bit by working for neighbours (laundry for teachers, repairs). This was usually badly paid too.

Many women did not do any income-earning work or did so to such a small extent that it is hardly worth mentioning. The choices of women in the slum were mainly determined by their access or lack of access to work for wages. I would argue that the main reason for the clustering of women in self-employment and in outwork is likewise their more limited access to wage-earning work compared to men. Besides the lack of alternatives keenly felt by women, they had certain special qualifications compared to men in their household work. They were able to prepare food and sweets and were probably accustomed in the countryside to the administration of the family income. They had great reserves of patience, and in the case of middle-aged women, a broader social network in the slum.

Still, self-employment and outwork appeared to demand as much time and effort as wage-earning work if the income was to be comparable. The reason for women's clustering in this kind of work is not therefore its compatibility with household work and the care of small children.

In the analysis of the economy and the labour market in Third World countries several distinctions have been made. Roberts (1978) has pointed out the interdependence between the small-scale sector and the large-scale sector. The links can take the form of sub-contracting and outwork, or of credit and standing agreements on the sale of output and services. Such work also went on in England at the beginning of industrialization; but if we compare this state of affairs with the situation today in Third World countries, two main differences are the great disparity in productivity between the small- and large-scale sectors and the existence of a centralized state in Third World countries today. The state in the Third World countries intervenes in the economy by legislation on the labour market and in other respects. Whereas the large, often foreign-owned, companies have to observe this legislation, the enterprises in the small-scale sector can usually avoid this, and in this way they can be competitive even when their much lower productivity is taken into account.

> The small scale sector of the urban economy survives in the interstices of state regulation. Small scale sector enterprises make a profit, partly because they lie outside direct state regulation (Roberts 1978, p. 133).

The concept of the formal and informal sectors is utilized in small-scale studies in an IDS (Institute of Development Studies) Bulletin (vol. 12, no. 3) and here the informal sector is defined as having the following characteristics: a) non-permanence and casualness; b) lack of company and/or government regulations; c) taking place in small-scale and less capitalized establishments, relying on household labour (Heizer 1981, p. 3).

This definition is difficult to use as its contains several elements. One or more of these corresponded with the jobs all my women did (with the exception of the potter). All three (or four) criteria were not necessarily found interconnected. In construction and with the transnational firm, for example, there was a high organic composition of capital; with the transnational firm there were company regulations, but the laws of the land were not observed and there was a strong element of non-permanence and casualness.

Both these concepts, of large-scale and small-scale sectors, and of the formal/informal sector, are hard to apply to the empirical material. In a sense the simple fact that the point of departure for this study is slum-dwelling could be used to argue that all people in my slum houses were part of an informal or small-scale sector. But on the other hand several of the men had jobs in the large-scale or formal sector and some of the women worked in enterprises which used high-level technology (in construction). They built motorways or high-rise buildings in the centre of the city and could hardly be seen as left out of the formal or large-scale sector.

The distinction between the two sectors of the economy has been developed in discussions of the functions for capital accumulation of the small-scale sector. It has been argued that cheaper products can be produced through sub-contracting to firms not forced to observe the legislation and able to pay lower wages, and this seems highly probable as far as the work going on in my houses was concerned. The possible drawback with this way of organizing work is the decrease in the control of the work process, resulting in a bad or unstable supply of products/raw materials. This was what the Chinese buyer of plastic complained of, and the same problem must arise with outwork since the women's inclination to work is mainly the result of their lack of alternatives.

It has also been argued that the informal sector keeps down wages by providing cheap goods or by providing a possible way for women to earn something, thus enabling enterprises to pay less than a family wage to men. But as Moser and Young (1981) have argued, the last argument is doubtful since men's wages are only in a few cases enough to cover a whole family's expenses.

The argument that the informal sector keeps wages low by providing cheap commodities, thus lowering the cost of living for workers, has been much discussed in Thailand in the sense that one major argument for the rice premium is the low wages thus made possible — an advantage both because it attracts foreign investment and decreases state expenditure on salaries.

Besides a stable food supply, accommodation is probably one of the most important items of expenditure for workers and lower paid employees of the state. The problem with keeping down prices by some sort of government action is, however, that there is usually a clash of interests between the government's wish to keep down the prices of the more important items of expenditure for workers and the interest of those producing (or controlling) those items in maintaining higher prices.

In the case of the rice policy, this problem was initially partly solved because the policy was forced on the government by the Allies during the war (especially Great Britain), and partly because the rice millers, whose profits were thus cut down, were mostly of Chinese origin and had very little political influence at that time (Skinner 1958). Later oligopoly in the trade has made it possible for the big traders to make a profit despite the premium and the peasants/farmers who pay the price have very little if any political power.

In the case of housing a struggle is going on at the moment; even if government agencies such as the NHA advocate a solution which keeps housing cheap, the interest of landowners (private or public) in exploiting rising land values is strong, probably much stronger than any vague intention to keep down workers' expenses.

The possible functions of the informal sector for capital accumulation seem mainly to be connected with sub-contracting and less with the production of cheaper goods for consumption among workers. The main reason for the existence of this sector seems to be the lack of other opportunities to earn an income, and this lack of opportunities is decidedly greater for women than for men, and again for older than for younger women.

An informal work sector outside the legislation of the country is also growing up in Western Europe today, produced by the growing economic crisis and unemployment. Work in the informal sector is not necessarily easy to do at the same time as taking care of a family, and the clustering of women in this kind of work seems mainly to be explicable in terms of their more limited access to wage-earning work.

7. Prostitution

The self-employed women in the slum extended services normally free from the family sphere to the market, where they could be sold. In my houses it was first and foremost the production of food and the administration of money which became saleable commodities in this way. However, two women were former prostitutes and one woman in a house just outside my area worked from the slum as a prostitute and another woman was considering it.

The sale of sexual services by women illustrates the interplay between women's difficult economic situation, their economic dependence on men, their sexual subjugation and the social definition of women's sexuality. These factors are mutually reinforcing. Almost all women in the slum were economically and socially dependent on men and on the sexual services they provided for men. This was true whether they were wives or minor wives; if they were, as often, dependent on a protector in the economic sphere, or if they were prostitutes.

The problems raised by women's economic dependence on men were illustrated by their deliberations about escaping from their men. Sămphaw gave this idea serious thought after a major fight with her man, where she had received serious bruises on the face, the thigh and the legs. She did not see work as a realistic alternative. Given her daughter's experiences and her own relatively weakened physical capacity this was a pragmatic enough attitude. She considered performing in the Likee plays, as she had done when she was young, but was aware that her chances, at the age of forty, were now small. It would also require investment in costumes and make-up, and was an insecure career; but also a tempting option, she thought, because of the freer, more varied and more amusing life. Her husband had said that no matter where she ran off to he would find her and bring her back. She also considered becoming a nun, but shied away from giving up her femininity — symbolized by the cropping of the hair — and from the rather hard and restrictive work. She could see no realistic choices open to her.

A younger woman, Ùbon, was thinking along similar lines and wondered whether she should become a prostitute and go to Pattaya to work. She had discussed it with women who had worked in Pattaya before and was drawn by the high incomes and gifts, and Bunryang had assured her that she was young and pretty enough. She had also talked to her mother and to Àat's and Praanii's mother about it and both of them had advised against it. But when her husband scolded and threatened her she would think about it again.

Women's Work for Incomes

The two women who were former prostitutes both said that they had run away. Bunryang had run away from her husband who had many minor wives, which made her very angry; she was perhaps also glad to escape from her life as a stay-at-home housewife and from taking care of children, which she was very tired of. Cíab had run away from her in-laws: her husband was a soldier, deserted, went to prison and became a soldier again; deserted again and went to prison; the process kept repeating itself. In the end he found a solution by becoming a monk and Cíab was left completely on her own again.

The difficult economic conditions drove women to prostitution. Cíab is an extreme example: she came from north-east Thailand, and told me about conditions there. She had seven younger sisters and brothers and several relatives who worked as agricultural labourers and in construction work (there was a US-airbase and road-building not far from her village). Despite an irrigation system the ricefields were often flooded (more than, and at other times than, they should have been).

The family was paid for the work in the ricefields with rice, but not enough; so they frequently had to borrow rice from the landowner for their own use. Debt and interest aggravated their poverty. Cíab described the situation of starving peasants.

> One fish, unsalty and delicious, that we find ourselves. Then we go and sell it to buy this salty Tu fish.
>
> So we go and sell our delicious fish; we get as much as 20 baht for one delicious fish: one fish weighs many kilos. And so we don't eat the delicious fish, right? We enclose them in a container, and soon we go to the market, then we go and sell them to people.
>
> And then we buy salted fish, so we can come back and eat them with rice, and then we go and catch fish again. Just think! Instead of eating the fish we find, that we catch ourselves . . . Well, starving people . . . 10, 11, 12 persons and two small fish. And then only two pieces per person, just tiny little pieces like this, and we eat one bite, two bites and it's finished.
>
> Then I just wonder why we have to starve like this, why we have to be poor, why we can't eat the good food, but have to go and sell it, and we get no good food to eat. I think about this . . . If we get the delicious fish, if we eat it, then we don't have rice. Will we be filled in the stomach then? We must buy rice; we must sell the delicious fish so that we have money to buy rice to cook.

When Cíab went to Bangkok, it was with a broker. Today there is much talk of brokers buying children in the provinces, but Cíab's parents actually paid her (the broker).

> Then I come to Bangkok. I come, and then I have no chance of going back. Difficult, very difficult . . . Then I have this boss and face [broker]. She takes me to find work, like this. We gave her money at our house, we gave her 200 and then she took me to Bangkok: everything was finished already.

Cíab, who says she was 10–14 years old at this time, stayed in Bangkok and was put to work at a little stall in the market — "I went to work to wash bowls and plates." Cíab's ideas about figures are still rather vague and imprecise, but she earned so little that a whole month's pay was docked if she accidentally broke a plate, she says. In practice she was working for her board and lodging.

She met her *feen*[1] at the stall: they didn't marry, but she moved in with him, and bore a child.

> I went and stayed at the house of my *feen*, I went and stayed with the father and mother of my *feen* . . . He was still a soldier, he was still a soldier then. Money, gold, I didn't have any then. Then I worked, I did work in the orchard, in his father's and mother's orchard. I lived and ate with his mother . . . I didn't have to use any money. My *feen* didn't have any money to give me, he was still a soldier.
>
> Well, if I needed money I went and asked his mother for 10 baht, 20 baht . . . It's not a body of my own [I'm not independent].
>
> I went to other people's orchards, then I cut grass in other's orchards too . . . Then I could get money, then I had to give it all to his mother.

Cíab bore the child, and the *feen* still alternated between being a soldier and being in prison because he deserted. She and the *feen* fell out: she was thoroughly tired of living with his parents, and could see no prospect of his coming back home again.

> If I stayed with my *feen's* mother, I would be in terrible difficulties. Firewood, just full of firewood, I carried firewood every day. And then this *feen*, he made my heart hurt. I tried not to run away from him, I wanted to bear it and stay. Oh, but to stay with my *feen's* mother, I couldn't bear it. I didn't have a *feen*, why should I let them use me? And then my child fell in the water and died . . . So I escaped, ran away from him, escaped to go and find money [in prostitution].

Cíab was still only a half-grown child. Their own child drowned while her in-laws were taking care of it, and her *feen* went to Surin to tell her and her parents. However, she herself was still in Bangkok. When her *feen* told her parents about it, he said that Cíab's child had fallen in the water and died. Cíab's father believed that it was Cíab who had drowned. She said, "Father thought that I didn't have a child yet. Then my father thought that I had fallen in the water and died."

Cíab's *feen* now became a monk — partly to avoid the army, partly as penance for the child's death, to wash off the sin for the child. Cíab, who was at this point hardly more than sixteen, began to work as a prostitute. She had worked hard since she had come to Bangkok and barely earned her own board and lodging. She was completely defenceless, almost ignorant of figures, unused to money and without any knowledge of big city life.

Her first customer, whom she met at a restaurant, gave her 1,000 baht for a night plus food and drink. For Cíab as a young girl it must have seemed overwhelming riches. "I wanted to use this money. But still I didn't have a chance to use all the money yet because I was not used to spending money." For Cíab her poverty played a crucial role, but it was aggravated by her youth and helplessness. For her own part, she saw prostitution as the only escape route from her *feen* and life with her in-laws.

For other women with more experience, too, prostitution and the income it provides must appear a viable option. By working hard every day in a factory or at the market they can earn the same as they can get, with luck, for one night with a foreigner. Life as a prostitute was, however, hard enough in practice. Neither Cíab nor Bunryang had been self-employed: Bunryang had worked from a bar and the owner had taken 100 baht when she left it for an evening. Cíab had been badly exploited by a pimp. She told me about her experiences.

> Then he [her *feen*] went to be ordained. He was going to be a monk for many years . . . Then I had to go and find money to use. And then I went . . . went up onto the ship and then I had a child with a *faràng* [Westerner].

When Cíab left her *feen* she went to a bar, sat down at a table, ordered a little food, and a *faràng* came, invited her up to dance and took her with him to his ship when he had to go on duty. She did not know whether he would give her anything. "Then we went to the ship, then I went and got money. I still didn't put my heart to him [trust him to give her money]. I wanted to try, just for one day."

When they had slept together he gave her 1,000 baht and informed her that she was to come again at one o'clock the next night.

Cíab was afraid of losing the money. When she came the next night there were many women, "Oh, a lot of women went up to the ship. They had seen me the night before so they know I had money."

She was also afraid of falling into the clutches of a pimp.

> There was a person, a Thai person. He wanted to trap me. He wanted to get us to stay in his group, stay under his supervision. These people recognized a newcomer. I didn't accept having anyone to supervise me, then I wouldn't have any means.

At first Cíab had no possessions apart from the clothes she was wearing. She washed them (and herself) in the river or on a ship. She slept on the ships with the customers, on the river bank (the Port had as yet done little building) and sometimes in one of the other prostitutes' rooms.

> I had to depend on coming to sit and eat rice and curry [in a food-shop]. I had no house at all. I washed clothes on the ship, dried them and ironed them on board ship, the same piece of cloth all the time. I stayed and slept on the ship for one period, then I got dizzy. When I came ashore I had no place to stay.

After some time she came back to one of her *feen*'s relatives, an elderly single woman. She hoped to meet her *feen* there.

> I went to the house of Mother Kèe, but then my *feen* had been ordained already, a long time before. I waited embarrassed, embarrassed. Mother Kèe never said a word to me. I thought then my heart was broken, already broken.

Cíab returned to the harbour and moved in with one of the other prostitutes. However, in the long run she couldn't avoid having a pimp.

> Hmm, I had one person. He said he pitied me. He tried to persuade me to stay with him. I wouldn't go and he just carried me, just carried me . . . I met him at the rice and curry shop. His mother sold rice and curry. He forced me really, too.

> If I didn't go to the ship he just hit me. He was a pimp. A horseshoe crab, a water-bug [a parasite] a golden-winged water-bug.
>
> He wore gold of this size, that was the money I found but still his heart did not have enough.

The day the pimp had carried her home, Cíab's girlfriend, with whom she usually slept, came to fetch her. The *feen* stood with a knife at Cíab's back during the conversation.

> People said I had a small body like a child, like this, they said so, everyone, that I looked like a child. They didn't believe I was a prostitute, didn't believe I already had a child. I didn't open my story to them. I was still a child, I didn't know anything, then I still didn't know anything.
>
> The pimp, he got me to stay in his house, he was going to stab me, stab me to make me stay in his house. And the person I used to go and rest with, she followed me then, she came and found me: Go back home, she said.
>
> I'll go back home or I won't go back home, that's not important, I said.
>
> Will you go back home or not? she asked.
>
> I told her if I want to go back home . . .
>
> Just tell me one word, she said. Will you go back home or not?
>
> This woman didn't know that the person [the pimp] was holding a knife at my back. If I said I'd go back, then he would stab me to death. Then I said: Just a minute, I'll go back home, but I won't go back at this time.
>
> I was afraid of the knife. Just then I didn't dare say anything. But that woman didn't see the knife. So I stayed. Then I went to talk to his mother: Mother, I want money.
>
> Then she went and told her son Pao: Pao, she wants money, she wants to go, I don't know where.
>
> Then he came and kicked me: Go where? he said. Do you think you have a lover?
>
> I talked to him nicely, asked him to talk to me nicely too: I don't want to go. I want money attached to my body [jewellery or pocket money].
>
> Let's go and buy gold, let's go together.

So they bought a gold necklace, but the pimp kept it.

Cíab worked for this pimp for several years. Childbirth and childcare are just as much a problem for prostitutes as for other working women. Cíab became pregnant again but was unwilling to talk about it; "It doesn't have any story at all."

She had her son by Cæsarean operation. A year or so later she was made pregnant by a Yugoslav. She saw him when his ship came in and three, six and nine months later. He wouldn't have her sleeping with others during the pregnancy and gave her some money, but nowhere near enough for the pimp.

Language problems and Cíab's innumeracy, however, led to great misunderstandings. The day she gave birth she was with him on board ship. But then she told him she was only eight months gone, and he was disappointed, she says, because he thought it was not his child, but still he gave her a largish sum of money. She hid the fact that she was having labour pains and went straight to the hospital, where she gave birth to a girl by Caesarean operation and had herself sterilized.

Her story now becomes difficult to follow. The pimp fetched her from the hospital and sent her to work, but at one point she succeeded in getting home to Surin with the two small children, whom her parents and later her brothers and sisters took charge of. From there she went to Sattahip (to the American base).

Judging from Bunryang's description, it is hard being a prostitute at Sattahip. There is strict supervision of the women, and they do not keep their earnings for themselves: Bunryang went on to Pattaya as soon as she saw how conditions were at the base. Cíab couldn't look up the father of her daughter because she was working at Sattahip: still, she thought the daughter looked so much like him that he would probably acknowledge her. Cíab gives a thorough description of her daughter and fantasizes a lot about her and the father: it was a big experience in her life to have had such a beautiful child, and with a man who was interested in the child.

Cíab carried on as a prostitute. She had other pimps, was severely exploited and never saw her children. Now she is starving, worn out and without hope for the future. Extreme poverty drove Cíab to prostitution. She has never been able to fend for herself, and in those situations where she has had work she has been cruelly exploited. Her attempts as a young woman to return to some legitimate society were pretty hopeless. She visited Mother Kèe and hoped to meet her *feen* there. She did meet him at intervals of several years, but got no support from him. And Mother Kèe turned her back on her.

For a time she lived with an elderly Chinese who had a little stall near the ships. He didn't demand that she work at the harbour, only that she worked for him at the market. But she felt that she was being pushed around, criticized and scolded a lot, and gave up the idea of staying there. Poverty and exploitation, loneliness and helplessness in the big city shattered Cíab's hopes.

Poverty and the difficulties for women of fending for themselves and their children can be insurmountable; but they are only some of the factors that drive women to prostitution. Another side of the problem is the dominant view of sexuality, and of women's sexuality in particular.

Sexuality is seen as a dangerous force: civilization is seen as something predicated on the control of sexuality. In an ancient text the end of the world is represented as the decay of the control of sexuality.

> When human beings are no longer ashamed of their evil deeds, when they no longer fear their bad *kharma* then they lose their good customs and couple with mother, daughter and sister without the least sense of shame ... so that the age of man in the end is no more than ten years. Boys and girls who are only five years old live together and couple with one another (Malaya Sutta, quoted from Skrobanek 1976, p. 13).

In Buddhist thinking,

> a being is born as a woman because of bad *kharma* or lack of sufficient good merit. Buddhist cosmological texts place women at the lower end of the ladder in the more corporeal, the less spiritual part of the human spectrum (Thitsa 1980, p. 22).

Sexuality is dangerous and must be controlled, and since the man is the wise and more spiritual being, the woman more of an instinctive one, with a dangerous sexuality, it is he who must control woman's sexuality, which poses a constant threat to him.[2] Men's control of women's sexuality is understood as a sign of their spiritual power. If the control of women's sexuality fails it is supposed that the women will take to loose living and prostitution.

Nǔu experienced this when she was working at a factory with her three older sisters when she was 15-years-old. She and the owner's son fell very much in love with each other. But he had had another girlfriend, who visited Nǔu and told her to go away. Nǔu was almost unable to do so, but left the factory. The young man wept and accused her sisters of wanting to separate them. Nǔu went to a relative and sat in his house for a month, pondered her sorrow and misfortune, cried and languished.

> I went to stay, to rest. When I saw a man like him, a man who wore a striped T-shirt like this, then I missed him, then I sat and thought the distance to him [missed him]. My older sisters, they knew, then they said this . . . if I ended up like this with him, then they knew that I loved him, they were afraid that my heart would break, that I would go out and *paj thîaw* would become a bad woman . . .
>
> But my mind and heart are not like that: what needs to be cut must be cut.

Nǔu's sisters were not alone in this view. In descriptions of prostitution in the press the explanation journalists propose most frequently is that the young woman has had an unhappy love affair and therefore gets involved with prostitution.[3] It is assumed that a woman's sexuality, when first aroused, if it is not subject to parental control or the control of a fiancé, will lead her off the straight and narrow and into unbridled promiscuity.

The assumption that women cannot control their own sexuality also underlies reactions when young women run off with their sweethearts.

Ùbon was an example of a woman who had failed to observe the generally accepted rules of good behaviour by moving to her *feen*'s house without a proper wedding in her own home; she came to be characterized by those around her as a loose woman. These examples show how women in some cases set aside or are forced to transgress the general rules of good behaviour and reject parents' and men's control of their sexuality. In such cases it is assumed that they are, or will become, loose-living and these expectations from those around them can easily drive women to prostitution; the expectations can become self-fulfilling prophecies.

In other cases women made more conscious efforts to manoeuvre beyond the usual strict control. One particular woman — Kèe's sister — had a good, regular job and a tidy fortune and renounced sexuality and love. This was accepted and respected. The problems arose for those women who on the one hand would not tolerate heavily repressive treatment, and on the other hand would not give up their love life.

Dam, Nǔu's elder sister, is one example. She had been married in Si Sa Ked, but the husband was a heavy drinker and beat her when he was drunk. Dam left both him and her village. In Bangkok she learned to sew, and she was good with figures. Here she found another *feen* and became pregnant by him. But he had many minor wives and had no intention of taking on responsibility for her and the child. She left him and had an abortion performed by a traditional Thai doctor whom Sămphaw knew. She presumably became sterile on this occasion, as she never became pregnant again afterwards and did not use contraceptives. As long as Dam did not have a steady *feen* the other women considered her to be loose-living: Tíg made fun of her with expressive gestures and "decent" wives and girls turned their back on her and would not speak to her.

But on the *tham bun* trip to Phitsanulok she met an older dock worker whom she was very taken with. It was true that he was married, but she told me about his good nature and generosity. As soon as she had a steady *feen* she was accepted in the slum and could sit and talk with the other women who had previously turned their backs on her. Dam was not too badly off economically. She only had to take care of herself and help her mother in Si Sa Ked: she had no children. Yet she was dependent on having a *feen*: her social position in the slum hinged on having a steady relationship with a respected person.

In the slum context there were great differences between evaluations of the various types of relationships women had with men and the economic factors connected with the relationships. There were women who seek food, as they said of Cíab. There was one woman who liked to *paj thîaw*. There was no doubt about the way she had her fun: she took her customers back home to the slum. But although the whole slum sizzled with anger over her behaviour at one point, the motives attributed to her remained the same. There were also women like Dam, who tried to retain control of their own love lives: they were considered to be loose women until they found a steady *feen*. Women who worked their way up in the social hierarchy and lived like Dam could gain respect.

As for the minor wives, people were sorry for them if, or rather when, men pushed them around and confiscated their money; but the minor wives who had intimate relations with the husband were hated.

In a society where attempts to avoid the control by men of women's sexuality lead to such strong reprisals, and where women are so economically and socially dependent on men, the boundaries are vague between various types of economic dependence and avoidance of control.

For women in the slum abstract moral norms existed, but took second place to personal sympathies and antipathies in determining how women were judged.

8. Urbanization and Women's Work

Urbanization as a concept must include not only migration from countryside to city but also the simultaneous changes in the relations of production. Wage-labour grows more widespread both in the countryside and in the city eventually becoming the typical form of work.

In the Thai countryside wage-labour was already quite common at the time of migration for the women in my houses; in the city this form of work for an income was by far the most typical. Piker (1975) points out that in his village (Ban Qi) in Ayutthaya province roughly half of the inhabitants earned their living from wage-labour or from services paid by the other half of the inhabitants who still had access to land. The penetration of wage-labour in the countryside goes hand in hand with a loss of land for the peasants usually combined, among other things, with a population increase that leaves many peasants with no access to the most important means of production, land.

Among my women only a few had access to land up-country and in several cases their parents or relatives living up-country did not own land either. The peasants' loss of or lack of access to land, the spread of wage-labour and migration to cities are, of course, necessary conditions for industrial production. Indeed Marx argued that as long as workers had access to land from which to get a living they would not be willing to work as labourers in industry.

The processes of penetration of capital–labour relationships in production have been long drawn-out in Thailand as in many other Third World countries. The Thai economy was opened up to the world market in the middle of the last century; but for a long time the peasants were only (and in some places still are) indirectly subsumed under capital.[1] It is only in the last 20–30 years the parallel processes of the penetration of wage-labour and loss of land for peasants have reached degrees which have produced large-scale migration.

In order to see how urbanization has influenced the work of women, a comparison with conditions in a village may be useful. I have chosen the village which the Potters (1977) have analysed and named Chiang Mai. In this village the old relations of production are not yet eroded although it is situated not too far from a market. I have chosen this study mainly because the Potters' analyses of the everyday life of peasants and farmers are detailed and they have argued very convincingly for the actual kind of social structure in the village and, as the first, shown the interplay between men and women in the social structure in (great parts of) villages in Thailand.

In Chiang Mai rice production was the main economic activity. Other economic activities included the cultivation of cash-crops, wage-labour, and trade. These activities were often carried out by individuals on their own account; the earnings were therefore personal and created some degree of conflict between parents and daughters.

The social structure was built around the female line of descent. When a daughter married, the husband would move to her home for a period and the young couple would often then build a new house near by, cultivating a bit of land of their own. In later times land became less available and young couples in some cases moved to new villages.

The division of labour inside households was clear. Work in the house (cleaning, washing and food preparation) was done by the women. In the fields some work such as digging ditches or ploughing was exclusively men's, while weeding was mainly women's work. Most work, however, was done by both men and women, but in slightly different ways.

At peak seasons of sowing, transplanting and harvesting exchange of labour was common. The people involved in the groups working together came from households which were related to the middle-aged couple, who were owning land, as their kin (both female and male lines), as political allies of the husband or as neighbours. The more influential the family, the more people joined in exchange labour. The amount of labour was counted and reciprocated. Potter claims that the work could as well have been done by each family separately but that people preferred to work in groups to make the effort less boring. Women in my houses often claimed that, difficulties notwithstanding, work up-country was fun, explicitly naming the working together in the fields.

The purpose of the work was simple and known by all: to expand the well-being and wealth of the household in question. There seems to be little ordering about of other people in the countryside, since everybody understands the aim of the work and has an interest in the outcome. Norms are strongly against the showing of anger since it is debasing for the person showing it (Mulder 1978); young people are supposed to help and obey older people, but the atmosphere is kind and not dehumanizing.

Men and women inherit equally from their parents and thus both man and wife own land. Both sexes work together in the fields and contribute to the wealth of the family. Men have the greater authority, but men and women seem to have a shared interest in the household's growth and there are no reports in the Potters' works about husbands' lack of responsibility for the household or squandering of the household's incomes.

According to my women's stories men and women got the same wage when working as agricultural labourers (roughly 30 baht a day, that is half the minimum wage and the same as many of the women got for wage-work in the city). In joint enterprises such as rice-growing or brick-making incomes were either pooled and usually administered by the wife/mother or they were divided equally between the sexes but with children getting half the amount of adults. But in individual undertakings (trade and the like) the incomes were in principle personal, according to my women; in the Potters' village these earnings were disputed.

Up-country, then, women had access to the main production resource, land, and they contributed to their families' well-being and wealth by participating in production as well as by working with household chores. The division of incomes between men and women was relatively equal and not disputed.[5]

The conditions of women's work in the slum were quite different. Neither men nor women had ownership of or access to the means of production (except for some of the self-employed men and women) and certainly no access to land. The main resources for the livelihood of families were no longer their access to land but their possible wages or incomes; in this respect women were left with much worse access to resources for survival. They were working in a secondary labour market under bad conditions, with low payment and small prospects for future betterment. When they got older they would most probably have to earn a living from extended household activities or depend on their relatives.

There is a common concept of women as mainly or only concerned with the work for the family, the household chores. This concept is widely spread and to a degree internalized among men and women and is a basic assumption in cultural institutions such as Buddhism and in the mass media. The division of labour in families in a way where women are responsible for children and for the daily maintenance of adults and children is sometimes thought of as a global phenomenon; this division of labour is then seen as a main cause of women's subordination.

Both feminists and Marxists have argued strongly against biological explanations of the differences between the power and position in society of the two sexes. Some have argued along the lines of Rubin (1975) that the socialization of boys and girls creates the different gender characteristics. Rubin relates these to the Oedipus complex in early childhood and argues that this is not an outcome of biological but social conditions although the definitions of gender roles and women's subordination seems in some respects similar in nearly all societies.[2]

It has been argued, too, that women's care of children make their contributions to the production of food and necessities for the family less than men's contributions; but this has been shown not to be the case (in many societies of hunters and gatherers as well as in horticulture, women's contributions of food often outweigh those of men). Rosaldo points out that even if women's contributions to the family's livelihood outweigh men's they are not valued as much.

> What is perhaps most striking and surprising is the fact that male as opposed to female activities are always recognized as predominantly important and cultural systems give authority and value to the roles and activities of men (Rosaldo 1974, p. 19).

If women's subordination is a global phenomenon it seems it can only be explained by universal facts. The outstanding biological difference between men and women is women's ability to procreate, to become pregnant, give birth to and suckle babies. This ability has been widely used to explain women's subordination; but it seems rather problematic to explain women's lesser status and power in this way. It does not seem reasonable that this ability to create new human beings with very little help from men accounts for women's universally inferior position.

The global existence of subordination of women is at the moment being questioned. Etienne and Leacock claim that such global subordination of women is very doubtful and especially so in societies with a low degree of hierarchy and no state organization. They discuss some classical texts in anthropology (Lèvi-Strauss (1969) and Rosaldo (1974)) and discuss the possible biases in anthropological research: the Western obsession with power relations, the westerners' first meeting with pre-colonial people who were men and the Western bias on the question on women's proper roles. They try to substantiate their claim that,

> In sum the entire conceptual framework of anthropology and as a result the data on which generalisations were based suffer from ethnocentric and male-centered bias (Etienne and Leacock 1980, p. 4).

In their collection of studies they document several cases where women and men both had social power and where their roles were complementary, and they document how Western colonialism in nearly all cases diminished the power and role of women and led to deteriorating situations for them.

A division of labour between the sexes where women cater for small children and often for older ones and adults too, seems to be widespread though not universal. It seems to be partly related to the fact that only women can give birth to and suckle babies. But it in no way explains why women's subordination should be a global phenomenon. Even if the division of labour shows some traits of similarity in many societies the labour women do might be and is valued more highly in some societies than others. Women in some societies can wield social power.

The concept of women's subordination seems thus rather broad. Power relations and roles in society between men and women may vary considerably and may be complementary instead of out right domination-based.

The concept of women's proper work as the work of creating and maintaining human beings in the family is dominant in Western (and indeed industrialized) cultures. In traditional Thai-culture women were, as we mentioned, expected to work with human beings as well as in production and they did so in village society. In the slum, however, the difficulties in doing both kinds of work were much greater and it seems women's situation relative to men's deteriorated after migration. The capitalist way of organizing production made the position of women relative to men worse even in the Thai context where (young) women's labour in industry was a desirable commodity and where norms prohibiting and devaluing women's work for incomes did not exist.

A similar deterioration in women's position has been demonstrated in other societies after the introduction or penetration of capitalist relations of production; classically in England where the expropriation of the common land in villages at the beginning of industrialization was an expropriation of the land utilized by women for subsistence production (Pinchbeck, 1981).[3]

It is often pointed out that the division of labour in capitalist societies is similar to the division of labour in traditional (pre-capitalist) societies. Thus Mackintosh writes,

Historically as wage-work has spread, capital has seized upon the pre-existing division between men and women, and has incorporated that division within its own workforce to its own advantage (Mackintosh 1981, p. 6).

This seems true in Thailand, England and many other societies inasmuch as women often worked at caring for human beings before capitalist relations of production became dominant. It is, however, wrong in the sense that they did much other work besides. More important is the fact that the work in looking after people went on in a different context before the penetration of capitalist relations of production.

The aim of the work was, other than in capitalist societies, to maintain the human beings, to create as much wealth for the household (or social group) as possible, or to enhance its power and status in the community. In some societies, as in Thailand, part of the product was extracted by a ruling class (the *sakhdina* class); but the main aim of work was the wealth of the unit organizing it, the household, which both catered for human beings and produced things and was responsible for both kinds of work.

Capital organizes production in a radically different way: the work goes on (typically) in factories and the purpose of production is the creation of value, to extract profit for the expansion of the business. Capital values work done in the factories by paying wages to workers in exchange for their labour power. The production of human beings goes on in families or households and it is not provided for by capital. Marx expressed a common viewpoint when he wrote,

> The maintenance and reproduction of the working-class is, and must ever be, a necessary condition to the reproduction of capital. But the capitalist may safely leave its fulfilment to the labourer's instincts of self-preservation and of propagation (Marx 1965, vol. 1, p. 572).

This radical division between the work producing human beings and the work producing things has grave consequences for women's work.

The work producing things is termed production since it is by this work that value is produced. The work is paid and it is (to a degree) respected. The production of value is the whole *raison d'etre* of capital. Work producing human beings is termed reproduction. It is not valued, it is not paid and it gives little prestige.

Both kinds of work of course need creation as well as maintenance, but the valuation modern societies give the two kinds of work is reflected in the terminology.[4]

The division and radical separation between the two kinds of necessary work can be termed the domestication of women.[5] It is linked to the very nature of capital accumulation and the consequences for women's work and position in society are grave.

Women's access to work with the production of things, work that generates income is diminished and the result is that women either do not participate or suffer an intolerable double work burden.

The organization of work is done by two separate units: the household and the factory. Work in the factory is organized with no consideration for women's work for the family. Time-schedules, working hours, even the planning of overtime, are done without consultation with the women or considerations for the work burden in the family. The purpose of work in factories is in no way connected to the actual needs of human beings. Production is planned and implemented from the point of view of furthering the accumulation of capital and not from the point of view of creating useful things. The purpose of work in the factory is to create profit for the owner. This has relevance for the women since low wages, lack of investment in working conditions and lack of expenditure for social benefits will increase profits. Capitalists have an interest in splitting the workforce along whatever lines it is possible to do so; they therefore exploit (among other things) gender divisions. The purpose of work in the household is of no relevance for the factory and the extended household activities seem likewise to be of no concern to capital.[6]

One effect of this is that women's dependency on men's earnings increases. They are no longer able to earn approximately as much as men, and they no longer control any important resources for the production of things. Their livelihood and daily life thus becomes dependent on their husbands' (and sometimes children's) incomes and on the division of incomes in the family. Since most women's incomes were too low to support their family this was the case whether the women had incomes of their own or not.

Women's need of the family or extended family had not diminished in the slum. They were dependent on the earnings of their husbands and they were dependent on female kin to look after children if they were going to work.

It seems, however, that men's need for the family and extended family was diminishing. They no longer had any relevance to the production of things and incomes. The family still rendered important daily services to the men; but most of these services could be bought as commodities. The main reasons why men should maintain families were the social psychological satisfaction of having a family, of the relationships to the other members of the family — among these the wife — and the need for a sphere where their control and their humanity was reflected among other people.[7] The combination of these two factors (women's growing economic dependency on men and men's social–psychological needs) made the women economically dependent on their sexuality.

Since all other aspects of life were becoming commodities, sexual services tended to be saleable too. Prostitution has grown and taken more commercialized (and exploitive) forms; but the commercialization of women's sexuality can also be seen in the changes connected with the bride-price.

Formerly and up-country a prospective husband would pay something to the mother of his wife-to-be. This was his payment for his incorporation into the spirit-group connected with birth, death and family matters, spirits which are inherited by the daughter from the mother. Since the husband usually leaves his own family at marriage he has to be incorporated into the new group. This incorporation takes place at the wedding ceremony.

The women in my houses had mostly paid a bride-price to their mothers too, and they simply explained this by saying, "She has brought us up. She has worked and fed us, and she must be paid for her efforts."

The bride-price has risen much in later years, the women said. The highest bride-price paid in my houses was paid for a young woman who at the moment was going to the university and expected to go on with her study. Her father told me about the engagement and when I congratulated her she answered, "It is not my *feen*. It is my father's."

The fiancé had paid 30,000 baht at the betrothal, the remaining 10,000 plus 6,000 baht of gold had to be paid when they married.[12] This was the only house where the bride-price was paid to the father in the house.

Women's sexuality is not always controlled by themselves. Others, as in this case a father, in the cases of prostitution a bar-owner or a pimp, try to get the benefits. But it seemed that all married women were economically dependent on their husband's feelings and on their sexuality and most tried to manipulate their husbands' feelings as best they could. This was the only power left to them.

It should not be denied that the life in a big city opens new possibilities for women; better access to education and contacts with many people at school, at work and in the slum. The better access to health clinics is maybe most important in that it opens new possibilities for birth-control. But it cannot be denied either that for most women the possibilities were hard to exploit since the conditions of their daily lives, the forms of and access to income-earning work and the conditions of their work for the family had changed in ways that made it difficult for women to take advantage of the abstract possibilities of the city.

The women in the slum did not feel their work for incomes to be important except as a source of money, as a necessity; they reacted to cheating, low payment and arbitrary discipline. But their lives in the slum, the time free of work, were most important to the women — their relationships to husbands, parents, sisters, friends and children. This is common for all workers, men and women. Life is not the time which is sold but the time you dispose of yourself, the relationships you build up for yourself. But this is even more the case for women because they are domesticated and made responsible for the children and the home.

Thus Nŭu told long stories about her love affairs, her husband, her child, her sisters and mother. Her evaluation of herself depended on such relationships. I asked about her work and she told me about it. But her main concern, the themes she chatted about from day to day, was her relationships to husband, friends, family.

In emotional terms the emphasis on life outside work is easy to understand. In economic terms these relationships were important too. Even Nŭu, who was lucky and worked in a factory which paid her the minimum wage, lived in great poverty compared to other women in the slum. Her husband did not give her any of his income — she had to support herself and her child on her earnings. Her mother and sisters did not live near her house. Thus she had neither her husband's support nor family and kin to rely on.

Part 3:
Women and the Family

9. Caring for Husband and Children

Women in the slum worked for the family: for husband and children; for the sick and the old; and with the day-to-day work of the household. This housework was defined as the women's responsibility. "Here the women get up early in the morning and get everything ready for the men," explained Sŭu.

Women found this work more or less fatiguing. Kàj, a strong and self-aware woman in her forties, shouted to her ten-year-old son, one day when he had stolen five baht from the housekeeping money to play cards with his friends, "Oh, it's my evil fate to have been born a woman! It means that I have to look after you and your father — and you're as bad as he is!" Similarly, men took it for granted that women saw to the house and children. A man could come home drunk and shout, "Where's my wife? Isn't she supposed to be looking after the house and children?" and the wife would come running right away from the neighbour's house where she had been sitting talking, and serve some food and whisky for him.

This was perhaps clearest in Sămphaw's case. Her son had had a child with a very young girl who had to stay in hospital after the birth. The son had a row with his father-in-law and moved home to his mother. He had no regular job (he played the guitar at festive gatherings at scattered intervals) and was thus able to spend his time as he wished. Sămphaw's husband said that she should take care of the grandchild. Sămphaw told me, "Look at me. I'm not a grandmother yet. I won't look after the child."

But she had to do, while its mother was at the hospital. Her son was happy to have the child and proud of it, and he helped her now and then; but it did not occur to anyone that he could have looked after it himself. Sămphaw did it while he sat practising on his guitar.

There was no doubt about men's control over women's work. A middle-aged woman could go off to the country to visit her mother only if her husband would accept her daughter to keep house in the meantime. Men could help, for example, with the salad that went with their Thai whisky, by draining the water off from the rice, and the sons could fetch water. But there was no doubt about who was responsible for keeping house.

The daily work for the family included cleaning and washing clothes, shopping and making food, care of children, and for most women seeing to it that there was always someone in or near the house. Very few of them ever let the house stand empty for fear of theft of clothing or other possessions. There were also a number of smaller activities, each of them less time-consuming in itself, which mounted up together to a considerable pile of work: repairing clothes, bailing or dredging the water out of the small gutters around the houses, chopping up firewood, burning rubbish, washing big clay pots in which the water was stored, and often the making of special Thai confections — Thai iced coffee, ginger juice, rice scones and salads.

Physical conditions in the slum made the work difficult. The dirty walkways (which some of the women washed) and the mud beneath them meant that children got dirty. They played under or fell down from the walkways, trod or fell in dirt on them, or one of the dogs ran down in the mud and made a mess of everything. Children were washed and had their clothes changed at least two, often three, times a day. Grown-ups, too, bathed and changed their clothes twice a day. All the cleaning work was increased by the mud and dirt under and on the walkways.

Shopping and cooking were much more demanding than in Western countries. It was a long trip to the nearest market and women would sometimes go to markets that were farther away to shop cheaply. Thai food is made with many ingredients and the raw materials are unprocessed. It gets very hot, as the food is made over an open fire in a chafing-dish in most houses (a few, however, had an electric rice boiler).

Water was by far the greatest problem. There were water-pipes by the houses, but there was no water in them. They ran out under the mud. Supplies varied and there were no reasonable explanations for the lack of water in the pipes. A Dutch student group made a technical survey and discussed the problem with the elected village leaders and other tenants. But the water-pipes they installed contained no water either. The women in my slum thought that the problem was because of a debt of millions the slum owed to the Water Board; but the rich man, who had a well, where there was almost always water, thought the problem was a technical one. The staff of the NHA and the Prateep School could not explain the lack of water.

For a period a water-wagon with long pipes came to the slum. Here one could buy water for five baht for a clay jug (*tùm*), and it was delivered straight to the house by an elected village leader and a driver. In the warmest month (April), however, it disappeared. The van with the pipes no longer came, nor did any other supplies come.

Each woman had her own explanation: there was a drought in the north-east and the van had been sent up there; people spoiled the pipes to get free water; people harangued the suppliers and complained over having to pay.

The women tried to get water in various ways. Some had a contact at the harbour or the slaughter-house and fetched water there. Some obtained or borrowed a small cart which could carry several oil drums. At one place in the slum a family had made a trolley which ran on the train rails to the harbour. Some carried water long distances. One family which lived several hundred metres away had water and sold it. It was pumped through long, thin, green plastic pipes, but there was a great deal of discussion about the price. People thought that water should be free, criticized the fact that it was being sold and cheated as much as possible.

Sŏmcìd went to the Port and asked on behalf of our walkway why there was no water. The Port Authorities said that the van with pipes came with free water. But some of those who delivered it had demanded money for it. People kicked up a row and the Port did not want trouble. So they did not send any more water in.

Sŏmcìd bought a tank-van with water for 180 baht and tried to ensure that her own house and her closest neighbours and friends got water. Everyone tried to help themselves, so it was a question of how quick you managed to fetch it. The week after Kèe's husband bought a similar water-van.

A month later, the Port began to send tankers in with water, but now without pipes, so that the water had to be carried from the gravel road in to the house (200–400m). This was heavy work.

Every house had a yoke and two large buckets (old, but cleaned and often painted oil drums). Each drum could hold about 20 litres. To fill up a normal *tùm* you had to go three or four times, and most houses had from three to six *tùms*, the contents of which were used up in half a week. The *tùms* were scrubbed out at (long) intervals. This was difficult because they were too heavy to turn over, so all the water had to be bailed out. The women complained a lot over fetching water and showed me sore and swollen shoulders.

The neighbourhood and the elected village leaders in the slum could not organize a water supply or distribution. Nor could anyone in my houses speak up on behalf of the walkway. Sŏmcìd could, because she was a teacher and respected; Kèe's husband could because he worked for the Port, driving goods for it in his lorry. But the distribution was completely disorganized both when they got hold of a van with water and when the Port sent the pipeless tankers in with water. Neighbourly relations and kin did not reach far enough out of the slum and formal organization did not penetrate far into the sphere of everyday details.

Heavy rainfall also created problems. Almost all the roofs were full of holes so that everything got wet. There were many colds after a rainstorm. Two houses had roof gutters and a stub of pipe so that rainwater could be drawn off. This was easy, and the opportunity was used; but the roofs were never washed clean by the water, and the water continued to be cloudy.

Housework was the mother's responsibility, but others helped. Grown-up children could help fetching water, if they felt like it. If the mother was too old the oldest daughter took over, but grown-up sons also carried water.

Cleaning was the housewife's job. The washing of clothes was done by each grown-up him/herself, but the mother washed the father's, small children's and old people's clothes, if necessary. Young men liked to try to coax their sisters into washing their clothes, as far as I know with no success.[1] Children went on errands, put the rice on (but did not drain off the boiling water) and washed up. Girls of ten could make plain food. Husbands and others often helped a little making food; this was often a joint activity, where everyone wanted to do a little. Men also helped to make the strong salad they ate when they were drinking.

But in general they expected and got the women's services and had their food served when they were drinking with friends. Some daughters and one wife went to visit others if they thought the husband was drinking too much and too often: they made themselves invisible.

Children, pregnancies and childbirth were demanding for the women: they required their continuous physical presence. Children were generally loved and valued greatly. If a family broke up, whether the husband and wife left one another or a mother and daughter moved away to different places, there was much discussion of the children, as both sides wanted to keep them. They were expected to be of some help at an early age: to run errands and wash up; middle-aged women whose children did not live with them felt lonely.

All children of school age went to school. There are four years' compulsory schooling, but many carried on longer. Some children went to creches or kindergartens. The parents had to have a registration card so that the children could go to school. Two women (the former prostitutes) had no such card. The husband of one, however, had a card, and the other one's son was well below school age.

Among the children and youths there was one who worked for an income. This was a fourteen-year-old girl, Phen, who worked at the transnational factory, liked it, and handed over her whole income to her mother. Another girl of sixteen went to school but functioned in practice as a maidservant at home: she lived in the rich man's house and was the daughter of one of his minor wives. She had a bad relationship with Claw and took a large share of the household work — went shopping, made food and did the cleaning. She had to take a lot of orders and instructions from the rest of the family.

None of the other children had jobs. They helped with the housework, were taken along to a construction site with their fathers or helped the neighbours to wash plastic; but they did not have actual income-generating work.

Boys were held in high esteem by their mothers. When they grew up they would become monks or novices for a period and thus win religious merit for their mothers. Several women kept on having children in the hope that they would have a boy. Some women called their small sons "father" as a nickname. It was boys who were sent to creches or kindergartens. A father's favourite child, on the other hand, would often be a girl. She would get extra pocket-money and more schooling.

All women except one in my houses were aware that contraceptives existed. The older ones had rarely used them, but the young ones did, in the form of the pill, coil or Depo Provera injections. Two were sterilized, several knew about condoms, but they were never used. None of the women were aware that there was any danger to women's health connected with any of these. Although everyone knew that contraceptives existed, women often became pregnant without wanting to. One of the women, who was very tired of having to look after children and the house (and tired of her husband) had had several abortions.

Abortions are disliked. As Buddhists most Thais consider it wrong to take life. Abortions are forbidden in Thailand, but accessible: it all depends on how much money the woman can get hold of. One woman told me about her abortions: the first two were successful, the third unsuccessful; she was now pregnant again.

> The first time it was not in a clinic, it was in an ordinary house. He was not a doctor. He brought the medicine to put it in the vagina.
>
> I don't know what kind of medicine. It was like . . . he put it through like when you give a kid an enema. Like that.
>
> Then when he had given enough, he told me to go back home. Oh, when I sat in the car going home, when I was on my way, it looked and felt as if it was coming out.

But it didn't.

Then, later, he put in more medicine, he put it in the same way. He sticks it in so the blood-clot breaks, just like that.

So I eat medicine to push it out. I don't know what kind. I ate everything he told me. It was liquid medicine. You put it in liquor and drink it. I took the medicine for months. He didn't tell me it would take months before it came out. I had a stomach-ache, it was like . . . when menstruation comes, like that. So I think it'll come out, but it takes more than a month before all the blood comes out.

Before each lump comes out it is very painful, very painful. Believe me, each time it was more painful than the delivery of a baby.

For this treatment she paid 1,200 baht, and had to pay for her own medicine.

The next time she tried to have an abortion she was able to get enough money — 3,000 baht — and she had the foetus removed by suction at a clinic. "This time it was not dangerous at all. It didn't hurt at all." The third abortion had been unsuccessful. She had only been able to get two sums of 200 baht, and for these she had been given two shots.

Though I had the injection, it didn't come out, so it never would come out. After the injection he pressed it to get it out, and he said I should let the doctor-who-follows-the-house [a local practitioner of traditional Thai medicine] press it out. He tried, but it did not come out.

Her husband wanted the child — he hoped it would be a girl, so that they would have two sons and two daughters. The mother was in despair at the thought of another child and hoped her mother would look after it, just as she looked after the daughter she already had.

Rumour had it that two other women had each had an abortion. One of the middle-aged women in the slum knew of a traditional Thai doctor who could induce an abortion by pressing the foetus out. Some children were born very much against the parent's wishes. In some cases their mothers accepted them: a 14-year-old girl and a woman in her twenties who had become pregnant for the third time kept the children and tried to live with the extra burden. Other women could not cope: this led to two adoptions, in both cases boys, during the years just before I lived in the slum and while I lived there.

Cíab told me how she had been given her adoptive son — now six months old.

His mother had this child. Then she came and sat in front of my house, carrying the child. She didn't dare go in. She said that I had always said I would take the child, and now she had come to give it to me. First she said she had wanted to squeeze the child's throat, break its neck. She tried to have an abortion and the child didn't come out. She ate medicine to kill the boy. But she didn't succeed. So she wanted to hire somebody, a masseuse, to break the child's neck.

The mother told me this, then she said: Can he stay here or not?

She said her husband kicked her, kicked her in the face until she was black, blue and green. Her husband kicked her in the morning, kicked her in the evening, they kicked each other until she gave birth. Her husband, but not the person who was the real father.

While she was still pregnant I told her: You don't have to go and hire somebody to break the child's neck. You have the child and when it's out, you come and give it to me. I want a child.

But I said it playfully. It was a joke. She took it seriously. When the child was only three days old she went and asked people, who wanted a child? Then she asked me: Will you feed the child for about ten days, OK?

She just dumped the child on me for good. Then she came, and I thought she wanted the child back. She said: You'd better feed the child for a long time, then you won't regret having to give him back. It's true, I fed the child; and I loved him a lot, too. Nobody else wanted him, now he stays with me. My *feen* curses me: Why do you feed this boy?

Cíab used what money she had on the boy, had even had him in hospital when he was ill, and always carried him around. She had taken him over, loved him a lot and did not want to give him up now. A family had asked to take him over, and was willing to pay her a sum of money to make up for the time and money she had already spent on him. But Cíab would not part with him, and repeated emphatically that she would *never* sell a child.

Kèe had also adopted a little boy. She had two girls and was pregnant again when a relative of the boy's mother came and asked if anyone would have the boy, Kèe said, "He was so small you could give him a bath in a drinking-bowl" (i.e. a bowl about 25 cm diameter). She had had him in hospital to have his blood changed, she said. Now he was living with a brother and his wife near her mother in Korat.

Lee had two adopted children, a boy she had taken in before she had children herself, and Sŏmcìt, her sister's daughter, who had lived with her since she was small.

Another six children lived with relatives in the slum. Sĭi had two grown-up sons who were in prison. The wife of one of them died and left two children, the other left a child in a restaurant, where a resolute relative found it and took it back to its grandmother.

In the rich man's house, besides the young girl who kept house for him, lived her younger brother. The family had also taken in a little girl. She was the daughter of the man's brother. This brother had been a caretaker and collected the rents on the land the family had bought in the provinces, and which local peasants had first rented, then seized for themselves. The brother was killed by the peasants and his wife came back to Bangkok, where the rich man's family offered to take care of her daughter. The girl was now six-years-old, and had lived there for two years. The family all vied with one another to play with her and cosset her.

Other children had their parents or at least one of them, living in the slum. Children from seven houses lived with relatives in the country — mostly with mothers, a couple with mothers-in-law, and some from split families with the other parent. The relationships between adults and children were warm and showed little evidence of possessiveness. For a Westerner it was surprising that no force or even strong persuasion was used with children.

No one considered it surprising that an eight-year-old girl could say that she did not want to go home to the village with her mother — or that her wish was respected. On the contrary, there were several examples of children of five or more living somewhere becaused they wanted to — against the wishes of one or both parents.

Parents were proud of children's initiatives — for example of a girl barely three years old washing clothes or powdering her drunken grandfather while he was asleep. Children were imprinted with respect for their elders at an early age and older children would give younger ones information about all sorts of things. Children were always polite to adults.

During the six months I lived in the slum I heard hardly any children crying, apart from Nŭu's daughter. Considering how densely crowded with dwellings the area was, and how poor its play facilities were, this was quite incredible. Apart from the schoolteacher, I never saw an adult strike a child.[2]

The friendly relationship between mothers and children and the lack of possessiveness also formed the background for the easy-going and graceful way daughters treated their mothers and vice versa. They could all talk and make their points without quarrelling, even when their views were completely opposed. Mutual respect and acceptance of differences made for smooth relationships.[3]

An example may perhaps illustrate the relationship between adults and children. Nŭu worked in a factory, was married and had a daughter just three-years-old. During the first year after the girl was born, she lived with her mother-in-law in Bangkok, and the mother-in-law looked after the child. Nŭu did not like this. The mother-in-law became irritated if the child cried and did not pay enough attention to the baby.

When Nŭu and her husband moved to the husband's sister's house in the slum there was no one to look after the baby and she was sent up to Nŭu's mother in Si Sa Ked. Nŭu missed her a lot, and when her sister Dam came to Bangkok she had Nŭu's daughter with her. So then Dam lived with Nŭu, where she took care of the child while Nŭu was at work.

Nŭu's husband did not care for this arrangement. "Why should we feed her?" — and Dam had to move.

So the baby had to go back to Si Sa Ked and Nŭu's mother came on a visit to fetch her. She lived with her grandmother for a few months, but Nŭu missed her, and when Dam went home on a visit, and I went with her, we brought the child back with us. The grandmother in Si Sa Ked was very sorry to part with the child. She thought the little girl was much better off in the village. There she could move about without restrictions and everyone would take care of her; no one would scold her.

In fact, Nŭu's grandmothers, both maternal and paternal, lived just across from Nŭu's mother's house, and they vied with each other to take care of the girl. They were both old women; the paternal grandmother was bent almost double from the hips up, but they were both agile and got up and down the stairs of the houses without difficulty.

When we had to leave there was a rather depressed atmosphere between Dam and her mother, who did not want to part with Nŭu's daughter. The little girl had her

Woman and the Family

best clothes on — a nylon frock, white shoes and socks and ribbons in her hair. The two great-grandmothers knelt on the floor on either side of her. They each tied a piece of cord round her wrists and said, "Journey far away, have a good life wherever you go, don't forget us and come back healthy and happy."

Back in the slum the problem of looking after the child was pressing again. But Nŭu's mother-in-law came to Bangkok from Korat to help her daughter and keep house for her while she was having her third child. She could also look after Nŭu's daughter.

In the slum Nŭu's daughter cried a lot. Nŭu and Dam gave her a lot of attention, but presumably she was having difficulties adjusting to the many changes: she could hardly speak Thai (having spoken only Laotian in the village) and was teased by the other children, who were far less gentle and hesitant.

The adults', and especially the mothers', love for the children was great, as was their respect for their wishes. But there was hardly any situation where the difficulties the woman had to struggle with emerged so clearly as in matters of pregnancy, childbirth and childcare. Easier access to birth control for women was a great step forward. Yet many got pregnant without wishing to. As far as childcare was concerned, the women were completely dependent on relatives, or, failing this, neighbours and for those of them who had no such secure network to fall back on the problems were insurmountable.

10. Patterns of Settlement

In the slum there was much emphasis on the individual. Women said that they did what they liked and what they thought was reasonable; young couples said that they settled down where they wanted to and where there was room; older people said that they moved in and lived with those of their children they loved most.

The attitude can be summed up in the saying, "The Thais are a free people."

The actual pattern of settlement in the slum presented — at least at first sight — a rather complex picture. Taking as our point of departure a person under sixty years of age, and defining a family as one or two parents and one or more children, we can say that 33 families lived in the slum. Some of these nuclear families had a house to themselves; some lived in a house with kin and some lived very near their relations.

I have defined an extended family as a family where three or four generations live in the same house or near one another (in a little independent house on the other side of the walkway, beside or behind the parents' house). In my 24 houses lived 11 extended families comprising 21 nuclear families (persons over 60-years-old are included in the generational definition, but are not counted as defining a nuclear family). Nuclear families with grown-up, but as yet unmarried, children lived in four houses. In two of the houses lived a brother and sister, each with their spouse and children. Another sister had a small hairdresser's shop beside her sister's house.

Nuclear families lived in six houses. The settlement pattern looks as follows when schematized.

Table 10.1
Family settlements

Family type	Living near or with	Old/dependant
Extended:		
4	Married sons & daughters	–
1	Married daughters	8
1	Married sons	–
3	Other relatives	–
Nuclear:		
4	Unmarried adult offspring	1
2	Other relatives	–
6	—	1

How far a nuclear family functioned as a household or not was dependent on whether it was concentrated in the same house — in which case a mother or grandmother in her forties or fifties would be responsible for the running of the household. But it was also dependent on whether the extended family was related through the women or the men. If it consisted of a female line (mother and daughters) with husbands and children, it usually functioned in practice as a household, or at least with a great deal of cooperation between the nuclear families involved. If the extended family on the other hand consisted of parents, their son and his wife, there was no cooperation between the nuclear families in the normal run of things.

Among the families there were six single parents. A single father and two single mothers lived in extended families, two single mothers and one single father in nuclear families with grown-up children. Added to this there was one minor wife, and Cíab, with her wreck of a husband. Four of the women had been married more than once: two of them now lived in a marriage which had lasted more than ten years (the prostitutes are not counted here). There was thus a considerable degree of stability in the families.

During the six months I lived there, one family moved away to one of the Port's houses for workers, and the wife's younger sister moved in with husband and children to live with the original family's unmarried grown-up son. Another family was split up so that the mother, grandmother and two grown-up married daughters with children moved away to live by themselves — the daughters each to her own small house. The father, a grown-up married son and a grown-up divorced son with three children stayed behind to live by themselves. Although stability within the families was great, there was all the same a certain turnover as regards individuals: in all, 18 people moved in or out of my 24 houses in the course of the six months.

People in the slum were inclined to prefer living in large families or with kin nearby. Middle-aged parents had an interest in having their grown-up children living at home and they did what they could to ensure that they also lived in or near the house after they got married. For practical day-to-day purposes the grown-up children's presence meant help for the parents with household work, and often also an economic contribution. When the children got married this sort of help was less certain; but most of the daughters would at least do their best to help their parents in their old age, and often before this, too, on a modest but regular basis. Sons were a great help, especially in situations of need: with funeral expenses when the husband died, if a palm-leaf canopy had to be replaced with corrugated iron and so on. Some of the households could hardly have been economically viable without the pooling of several large or small contributions.

Similarly, it was an advantage for most young couples to live with or near one of the parents. In many families economic considerations were important to the young: they would hardly have been able to maintain an independent household on the man's income. For the women, living near their mothers meant that they had someone to look after their children when they went to work. But it was also true that the daughters would have missed their mothers if they had had to live elsewhere. For both men and women, living near the family meant consolation, support and perhaps allies in cases of marital conflict.

Patterns of Settlement

However, when we look at patterns of settlement in those families where the grown-up children had *not* migrated to Bangkok, but had grown up there, it seemed to be commonest to settle with the woman's family.

In Chalŭaj's family there used to live both a married son and daughter. But the son got married a week before I made my survey. His fiancée had run away from home because her father would not accept Chalŭaj's son, and she had come to Chalŭaj's house. They had been married at the end of May. Chalŭaj's married daughter Túg, had always lived with her mother, and her husband gave Chalŭaj his income. Their only child was the same age as her youngest brother (about five).

In Sămphaw's house a married daughter and her husband lived with two children just opposite, another daughter had lived with her husband just across the walkway. She had run away with her husband, but not to his parents. There were no problems involved in their choosing to live near Pùu's parents once the wedding had taken place.

The son lived, as we have seen, with Sămphaw too. But there was an attempt to freeze his wife out. She was the same age as Túg (Sămphaw's youngest daughter), said Sămphaw. They had moved in because the son had quarrelled with his father-in-law who had a food stand at a market, and both demanded a wedding and that the son take part in the work of selling food. But he was neither able nor willing to pay the bride-price, nor did he want to work at the food stand.

Near Sĭi's house lived both a married son and a married daughter: both couples had children. But in this case the daughter-in-law *also* lived near her own mother's (Khìad's) house. Khìad lived with her husband, her children and another married daughter with children.

Nípapheen and Sŏmsùg each belonged to a branch of the split family. Six months before, Nípapheen had moved in with her *feen* in a household consisting of a married couple of about 65, the mother's mother, two grown-up daughters — both married — and two grown-up sons, one of them her *feen*, the other an older divorced brother with three children. As in Sămphaw's family, the members of the household refused to accept her, especially the women, who moved away. One daughter lived in a little house nearby, and her mother and her 80-year-old grandmother moved in with her. The other daughter had recently married, and she and her husband got their own room nearby. The women cooperated and helped one another, and the father, the brothers and the new daughter-in-law lived together.

Dèeg lived with her husband and youngest child (10-years-old), and her son lived with his wife and three children just behind the house. There was virtually no cooperation or communication between them. Another son lived with her during the first months of my stay. He had a pregnant wife of whom he was very proud. His wife was afraid of childbirth, and when the time approached they moved home to her parents. Her husband could then work in his father-in-law's shop.

Phád lived with her husband and his mother, and sometimes his brother. She was far gone in pregnancy, and had moved to Bangkok from the provinces when she got to know her husband-to-be. The mother had moved in from Korat three months before (because another son was going to continue his studies in Bangkok).

Kèeb lived with one married and one unmarried daughter. She was in her forties, and looked after the daughter's child and the household. In this family the mother managed the collective income. The mother had two grown-up sons and one of them got married in June. The couple built a house beside Kèeb's and just round the corner from the woman's parents' house.

The young couples in the slum settled down near the wife's parents. In some cases they lived near both the husband's and the wife's parents — but day-to-day cooperation was a matter between mother and daughter(s), not between mother-in-law and daughters-in-law.

In two of the cases where the young couple lived near the husband's, not the wife's parents, the wife's mother was dead. In the one case the wife had moved to Bangkok a year before, in the other the mother-in-law had come three months before. In two other cases the young girl had run away — that is, had fled to her fiancé's home, and the couple had stayed there until the wedding, or until pregnancy was well advanced. A similar temporary settlement with the man's mother was the result of a quarrel with the girl's parents when her *feen* was unwilling to get properly married to the girl or work at the father-in-law's stand in the market-place.

A number of nuclear families also lived in the slum. Some of these had grown-up, unmarried children, and a couple of them were the families of siblings. If we look at the true nuclear families, Kàj's was the one which most resembled a Western one. She had been married once before, and had two grown-up daughters from that marriage. They lived in flats in rehousing projects near their father, where Kàj had let them stay when the marriage broke up. Now she lived with her husband and a boy of ten. Her mother had died when she was a child, and she said that she had no family.

Among the others we can mention Pheen, who was a Christian, and not a proper Thai, according to people in the slum. She kept up close contact with her mother and had converted her to Christianity. The mother visited her, but would not live with her because there was no work for her to do in the slum, she said. Pheen's children went to school and Pheen had no income-generating work. Dèeg (like Pheen) had moved to the slum less than a year before, and the last three nuclear families were those of the two prostitutes and a minor wife.

Three of the six nuclear families here were families where the woman of the house was alone or very badly off; in four of the six the woman had no family or had very poor or tenuous relations with her parents.

Older people who moved in with their families in the slum moved in with a son or daughter. Several factors were important for their choice: which children they liked best, the practical situation of the family (Sìi's father did not move in because he could not go to the toilet): and economic considerations — it is of course more pleasant to live with a relatively well-off family, and finally, of course, the choice depended on which of the children would have them. There was no indication that the old lived most frequently with the youngest daughter, or expressed any wish to do so.

The complex picture of the settlement pattern grows a little clearer when we consider settlement in the slum among the young couples who grew up in Bangkok and can settle there as they wish or as practical and economic considerations allow.

Among these, settlement near the woman's parents was preferred. This conclusion is supported by a consideration of the emotional relationships between mothers/daughters-in-law and mothers and daughters respectively. In all cases where a family lived with the husband's parents there was either open conflict or an avoidance relationship between the women, whereas mothers and daughters had relationships of close day-to-day cooperation and expressed warm feelings for one another.

In the villages in Thailand the most common form of settlement is that the young couple moves to the girl's parents' house when they get married and afterwards move to their own house in the neighbourhood, where they stay. Here the extended family cooperates in everyday work, both household work and the cultivation of the ricefields. At harvest-time, periods of transplanting and sowing, work is done in mutual help groups. These consist partly of the man's political connections and neighbours, partly of the group defined by the female line of descent. In the slum this settlement pattern came naturally to the women. But there were several factors which contributed to changes in the pattern.

First, there was the question of space — there was not always scope for extending the family near the mother's house, although some families in such cases cramped themselves together more to make room for a new family. Secondly, migration itself entails that the woman moves away from her mother. Among the 24 women who had migrated to Bangkok, there was only one case where a whole family had moved at once. The women maintained contact with their mothers in the country even after as much as 20 years in the slum.

Another factor which counteracted settlement with the woman's parents was that fathers tried to keep their daughters under control. They attempted to monitor their grown-up daughters' circle of acquaintances, and especially to prevent young men from visiting them. In most cases they rejected offers of marriage to the daughters, who would thereby be forced to run away with their *feens*; and since the usual procedure was simply for the young couple to go to the man's home, they often stayed there, at least until the birth of a child was imminent. We may add to this the fact that men's power and scope seem to have been reinforced in the city. In the villages there was no special advantage for a man in moving to his wife's home or near it. He would be subject to his father-in-law's authority for years to come and would have no kin of his own to support him. Potter (1977) describes an avoidance relationship between fathers-in-law and sons-in-law, and the wife as the one who mediates between them.

In the slum similar factors are at work. It is an advantage for both the woman and man to live with or near his/her own parents. If men's position in relation to women is strengthened in the slum, they will in many cases be lucky enough to be able to settle with their own parents and to avoid moving in with the young woman's.

In the villages, sons and daughters inherit equally, and sons-in-law will, through the wife's inheritance, be provided with land which is at the family's disposal. One of them (if all the daughters are married) will presumably take over the father-in-law's role as head of the house. In the slum, there is not much to inherit, and much less authority to take over. When we consider these factors and the practical restrictions in the form of lack of space, it is quite surprising that the settlement of young couples with the woman's parents has been kept up to the extent it has.

11. Social Relations within Families

The social relations within the families were based on the dimensions of age and sex, men and older people having higher status. This was built into everyday habits such as forms of greeting and language in general (such as choice of personal pronouns). Men were supposed to be the heads of households and controlled the most important resource of the household, the money income. Men usually had higher incomes or the only incomes.

Men's control of incomes

In four families a middle-aged woman administered the incomes of the whole family: in one family a son and daughter-in-law gave the mother of the husband their earnings; in one family two daughters and a son-in-law gave the mother of the wife their earnings; and in one family an adult but unmarried daughter maintained her mother and two younger brothers with some help from a married brother. In these three families the middle-aged woman was unmarried (either divorced or a widow). One of the families, however, was large: a middle-aged couple, three daughters (one of them grown-up), three sons, a son-in-law and a daughter-in-law. The middle-aged mother administered all of her children's incomes along with her own and most of her husband's. In this family no one had a big income; many small ones were pooled, and the men did not earn much more than the women (one daughter earned the minimum wage, the mother lent out money and the men worked as carriers).

In nuclear families the wife administered the income. The use of surplus was decided on in common in two, and in one the wife got a fixed amount, the husband the surplus. In four the wife got nothing or very little from her husband (Nŭu's, Cíab's, Tĭm's and Bàd's).

In 16 families the wife got a more or less fixed amount of money and the surplus was utilized by husbands, sons and daughters as they saw fit. In ten of these sixteen families wives complained that their husbands utilized the money for minor wives, gambling or *paj thîaw* (restaurants and so on).

The women who earned money and were mothers all used their incomes on necessities for the family and the remaining six women earning an income were young women living with parents or in-laws, all paying something to their mothers.

Three paid their whole incomes, to the mother, one her whole income to a mother-in-law, and two only part of their incomes.

An example can be taken from a relatively well functioning family, Sïi's. She lived with her husband (a second marriage but of more than fifteen years standing) intermittently with between one and three unmarried sons and one married, and three grandchildren by other sons. Her daughter Tïm lived opposite her house with her husband and three children, but the daughter had trouble maintaining her own family, as her husband gave her no money. Sïi worked for her big family besides making and selling roasted bananas and rice scones. She earned 25-30 baht a day (plus what her family ate of her products) and got approximately the same amount from her husband. Her sons gave her money in crisis situations if they could afford it. Her husband and sons would earn 100-150 baht a day working in construction, on the average working 20 days a month, depending on circumstances.

Sïi thought her husband a really good man. He always gave her money if he had any, her grandchildren loved him much and considered him their father; he did not gamble too much, and when he did it was mainly to be together with his friends. He was often tempted to lend out money to other people, and she thought he ought to think of his family first. But he was a very good husband, she could tell him everything the way it was, and they did not get into quarrels but were like friends to each other.

Still, the control of resources within the family was the man's privilege. Sïi could hardly feed her big family on 60 baht a day, and very little, if any, surplus was left for her and the children's personal needs, while her husband had a quite reasonable surplus. The situation was extremely acute in the first month of my stay. Sïi had typhoid and had been given an injection and pencillin pills at the clinic. She could hardly pay the expenses and the children were given poor food — rice and raw cucumber. At the same time her husband went gambling, lost more than a 1,000 baht and unfortunately had to bribe the police to escape. Sïi did not complain. She thought of the lack of income as a result of her illness and the fact that she could not work then.

Men's control of incomes and especially of the surplus meant that women and children lived in poverty while men were able to squander money on their vices. The following table sets out the control of incomes.

Table 11.1
Use of incomes[1]

Pooling	5
Only men had income	10
Wives' income	12
Only income for necessities	4
Supplementary to men's	8

Men gave a fixed amount of their incomes to necessities.
The surplus was used for Minor wives, 3; Gambling, 5; Restaurants, 3; Heroin, 1[2].

Men thus controlled the most important means of survival — the money incomes. Their main argument was that they had earned the income. They had worked hard to get it, and their work was independent of the family or household, the result of their own efforts. They had earned the income as individuals and thus could dispose of it as individuals. Their responsibility for the family, or their lack of it, was a personal question related to their characters, needs and dispositions. It was not a question for the family — although women might try to make it one — and it was not a question for any outside group. (It might well be true that the way to get any work at all was through family connections. Sĩi's husband, for instance, was often the one who found work for his sons as well as for himself. But the payment was still a personal income and disposed of as such.)

Men's control of labour and sexuality

Men controlled the main resources of the family, the money incomes, and they likewise controlled women's work in the sense that they had the right to women's services at home, as shown above. Most men did not object to their wives and daughters working for incomes as long as they took care of the household or arranged for it to be taken care of in one way or another.

When wives wanted to go up-country, either to visit their mothers or other relatives, or when they went on a trip to *tham bun*, they had to arrange matters with their husbands — to ensure that food was prepared, that somebody was in the house to look after family possessions — and they had to get the money from their husbands. In some cases such decisions were altered at the last moment because the husband changed his mind.

Women's whereabouts in the slum area were not subject to strict control in most cases. If they did not neglect the household and the care of husband and children, most men did not object to wives or daughters going for walks and talking to other women. In the evening and at night, of course, women had to be at home.

In three cases, however, husbands did object to wives sitting in a neighbour's house chatting, but the women and friends and neighbours reacted strongly against these restrictions. In a few cases, too, women refused to cater for drunk husbands. In one case both the wife and daughters fled the house in the daytime and went to friends so they could not hear the husband's calls for service. In another, a wife moved herself and her children into her mother's house at night when the drunk husband and his friends insisted on a third meal in two hours.

Men thus controlled the main resources of the family, the income and the labour. They also controlled women's sexuality. Men were extremely suspicious of wives' and daughters' flirtations. A man would become furious and very threatening on hearing about his wife's flirtation with another man. He would get extremely jealous if another man touched the upper arm of his fiancée, and men felt it to be their right to control any contacts their women might have with other men.

Men's sexuality was not subject to control. Wives might react to their husbands minor wives by trying to please their husbands, in the same way as they reacted to lack of economic support from their husbands — but usually they were in no position to take action over their husbands behaviour apart from leaving them. Even then husbands would threaten wives that they would find them wherever they went and bring them back.

Norms for men's responsibility for the family was weakly enforced if at all in the slum. Among the men, but certainly not among the women, norms might have been that spending money on drinks, gambling and especially minor wives was a sign of manliness and power. In the official culture an example of this attitude is the former Prime Minister, Sarit. The image he tried to build up in public has been analysed by Thak Chaloentiarana in *Thailand: the Politics of Despotic Paternalism* (1979). This shows how Sarit tried to win support by building on a modern version of traditional male values. He tried to pose as a *nág leeng*, that is a powerful man with strong feelings, a man of action, warm and supportive to his friends, fierce to his foes and a great womanizer. Elements in Sarit's image as a powerful patriarch were a strong emphasis on cleanliness, fierce persecution of minor criminals and a modern harem — a flock of more than 200 mistresses.

In traditional as well as modern Thai culture there seem to be differences between upper-class (and middle-class) concepts of gender roles and behaviour and the concepts prevalent among poorer people. As mentioned above, upper-class concepts a hundred years ago were very rigid, requiring the seclusion of women and a strong emphasis on virginity, although even here women usually had some education in secular matters. Peasant women had much more freedom. They managed the household and production, while men did corvée-labour, and they were the nucleus of the household and the bearers of the spirits connected with birth and death.

Men from the middle class today still seem to retain much more narrow-minded attitudes to their women. Fathers control young women's whereabouts much more strictly, concepts of women's work restrict women more to traditional, or rather Western, concepts of women's proper work.

It hardly seems an accident that the rich man in the slum was the head of a family where women were closely watched and the young were subject to control, while the man had many minor wives. This was clearly the most patriarchal family in the slum, the one where the women felt most helpless in the face of their suppression.

The household's importance for men

Men had greater authority in the household. But the household had much less importance for men in the slum than it had up-country. The household did not own or manage any property, land or other means of production. It was without relevance for production which created things or incomes. Nor did the household, seen from men's point of view, need any daily work or cooperation to be maintained. This was women's domain and men felt rather aloof from daily problems. These were not their business, as long as they, themselves and the children were catered for.

The household was no longer the nucleus from which men would make political alliances in the attempt to influence the board of a school or temple as it was no longer the nucleus where it was necessary for kin-relations to co-operate in order to produce or gain influence. The household had no value as inheritable property or as a responsibility to be taken over when the parents-in-law retired by younger men married into the family. Even if men had the greater authority in the household, there was very little in material terms to exercise authority over, and nothing to be taken over. Even as far as men's prospects for old age were concerned, the household as a unit held out very little promise: it might well be dissolved before the parents grew old. The important thing then would be either the man's own savings/investments, which were usually nil, or having one of the children in a good position in society. In most cases, this was a possibility beyond the reach or influence of a father, although his interest in his children's education could be seen as a factor here.

The authority men held in families and households was thus important in the sense that they enjoyed their women's services at home and that their freedom to utilize incomes and time off work as they saw fit, and to indulge their sexuality freely, was not curtailed. It might have had some importance too in that it gave the men a feeling of having a place or a situation where they were masters in their own homes.

But in material terms of wealth, inheritance, production or security in old age the household played a minor role. Nor did it require cooperation with others in daily life or in special situations. When men formed bonds with others as friends, by exchange of favours, by obtaining and discussing work, by lending money, in pastimes such as drinking or gambling, the household might play a role as the place where their needs were served; but the links to women in the household and their relatives were of little significance.

The household's importance for women

From the point of view of women in the slum the family and household had much more importance.

The household was of importance to most women in the slum as their main source of money. Most women were dependent on their husbands' earnings. Even the three self-employed women who earned decent incomes could only do this either because a husband had helped with the initial investment or because the earnings contributed by husband or children formed the capital they lent out at interest. Those working in wage-labour could only rarely maintain a family on their incomes. The household was thus of great importance as a major resource for survival.

The family, or the extended family, was also however, of great importance as a source of support when required. In everyday life mothers and daughters helped one another greatly. This was taken for granted and not talked about; but in extended families where a mother and grown-up daughters lived near one another it was often next to impossible to know who made the food and did the shopping and so on.

Some women, who did not have a mother living nearby, were close to neighbours, and help was exchanged between these instead (for instance the families living around Chalŭaj's household). Young mothers had their mothers to look after children when at work. Tíg's mother, Sămphaw, for instance, who complained about having to take care of her son's baby, had looked after, and still did look after, Tíg's children while she was at work. Among the women who had both children and work the mother would look after the child/children if at all possible. (There were exceptions, for example in Nŭu's family, and in the case of Bun, whose mother was dead and who asked a neighbour instead.) Mothers were often of great help in family crises or conflicts. Most fathers, I was told, would try to prevent their daughters contacting eligible young men. In three cases the father was extremely possessive — *huàng*. The feeling of being *huàng* indicates, I was told, that the father loves his daughter a lot, and this is good. But it also means that he wants to keep her for his own comfort and companionship and thus to prevent her finding a boyfriend and the young women thought this was bad. In any case the father has little opportunity to prevent young women from meeting potential boy-friends, since they go to school or work. What he can influence are visits to his house and this the fathers did.

In these situations the mother, who is supposed to help the father to keep watch on the daughters' acquaintances, did turn a blind eye to visits in the afternoon before the husband returned from work; in one case a mother even went on a trip to *tham bun* on which the young man in question had suggested the daughter go. Thus mothers often helped their daughters in practical ways to avoid their fathers' control.

Mothers were likewise a major source of support when conflicts with husbands occurred. Sĭi, whose daughter Tĭm got divorced while I lived in the area, waited patiently and did not interfere in her daughter's marriage although the husband did not give much economic or other support to Tĭm and her children. Sĭi looked after the children; they would often share a meal and Tĭm would usually fetch water for her mother. But only when her husband left her; drunk and angry, did her mother intervene — scolding him, protecting the children so that he could not take them away, telling him not to return and threatening him with a stick.

In crises mothers were usually of great help. The three women from my houses who gave birth while I lived there had their mothers come in from up-country to stay in the house, help with household chores and the newborn child. Other women had returned to their native village when they were about to give birth to a child in order to be near their mothers.

When a mother fell ill she would likewise ask a daughter to come and take care of the household while she was away. The same would happen if nobody was there to look after the house when they went up-country for a day or two.

The closeness of a mother thus meant a lot to a daughter both in practical ways, mainly at times of births and when childcare was necessary and in terms of support when conflicts arose with husbands or (in the case of younger women) with fathers. When mothers came into conflict with their husbands, daughters expressed sympathy, but could not interfere at all. They were supposed to, and mostly did, respect and love both their parents and conflicts between these were not disclosed to them unless they were absolutely obvious. Even when physical fights occurred the daughters did not intervene unless they were afraid the parents would kill each other.

Daughters expressed their love for their mothers strongly. Some young women said they wanted to live near their mothers; if they could not, they would miss them too much. The strongly expressed love for the mother might of course be more or less strongly felt; but it was the expression of an expected form of behaviour. One example was the university student in the rich man's house who had her own interest in continuing to study after her arranged marriage had been agreed. She told me about her studies, and explained how hard she worked. Her father had given her permission to go on to study for a BA if she got good marks. Then she said, "I do it for the sake of my mother. I do it to make mother happy. Now my brother has just failed his exam, I do it for my mothers' sake."

Younger women in the slum usually had their mothers living nearby, and cooperation in the everyday work for the family went on smoothly. The middle-aged women had usually migrated when young, leaving their parents. Some of them had come to Bangkok with a sister or maternal aunt and still more had lived with such relatives during their first period there. Now, many years later, nearly all the women whose mothers were still alive kept up contact. The most widely observed form of contact was the daughter's yearly trip home, if possible together with her own daughters. Some also received visits from their mothers in the slum. A few visited only at intervals of several years, but in these cases another family member — a daughter — would go instead. On such visits, gifts were exchanged: the middle-aged women would bring something more easily bought in the city and money, the mother from the countryside would give rice, fruit or vegetables. A few women had their children living up-country, at least for a period. But in so far as this meant a separation of mother and child it was not much liked by the mothers in the slum, as the separation of mother and child, when children lived with mothers-in-law, was disliked.

One thing that testifies to the importance attached to the female line of descent is the fact that every woman in my slum houses who had a mother living up-country, and had found a husband in the city, had returned home to her mother, held a wedding or asked forgiveness for running away, and paid the mother a bride-price. Usually, it was the husband who paid, but in some cases the young couple had saved together to be able to go back and re-establish or maintain proper relationships with the mother of the wife.

Since all the women in my houses, except one, had left their mothers (if alive) when they migrated, I found it very impressive that connections up-country were maintained to such a high degree. Many of the material interests which are the foundation of the importance of matrilineal descent up-country are eroded in city life with the atrophy of inheritance and common production. Yet relations between mothers and daughters are still strong, much valued and function in everyday life to a very high degree.

Relations between mothers and daughters thus ought to be good, warm and smooth. So ought relations between sisters. But in two cases sisters quarrelled in the slum. In both cases, however, they were very ashamed. One of them, a woman in her fifties, actually started to weep as she told me about the quarrel. (In both cases the women only told me about the trouble after more than an hour of interviewing in a situation where nobody else could hear). Both pairs of sisters had discussed who should take care of dependent parents. Unfriendliness towards sisters and actual struggles were disgraceful, the more so since they might create the suspicion that the women in question did not love their parents as they ought to, and did not help enough in their old age.

Relations between sisters were usually good. Sisters did not usually help each other with responsibilities as much as they helped their mothers. Only in one instance did a sister take care of a child for another sister, and only for a short period of time. Nor did they carry water for each other, although they might do so for their mothers. Their relationship was less characterized by formal commitments; but then they often had interests and daily problems or pastimes in common.

They often went *paj thîaw* together — going to visit a temple at the full-moon, going to see a Likee play or to a fair in the area or just going down to Checking Point, either to look at the children playing there and indulge in small talk with friends or to rent a bike or ride it for half an hour in the open space there. Similarly, sisters often went together to look for a job or tried to get work at the same place if possible.

Older women did business with sisters — one woman borrowed a house from her sister to start a beauty parlour and the sister living nearby kept an eye on what went on there if the owner was not on the premises. Or a sister with her family moved into the house another sister left to move in to the Port's staff housing scheme. In times of crisis sisters, aunts and grandmothers often helped. A young woman running away would rather return to a grandmother than her own family if her boyfriend jilted her. When Tĭm left home following her husband's return, she moved in with a sister of her mother. Sisters and mothers' sisters, sometimes grandmothers, were the relatives most immediately called upon if the parents and close relatives could not be counted upon in later life.

For women in the slum, then, the family or extended family was of much greater importance than it was for the men in the slum. The women's money income was dependent on the family. It was dependent on their husbands' incomes and their husband's support of their needs: whether the women had income-earning work or not, lack of support from a husband left a woman in a difficult economic position. The women's own incomes were likewise dependent on the family or extended family. Women who had children and wage-labour were dependent on female kin, usually mothers, to take care of the children while they were away. Women who were self-employed were dependent on their daughters' help for a lot of small things which had to be done in the business or in the household if the income earned was to be reasonable.

Older women who did not have a husband were dependent on children's incomes; while sons usually gave some money in times of crisis, and often gave higher amounts, daughters usually gave more systematically, including dependable contributions to long-term budgets.

Woman and the Family

Conflicts about settlement

Conflicts in the slum thus arose about who should live together. Men seemed to be able to ask women's kin to move out of the house — this happened in two cases. It happened when Nŭu's husband asked her sister to move and she did so, creating childcare problems for Nŭu. Nŭu's husband's sister's employee, a young woman working in the beauty parlour, then moved in instead. In the other case Chalŭaj's husband asked her mother and crippled sister to move out. They did, and were allowed to live in a small hut nearby in return for looking after the house of a single man when he was away at work or elsewhere. Chalŭaj continued to give them food, which she placed at their hut in the early morning before her husband woke up.

Women did not have the authority to ask others to move out, and conflicts thus lead to alliances between the women in the house against an intruder who might divide the loyalty of the men. In Sămphaw's family the members were divided according to gender. Sămphaw and her husband would often have rows, but all the children talked to both and loved both — they were heavily dependent on the father who earned the family income, who gave a fixed amount for the household and distributed gifts to his children. The two eldest sisters did not talk to the two eldest brothers. There had been many conflicts, some of them only dimly remembered; the latest had been the second eldest daughter's relationship with and later marriage to a man who moved into the house opposite Sămphaw's (he had rented a room in the house of Nŭu's husband's sister). The father did not like the future son-in-law and tried to prevent the relationship and the marriage and the two sons supported him strongly, while Sămphaw, and in particular the oldest daughter, supported Pùu.

The sons backed up their father, too, when Sămphaw had a flirtation with another man on a trip to *tham bun*, and the sisters and brothers in the family simply did not talk to one another. When the oldest son moved his very young wife and their child into the house, the women disapproved strongly. They did not speak to her at all, nor did they co-operate with her doing household chores.

The same patterns can be seen in two other cases where a new daughter-in-law moved into the house of the husband's parents. Ùbon told me about her relationship with her in-laws. She had migrated to Bangkok to avoid an arranged marriage and after six months work in a hospital met her boy-friend and lived with him. After another six months she went with him to his parents' house to meet them and get married. When she *wai'ed* (a Thai greeting expressing deference to seniors) her mother-in-law turned her face away — a very drastic and humiliating reaction.

Nevertheless, she moved into the house and soon became pregnant. While in confinement at a good and expensive hospital, she was afraid her mother-in-law would steal her newborn son. She showed a photo of the mother-in-law to the staff and warned them, "Do not give my child to this woman under any circumstances, please."

The mother-in-law came to fetch the boy but did not get him. She told the staff that Ùbon was just a "woman of that kind", implying that she was a prostitute, and that she would probably leave the child at the hospital. In actual fact Ùbon was very depressed, as her husband had not come to visit her and she thought about abandoning the child; but was influenced by the slogans hung on the wall. "Even animals take care of their offspring. You are a human being. Are you worse than an animal?"

On the seventh day her husband arrived and they went back together.

While she was pregnant with her second child she felt really mistreated, as she had to do all the hard work, such as fetching water; after three years she moved out. She stole her husband's money out of the house and bought a house. A brother and the father of the husband came and repaired it, and then she moved. The neighbours asked why she was moving and she replied, "This is the day of the abolition of slavery. [It was King Chulalongkorn's day]."

A brother of her husband moved to the new house together with Ùbon, and it was not until two months later that her husband moved in, because his brothers made fun of him, she said. In May, her husband's father moved in too, and the husband's family was thus split — the wife living with one of her daughters, the men moving to the new in-law.

The same kind of split happened in another family. A couple in their sixties, married since early youth, lived with the mother's mother and three children — two adult sons and one adult daughter. Another married daughter lived nearby with her two children; her husband worked in Saudi Arabia and sent money home to his family. One of the sons moved a girl-friend/wife into the family and this caused a split. The mother and mother's mother moved to the married daughter's house, the sister to her own small house with her new husband. The mother-in-law said,

> No, I do not have any disagreement with my husband. I moved on account of my red-haired daughter-in-law. Nobody can stand her. Just ask anybody, nobody can stand her, really.

In all the cases where women lived near or with their son's wives there were great problems, either open conflicts or avoidance relationships. Mothers-in-law and daughters-in-law were in no way shy about these conflicts. They would make a fuss, quarrel loudly and talk about it to everybody who would listen.

Both men and women were supported by their own kin, but mainly by their kin of the same sex as themselves. Thus women's harsh reactions to daughters-in-law (or sisters-in-law) who moved into the house led to these women's returning home for support — usually to their parents who lived close by. The relatively high number of young couples living close to the parents of the mother was thus a result both of the traditional way of living and of conflicts going on in the slum, occurring when women who were related to a young man reacted furiously to his moving a new wife into their house. As can be seen, the reactions were often strong enough to isolate the young wife; if she did not move out the family might split along gender lines — the mother and daughters living together, the husband living with sons and the new in-law.

Changes in family life

Up-country, according to Potter and Potter, the usual arrangement was that the new husband of one of the daughters in a family moved into the house of the parents for a period. The new couple lived with the in-laws of the husband and worked their fields. Later the young couple moved out, usually to a new small house nearby with some land of their own. In recent years young couples were more likely to move away, since there was often a shortage of available land. But the traditional form of settlement, which still functions to a great extent, is that parents live together with their daughters (in the same village or nearby) and their sons-in-law. When the parents die or retire, one of the younger couples, or the youngest daughter if unmarried, takes over the responsibility for the household. Inheritance goes to sons and daughters equally, but if the youngest daughter stays in her parents' house until they die she usually takes over the house.

> In a system like this, the wife is in a most important position. Her husband's status in the family is conferred by her. She has the job of mediating between her husband and her father, who are separated from one another by an avoidance taboo. She is the connecting link, bound to her father by one sort of love, and to her husband by another. There is a great deal of mediating to do since the father and the husband have interests which are frequently opposed to one another. The son-in-law, like any heir, is eager to take control, and the father-in-law is reluctant to relinquish it.[3] There is no relationship of long standing, as there would be between father and son, to ease the conflict, since the son-in-law joins the family when the daughter is an adult, and by her choice. The effect of all this is to give a woman an important voice in the management of family life, a position of power which comes from her place in the structure of the family. Thus, the specific kind of structure has the effect of increasing the importance of women, even though formal authority is vested in men. However, the rule of respect for seniors tends to reinforce the position of the husband (Potter 1977, p. 101).

If the social relations in the family and extended families up-country and in the slum are compared important changes become apparent. The household has continued to be important for the women; its importance has possibly even increased, since they are dependent on their men's incomes as well as on their female kin for organizing and doing their daily work, both the work of producing human beings and income-generating work. For the men, the household has lost much of its importance; it does not add to their income-earning possibilities, the organization of the household is of little or no importance either for their work for an income or their position in the local community. Thus women's power is diminished. They no longer confer authority within a producing unit or mediate any further inheritance.

Women struggle to build up or maintain households where they live together with their female kin, and they do this with some success as has been shown, since most of the young couples actually had their living quarters close to the wife's mother. The importance of female kin was in some cases greater than the importance of husbands, considered from the point of view of settlement. In others, women struggled to keep both husbands and female kin in the house.

Up-country women defined the group of people with whom men would work in their everyday life in production. Their presence conferred the control of the means necessary for production (land and tools) on men through their incorporation into the household. They held forth the promise of future inheritance and control, and with the coming of age and seniority the women's presence conferred authority over other people on the men.

Thus the diminishing role of the household for men entailed a parallel decrease for them in the importance of the women in the household. This is perhaps most clearly seen in men's attitudes towards the household and their lack of responsibility towards the family. In Potter's description the women have many suspicions that men might cheat them, for example; but no actual lack of responsibility on the part of the men is reported. Men are shown to be at least as eager to improve living standards and expand the property of the household as the women are. They do not squander the incomes of the household on expensive pastimes, and this seems reasonable enough, since they themselves can take advantage of the growth of the household's wealth. In the slum the men did not have a comparable interest in the household and its members, and since less importance was attached to the advantages women conferred by marriage, the women did not have the means or the power to increase their husband's responsibility towards the household.

12. Gender and Sex Conflicts

I have shown how changes in social relations within families increased the power of men and decreased women's. The importance of the family or household in material terms decreased for men, while women became more dependent on the continuation of the family. Besides this, a tendency towards increasing individualism seemed to be present. Social control of men's and women's behaviour was lacking and no communal institutions canalized cooperation between people in the slum. Men's attempts to control women mostly took the form of individual men's control of wives and daughters (sometimes mothers), whereas women tried individually to hold husbands' vices in check and usually supported one another only when conflicts were open and had become serious.

In such a situation conflicts between the sexes must be expected to be widespread and this was indeed the case in the slum. Only few families could avoid conflicts between husbands and wives, or fathers and daughters. It is often assumed, especially in the Asian context, that women submissively accept a deteriorating family situation, and mainly try to please their husbands and coax them into fidelity and responsibility towards the family. This was, however, hardly the case here. Women struggled to maintain their families, both with other women and with their husbands' vices. The conflict with female newcomers such as daughters-in-law has been described, and women also had to cope with minor wives, although a certain amount of discretion was usually maintained in these cases.

Women had a constant struggle coping with their husbands' gambling and the risks of police harassment. They came into conflict with husbands over minor wives and over their squandering of money on restaurants, motor-bikes and loans. Women struggled for some degree of independence, dignity and self-respect.

The understanding among the women of relations between the genders seemed to be based on an idea of equality. Some women would say, "If he can do it, why can't I do it?" Some women had divorced husbands, because they had a minor wife, as one of them said, "I don't want to be the first or the second. I want one husband and one wife." Although it was generally felt to be just that men and women should behave in the same way towards one another and that neither should have lovers, there was also a feeling that having minor wives was just the way men behaved.

Women used a variety of means to try to obtain some degree of responsibility towards the family from men. Some tried to manipulate their husbands' feelings; but sometimes conflicts developed into physical fights between husband and wife.

Gender Conflicts

Divorce was used as a threat by women, and in some cases the threat was carried out. Women usually had support from their mothers, sisters and neighbours, and from their closest friends, as we shall see in the three excerpts from taped interviews. The interviews are with members of the same family: it is a mother in her forties and her two grown-up daughters who speak.

No two women are the same; each of course, has her own personality. The three women chosen here were outspoken and explained their situations in detail. Not all families had such quarrels, but most had. In some, the husband's control of his wife's whereabouts was stronger, in some the daughters and wife behaved themselves. The problems with minor wives were very typical.

Sămphaw, in her forties, loved talking to friends and going to Likee plays. Her best friend was Lee. They had lived close to each other for twenty years, had husbands who worked as dockers and children of the same age. But she had many other friends and acquaintances in different parts of the slum. Together with Lee she had organized a *tham bun* trip to Lee's native village. Sămphaw and her daughters had made a beautiful money-tree with gifts for the monks and with her husband she had donated a large sum of money. She did not go on the trip, however, because her husband got very drunk while she was gambling the night before and took the 600 baht he had given her back again. She fought with him on this occasion and when we returned from the trip she came and complained, showed me the bruises and scars and told me about the fight. Sămphaw loved friends, she loved talking and chatting and she loved to go on *tham bun* trips.

As a young woman she had been a Likee player and she still loved to watch the plays, found the dresses very beautiful and enjoyed the coming together of large numbers of people. I have chosen her narrative because I find her love of life and her search for fun and happiness quite overwhelming.

In the part of the narrative given here she talks about this as well as about her conflict with her husband on this account, about her feeling of the lack of justice in the situation and, despite this, her continuing respect for the husband because he is the one who earns the money for the family. Sămphaw is not physically strong any more. She cannot read and write, and is — as will be seen — very imprecise with figures.

> Then we sit in a car to go and make merit [up-country]. We go to a temple over there . . .
> Then I come down from the temple. I play poker, you see. Just like that, I like to play poker. I play, and play rich, too [win]. Then I give him [A Likee player who liked her. They had met several times before in the slum. He was not her lover.] 50 baht to go and buy something to eat.
> Then I lose in the game, but in the early morning he comes and gives me money, gives me 150 baht to invest. Here it is, he says. Suddenly, 150 baht.
> I then strike it lucky and the investment comes back so I pay him his money back, the 150 baht. I make a profit, the money comes and goes, comes and goes. Then I say: Now I'm going down to wash my face, I'm going to the big pavilion. I tell him this: You mustn't follow me, Buntham. Otherwise people will see, there are many people here.

He says: well, other people may see, and so what? What does that matter?

I say: I don't mind if other people see me. But my son is here. If he sees, there'll be a big story [a conflict and fighting].

And the story was already there. In the morning time they wanted to kick, wanted to stab each other in the temple. Buntham and my son Kòb they start fighting. I go in between them, I try to block the way between them, I ask why they act like this, as if they were fighting over a woman. It's no good in a temple, I tell them . . .

When we come back and reach my house again, my *feen*, he sharpens his knife, a dagger as long as this. He says he will hit me, he will stab me in my face.

Well, I had escaped to go and *paj thîaw* at the temple. Then my *feen* comes home from work and doesn't see my face at home. So my daughter tells him I've gone, I've run off to *paj thîaw*. He gets crazy, very much, he drinks liquor, he cries out loud. I only stayed away for one night, one night only.

Then I came back, and my *feen* told that he would cut my face with the big knife.

Then aunt Lee heard this. When I got off the bus Lee told me quick, quick, quick. My bag was a big one, full of all my clothes.

Then I ran out this way, that way, and I just went into Lee's house.

So my husband comes and asks Lee very loudly: Lee Lee, have you seen Sămphaw or not? Lee says: I haven't seen her. Aunt Sămphaw, she is down at Akkamai [bus terminal], she's going to her mother's house. Ha ha ha, that's what Lee said.

So I stayed in Lee's house for many days, many days: five days, eight days. When he knew that I was staying in Lee's house, he came back. When he had calmed down, he came back to ask me to come home.

I still wouldn't go back. I told him: I won't go back. You've accused me like this before. I can't take it. I don't want to go back, because I want to finish with you. I told him that, but he didn't want to finish with me. He wouldn't give me a divorce.

He said so, and I said: You make me sell my face, make me lose my good name. I said this and then he said: From now on I won't say anything, not say anything. Then I went back, but after two days we had a big row with each other, we hit each other a lot, we fought each other a lot. We kept hitting each other, fighting each other. We didn't speak to each other; for as long as two months we did not speak to each other.

I didn't want to look at my husband's face. What was the matter with his face? I really hated it. When I took a nap, I slept in front of Aunt Ĭam's house.

Then my husband came. He sat down near me, and said: Here, just take this money, and gave me 2,000 baht. Oi! a lot of money — 2,000 baht.

I thought I wanted to escape, but it would be difficult with the children. And when the money was gone, where would I stay? What would I do? I was angry and hurt. But I didn't leave, I didn't go away.

He is very jealous. If anyone comes to talk, comes to speak, he curses them: come on, say it in front of my house here! You just go jib jib jib you can't, what's the matter?

I don't know. I'd never go and be a flower of gold [be promiscuous]. But he just thinks . . . I can't go anywhere, any day. I can't go anywhere at all, really. Have you seen me or not? Seen me sitting idle by my house? He is jealous. The older he gets the more jealous he gets.

I am not jealous. He has another wife and a child and still I am not jealous. But he is jealous. I can go nowhere. I can't stay overnight, no matter with whom. If people see my face, they have to see his face too. The people in the Port, they say he should not be so jealous of his wife. It's strange, strange.

I am not jealous; I am indifferent. My heart, it has died and hardened . . .

Aunt Kàj here, she knows the personality of Tíg's father. Aunt Lee here, she knows his personality. So when my friends go somewhere, they don't try to persuade me to go with them, to go anywhere at all. I get cursed, cursed, cursed, I don't like a jealous person, I don't like him being jealous. The more jealous he is, the more I like to have my own way. The more he is jealous the more I grow, really. I want to be myself then. To go, to go. I will make him see, you know, go openly before his very eyes.

These damned men, they like to come and see me. Strange. Liquor, I don't know how to drink. It was like this. When we came to a temple, then my friends like to deal out cards. When I sat playing, then these people saw our group, so they came and sat beside me, behind me, to watch me play cards.

I win or I lose and then the Likee people, they come and sat, then they ask Buntham. Then he told them who I am. That's only in the temple, he can't come here, they can't come here. He can come to block 6, but we can't meet. My husband tells me that if I go away he will follow me, he will search for me, look for me until he finds me. He will follow me and simply kill me. He is very jealous . . .

Then my *feen* went to gamble in Aunt Dèeg's house. I was bathing, I wore the *phâathǔng* around my breast to bathe. Then I went to call him. I called Tíg's father: Go back home! Whether you win or lose it's not worth it.

If the police arrested him it would be no good. I wouldn't draw the pot in the loan game, the interest was too much. I told him this, but he wouldn't listen, he said: Go back, go back.

Then I went back home and just a moment later Aunt Dèeg shouted out, she just came and told Sǎmphaw that the police had arrested him, they had already gone.

I myself still don't know the story of how the police arrested Tíg's father. Then I had to argue with the police. Dead damn.

When I went up the station, I put up my hair, I put on a hat to cover my hair, I took a bath . . . Then all the money, so many thousands, 7–8,000 . . . at the police station. I paid car fare too.

I made all sorts of food to give them, to give it to him to eat, enough for three nights . . . and then I went and paid over there . . . In all, it was as much as 3,800. The court fee . . . for the court fee. I paid as much as 1,300 . . . I paid the court . . . I didn't have to pay the police but I bought things for them to eat [and drink].

The court official asked: did you play high low or not? A big official, a big person like a judge. Play? Yes, I played, my husband said. All together six people, already. The court fee was 1,300 for the ringleader of the gambling, 1,200 for the owner of the house, and 800 for the customer... My *feen* was not a ringleader, but the police, they saw that. Tíg's father was a fat person, they accused him of being the leader. They were able to find money on Tíg's father in the gambling house, he had money, he had 200. They blamed him, accused him of being the leader. The real leader was Sii's son, my *feen* was only a customer...

The Port is terrible. The Port Police, they take everything. The fine was expensive. [Sămphaw did get money for the fine, by drawing the pot in the loan game. Since she had to get it she promised to pay 62% per week in interest. In order to pay she folded paper bags.]

Then he came back, he got released. We were going to celebrate, but his nerves broke down. He couldn't speak at all. The next morning he couldn't speak at all, he couldn't speak for five days. He didn't speak to people at all for five days. My heart was troubled. I asked him: Do you want to eat rice or not? Huu — he didn't speak to me, no speaking at all. No matter who asked him something.

He had never been in prison, you see. He had just been jailed for the first time, so his nerves broke down, right?

We didn't quarrel with each other. I still, I still respected him because he was the one who earned the money.

The day I came here [the day after her husband's release] I had already gone to pay the fine. I had no money, just one baht. My stomach was hard, I thought, I worried, I fussed around the house, I didn't want to stay at all.

I went to that house. My son, he asked me: Where are you going? Mother, Mother, don't worry!

Buntham, he came to block 6 and someone came to call me. Then I put up my umbrella and left. Tíg's father did not know the story, he was watching television... then I went to talk to Buntham... Then my husband's uncle came out of his house... OK, my heart simply sank down to my ankles. Then the uncle asked Sămphaw if she knew Buntham?... so I put up my umbrella and drew back...

I can't do it. He can do it. He has a minor wife... but he forbids me to have a friend. Why? He can't let me go. He can do it. He can go everywhere. But I am not allowed.

His minor wife — she can go everywhere, she can stay away overnight, three nights, four nights... she comes back, then they don't kick or hit each other. His minor wife, she used to be the leader of a brothel. That kind. Not a good woman. They have a child together. But if I try to do it, I'm not allowed. He tells me if I do it, then he'll have to leave his work for sure, have to follow me and find me.

If I want to go to my mother's house, he still doesn't let me go, you see? Usually at Songkraan festival I would go and see my mother. He wouldn't let me go at all. If I go, then he must go too. Last year he wouldn't go. He said he had very little money. I was angry. I quarrelled with him, I cried a lot, I sat and ironed my clothes. He asked: Where do you want to go? I said: I want to go to my mother's house. He wept. He said: If she sees your face she must see my face too. He said this: No, if we go we must go together. He said that, he cried and cried. He threw plates. Bang! he just broke them, broke them . . .

I like to go places, it makes me feel comfortable. Open ears, open head, open ears, open eyes. He wants to keep me in a narrow place like this. It makes me really angry. But last year, I went. This year, this year, this year I can't go. Too little money. Usually, to go to my mother's house I need 2,000, 3,000 baht.

Tíg is Sămphaw's oldest daughter. She has worked since she was a child and is a very active and rather determined young woman. She lives opposite her mother's house with her husband and two children. When Tíg had been married for nearly two years her husband was conscripted and had to join the army. Then he had other girl-friends while Tíg lived with their small son just opposite her mother's house. She worked to earn a living for herself and the son. She suspected he had other girl-friends, and one day she asked him in the middle of a meal. The spoon fell out of his hand, and she felt she was right. When she found a telephone number in his pocket she felt sure.

Then, the week after, he came home again on a Friday. He told me: Tíg, next Friday I can't come. The army has forbidden the soldiers to come out, he said. He said, We must prepare, must be ready for action. That's what he said, right? Oh, well, it doesn't matter, it doesn't matter, I said.

But I had already realized. Do you know what I did then? I forged a letter. I had a younger sister write that I was a woman, I wanted a date with him to see a movie. Try to imagine! Then, on Thursday, he came. But he had told me he couldn't come because of the army. He lied. When he got the letter he came.

I didn't know the woman, I didn't write any name, just a letter making a date with him. I wrote: Lég, private soldier, Som-Ran. Please come to meet me here at Phra Kanong for a date with me, 8 o'clock in the morning, Friday.

Then, in the morning, my husband dressed and left.

I dressed and left, too. When he first came in, I pretended to ask him: Hey how could you come? He said: It doesn't matter now. The army let me leave. But no, I thought that he'd got the letter . . . then he went to Phra Kanong. At 8 o'clock in the morning, he was standing waiting at Phra Kanong. I went too to see whether he would stand waiting at Phra Kanong or not.

And he really did stand waiting at Phra Kanong flyover bridge, but he stood on the footpath. Then we met each other. I asked him: What are you doing here? My husband spoke now without any sweetness: And what are you doing here? Why did you come? I said: To see a friend. Then he said this: You and I, I doubt whether we can live with each other. So we stopped talking and he went back to the army.

We quarrelled a lot, I wouldn't give in. Later, he came back home, but still he found new women, this time a prostitute. This time I pretended like this: Lég, today your friend, the black and skinny one, I don't know his name, came to wait for me at the lobster factory. He said you had another woman. You know, he has a lot of friends, so he couldn't know which one it might be. The black and skinny one, the description was just a guess. I said to Lég: He said that he sympathized with me. He came and told me that you have another woman.

Then he asked: oh really? Who told you? I said: I don't know. He came to tell me. Try to think hard. It must be one of your friends.

I said this, right? He said, he did not say anything, he was silent. Then, later, he said this: Ah ha! She's renting a house for me, to stay in. She also gives me 30 baht a day. She is only 14-years-old. 14 is a very young age. But there are prostitutes even younger, only 13, only 12-years-old. Just ask my sister. So he accepted, it was true, right?

Then I went to his camp. I asked Sŏmcìd, who is a teacher, to go with me . . . She was afraid that we could quarrel, would fight with each other. So when we arrived at the military camp she called out: Phîi Lég, Phîi Lég, Phîi Tíg has come. She has come. Lég asked: Hey, how did you get here? And I answered: I took a bus. I said this, right? Then he said: What did you come for? I didn't listen. I cursed him first, I scolded him loudly, I damned him a lot. He told me not to curse here, he felt ashamed, the soldiers came out to watch and listen. I asked him if he felt ashamed himself. In the end I said this: We have to go. We have to go to your mother's house. I wanted to talk straight with his mother, otherwise she would accuse me, blame me for leaving him when he was in need.

I myself persuaded him to go: We had better go to your mother's house. If we speak here, your mother will not know, she will accuse me that when you are in trouble, then I leave you.

I said this: This story, this conflict, let's go with it to your mother.

Then we went to his mother. She was sitting there and his younger sisters and brothers were sitting there too. Then I told her: Mother [in-law], this man, he is an ancestor of monitors.

It's a damned thing. I said: He is not a good man. Do not accuse me of leaving him. I did not leave him. He did it to me first. Money, I never get money from him. His mother's money which you said I should get, I never got them, I never got any. I still have to work to eat. And my son. If he wants to break up, let him go. Just bring the clothes for him. If he wants to break up, just let him break up, let him go, Tíg will let him go. The mother was calm. She said: Lég, is this true? Did you really do this? Lég then nodded his head. Then Tíg said: This man is a monitor. I cursed a lot, he is a monitor.

Before coming down from his mother's house I said: Lég, if you don't come home this Friday you don't come home ever. It means that you and I break up, you never step into my house again . . . and my son don't visit him, I can look after him myself.

I said this, but at that time I had got morning sickness, I had a stomach with my daughter. I didn't know yet, was just one month gone, but I felt dizzy.

Then I said: Even if I have two babies I can look after myself. You and I will break up. I said this, then Lég said: But Tíg, I didn't really like her. He himself he had no money, the woman paid, so he took the money, took the money.

I don't like it, I said: There's no point speaking nicely to me. I'm going to break with you. His mother told me: Calm down, calm down. Try to talk. As for Lég, his mother never scolded him, she just said: Calm down, Listen, listen.

Then I went back home.

On Sunday Lég came with all his clothes, he came home. I had made up my mind that if he didn't come home this week. I would break with him, just leave it at that. But then he came.

Now my husband doesn't have other women, other wives. There's nothing doing there! I would get very annoyed. He doesn't dare do it again, he doesn't dare, I would really curse him.

Pùu is the second oldest daughter in the house. She is an intelligent young woman with a relatively good education. She is one of the few women in the area who speak standard Thai. She was deeply in love with her *feen* and would talk at length about him: his tenderness, his generosity and his handsomeness. For various reasons irrelevant in this context he had to leave her two weeks after their marriage, but they maintained contact by writing and she missed him a lot. She felt cut off from the mainstream of society, and said that all her friends from school had jobs or families and she was searching eagerly for a job herself. She told me about how she met her *feen*, about problems with her father and her mother's compliance, and she told me in great detail about the runaway situation.

He came here. When I first saw him he had no hair at all. He had just left the temple. Mother said: Don't look at his face, it's frightening . . .

I was afraid of him myself, too. His body is so big. He is so big. His face was frightening. When he popped his face in to look at me I would hide inside the house. He lived at Kèe's house [just opposite her mother's and father's, where Tíg lives too].

One day I took socks to knit at Kèe's house, right? I sat knitting. After a while he brought Khǐaw, his nephew Khǐaw to sit near me and asked: Hej, how old are you?

Then I said I was 23 years old. He asked: Do you have a *feen*?

I said: No.

He said: Why not?

I said: Not yet.

He then said: Why not?

I said: I don't want to have.

He said: Why don't you want to?

I said: Staying alone is good enough.

He said: Not true, some day you must have one.

He said this, right?

Then talking coming, talking going he asked whether I was studying or had already left school. I said I had left. I stayed in school until year ten that's all, I said.

Then he told me his older brother [not his real brother] was arranging a *tham bun* trip to Ayutthaya the next day.

I said: No one is going to Ayutthaya.

He then told me my mother was going too. He asked me if I would go or not?

Then I said: I don't know. If mother goes, I go too. If mother doesn't go, neither do I.

He then said he would go and ask mother: But tomorrow you dress up, right? Dress up tomorrow morning . . .

Then when I woke up in the morning the buses were outside. Big buses: ten wheels, six wheels, something like that. People got all dressed up. Mother was dressed. Phîi Phiag was dressed, then he turned to look at me. I did not get dressed.

I pretended to sit in front of the house. After a while he turned to look at me. I ignored him, ignored him, but I had already ironed my dress the night before, right? Then I waited to decide. Should I go, or should I not go? Then I decided I had better go. It was Saturday–Sunday. If I stayed home I would have nothing to do. So I dressed up, went up in the bus, the same bus as him . . .

After this trip Pùu and Phiag became friends — went to the Zoo, to movies or to markets together. He spent a lot of money on her, for entrance fees, food, drink and gifts. She said to her mother, "If Father comes back I am at Aunt Deeng's house, see? at Udonsek. Mother knew."
But mostly they met in the slum and sat talking outside the houses there.

We talked every day, but father did not know. We talked on the days when father worked, right? On the days when father didn't work, we couldn't sit talking. When father stayed home, I had to go to bed early, because my father would kick me, he strictly forbade me to talk to Phiag he said: Don't ever let me see that.

Oh, if he saw it, it would be the end of me. Mother couldn't even stop him. He said that if other people in the village saw it, it would be ugly. People would gossip, you know, these people, whenever they see anything they have to talk. He was afraid it would give him a bad name, too, he didn't like his daughters sitting talking with anyone. He is possessive —*hùang* — you see? He is very *hùang*. It is not proper, it is ugly.

He did not like my *feen*, he did not like men. He said: This man will never get along with my luck . I didn't care. Well, if they did not get along I don't know. I thought, let's wait and see. He also said that he didn't know his head and toe [his background]. He said so many times: Don't mess with him. Don't pay any attention to him.

But in my heart I thought it had nothing to do with my father, it didn't concern him, right?

One day, my father saw us. He didn't go to work, he went and slept. I thought it was still the head of darkness. I didn't go to sleep, I didn't take a bath yet. I sat at Aunt Ĩam's house (her next-door neighbour). Phĩi Phiag rested on the other side of the walkway. So we sat on opposite sites of the walkway, not close, right? We sat at some distance, sat and talked, the talk was coming, the talk was going. Then Phĩi Phiag asked me how much my father and mother would ask for, if he was going to ask for me from my father.

I said, to tell the truth, my mother knew, but I was afraid of father, very afraid.

He had planned that if we got married he would buy a Saburu [minibus] to drive, he could pay by instalments. I said that was quite good. If we could get 100 baht per day, or a bit more than 100, that was good enough. That would be comfortable.

The talking came, the talking went, then father came out, he came out to pee, to the toilet.

Father popped his face out, I saw it and my face became pale. Phiag said: What's wrong?

Father, father came.

But father would kick me, you see. Father would beat me up for sure. My heart beat fast, my heart flashed downwards, my face was pale, my mouth trembled, I was so afraid. I was afraid of my father. I am so afraid of him. Mother I am not afraid of, but I am afraid of father.

He doesn't beat us but he kicks us, he's an old boxer, you see, he kicks the children very often.

In the old days we argued. I liked to argue, to have a say.

So I said Oh, Phîi, I called him Phîi, you see. Father is peeping at us. He said: Wait, wait, be patient.

I turned to look, but father was not there any more.

I said: Phîi, I think we better go to bed. Both of us. Then I moved to go to bed, but I didn't dare go up into the house, so I walked in at the back of the house, and then I went to peep to see what father was doing.

Father was sitting there talking with mother, talking about me and Phîi. I heard father say: Have they been talking for a long time? Do they talk to each other every day?

Mother, she said: Eh, how should I know?

I began to be heartsick, my heart trembled. As soon as father went inside his mosquito net I went inside my mosquito net, too.

When I woke up the next morning I didn't dare look at father's face. He knew already that I liked the man, he knew it at once. He would know how to find fault with me all the time.

He didn't ask me anything, but he would find faults with me. Mother, said said: You, watch out for yourself, your father, he already knows, he could figure things out, you see?

Next day, I was sitting talking with Phîi, then there was a man who brought a watch to sell. The body of the watch was golden, but not gold, you see? He sold it for 300 baht. I myself, I don't like watches in all my life I didn't really want a watch.

Then Phîi Phiag he asked: Do you want a watch?

I said I didn't. He said: Don't have any scruples. After a while, then, he took the watch, he fixed it up, set it for me, and then handed it to me.

I said: By death, why did you buy this? I am not going to wear it.

But he gave it to me, and I always wear it in my pocket.

After I saw he wanted to give it to me, then I appreciated it, I thanked him and *wai'ed*.

I didn't like the watch very much, but when I saw my *feen* gave it to me, I thought I should keep it, I would have it as a souvenir.

That day mother lost in the high low gambling. She lost 300 baht. Father he asked: Do you still have the money? Mother, she said: I bought a watch for our daughter.

She was afraid he would find out, she told me before: If father asks, where the money is, tell him I bought the watch for you. I agreed.

Then he said: Where is the watch? and I took out the watch for him to see immediately. He said: It is beautiful, keep it, child keep it.

When I did not have a *feen* I was his favourite.

In the evening, however, the father heard from his neighbour, the man Phîi rented a room from, that it was Phîi who had bought the watch for Pùu.

> Father, he called me. I didn't know anything yet. I walked face floating, eyes floating [happy, without worries] to pick up the watch and hand it to him.
> Father, he said: This watch, who bought it for you? Tell me, don't hit me in the eye.
> I am older than you. Take it back to him. I said: back to whom? To Uncle Phiag, he said. Then my heart trembled. By death, my heart wanted it. Should I return it to him? Should I not return it? I thought in my heart: No, I am not returning it, I am not taking it back.
> Then father said that if I did not return it he would stamp on it and break it.
> I did not give in. So I picked up my watch and sat looking at it again and again. Should I return it? No, I wouldn't return it. I sat waiting for father to scold me. But he didn't scold that much. He said: Whatever I say to you, you don't believe. I said, don't mess with him. He is just scattering seeds, hoping for results.
> I said: Father, you see only the bad side of people. Those who are good you accuse of being totally bad. How can you know that he is bad?
> He said: Soon you will dry your tears at our knees. I sat, I could not see any way, no way at all and I cried and wept, I sat crying harder than I had ever cried before. Thinking, again and again, I don't want to stay there. In my heart I did not want to live there.

Pùu's *feen* had seen and heard everything, and tried to talk it over with her the next day, asking her to move away with him to live somewhere else.

> I considered the situation . . . I said: I definitely won't go. I believe my father and my mother. I said I would never agree [to escape with him] because my sister she had already escaped. I felt sorry for my father and mother.

Shortly after Phiag proposed to Pùu that they should go and see a movie in the evening. She answered,

> Let's see. If father goes to work tonight I can go, but if father doesn't go to work I can't. Father went to work. My heart was beating fast and a little bit happily because never, never, had we been out at night together, only in the daytime. I thought, this is the night to go out.
> At six in the afternoon, I took a bath, I got dressed. But he had disappeared, and I thought he had cancelled the appointment. Then I wore a night-gown, the one he had given me. I sat on my mat, switched on the light in my room, and sat reading. I was waiting to see, I had opened the sliding door to see when he would come. My eyes, I used them for three purposes: looking at TV, reading and looking for him.
> At seven o'clock he came, wearing jeans, a T-shirt and woven sandals.
> So I thought, ah he is coming! ready! Then I wore a *phâathǔng* over the night-gown. He said: go, let's go, quick! Well, mother, she was not there either, she had gone to see a Likee play. Mother, she likes Likee plays very much, it is her life, her heart . . .
> My older and younger sisters and brothers sat watching TV. I didn't talk to them, I didn't care . . .

Gender Conflicts

Then I stretched out the mosquito net, I took off the night-gown I put on blue jeans, new blue jeans, a T-shirt and new shoes. I had never put the shoes on before. When I was dressed up, I picked up the watch. Oh, it wasn't beautiful, so I put it here in my pocket. I looked at my younger sisters and brothers. I looked the other way. I thought these damned children, soon they will know I'm going. Let's do this.

Then I took an old *phâathŭng* and wore it over my jeans. Then I laid the side pillow down in the net, and covered it with a blanket and switched off the light and walked outside. Then I ran, I ran away to meet Phîi Phiag outside.

It was late, there were no seats in the cinemas, and they had fruit and a meal at the market. Then Phiag, around midnight, suggested to Pùu to go by taxi to a friend of his living in the opposite end of Bangkok. Now they had really run away together. Pùu told me she only understood this when she heard the welcome greeting from Phiag's friend; but she must have guessed before.

They lived in the room for more than four weeks. Phiag tried to negotiate with her parents without too much success. Her older sister soon found out what had happened. Her mother stole her clothes out of the house for her, but then Phiag got involved in a traffic accident and they moved out of Bangkok to avoid prosecution. Staying in the countryside with some friends of Phiag, they floated lotus-flowers to read the omens for their future life together, and they had a row.

> Phiag said he wanted to go out with his friend. He didn't want to offend him. Phiag turned to look at my face, and I said, go! go! and so they went out and I lay down in a room.
>
> After a while, I heard his friend coming back again. He pretended and talked like this to me: He isn't coming back any more, I don't know where he is.
>
> I said: By death, you went out together, you should come back together.
>
> Phîi Phiag, he hid away from me, hid at the back of a coconut tree, a big one. Then I walked down to see, to look for him. It was Leeng Khratong [a festival held on the full moon of November when people float toy boats with candles and money in them in rivers or canals to ask for forgiveness and blessings from the Water Goddess and people light fireworks]. Then I met him and we had some fun there. He was drunk.
>
> Then he lit a firework, but he didn't let it go. He didn't throw it away. I said, let it go, let it go or soon your hand will be blown off. He didn't let it go, it exploded and I was frightened: Are you mad? You play like an idiot! I said that, it was ugly, and he got angry at me. So he walked upstairs, up into the house, and then he said: I won't stay any more. I asked for a little bit of fun and you wouldn't allow it. I just played around a bit and you scolded. You're small-minded, you know? I'm not going to stay here any more. And he took his luggage out immediately.
>
> I said: OK, take it, take it now. I threw the luggage at him. Threw his clothes. Then he folded them, folded them into his luggage.
>
> I myself didn't cry, you see. I was sitting laughing because I had never before had a quarrel like this. I was laughing.
>
> He himself, he cried, Phîi Phiag wept. He had a quarrel with me and he cried. Just then his friend said: Are you mad? Where you going? Don't go.

I said: Let him go. He has no strength. Oh, it's all right. If he goes, I will go too. Tomorrow, I will go.

Then he sat hugging his knees at the staircase, but I heard him buy two krathongs [small boats to be floated in the form of a lotus]. But quarrelling like this, I didn't have the heart and mind to float any more.

I thought I would have to go to live with my grandmother. I couldn't go back home, because we had not asked for forgiveness yet. Then I thought: Tomorrow, I will go to grandmother.

Then I got into the net to sleep. I lay down and I took a side-pillow to put in the middle. We should not sleep together, I did not want to sleep with him.

He sat thinking. His friend said: Are you mad? She didn't say anything much to you. He explained a lot of things to him. He sat thinking for a long time and then he got into the net. I had already been asleep then. So I stretched out the net, and I went to sleep close to the wall, outside the net. I hid myself, and he couldn't find me then . . .

Later, at midnight, he called me. He wanted us to go and float the krathongs together. I didn't have the heart and mind to float them any more, I said. So the krathongs were widows [unused and separated]. In the morning he called me to come and float them again, but I was passive.

Then he took the krathongs, mine and his, to float them together. I was just watching from the window. He lit up the candles and floated them, but the Krathongs did not float together, they separated suddenly.

Pǔu and Phiag did become friends again, and returned home the next day to Pùu's parents. Negotiations had been started through a neighbour and when they arrived Phiag paid the bride-price, 6,009 baht, and preparations were made for the wedding. "I was very glad. Oh, I was very happy to come home. I missed my home so much, missed my father, missed my mother, missed my room."

As can be seen from the narratives women were struggling very actively against their husband's and father's control and against minor wives. At the surface the women in the slum were very kind, smiling and laughing and very mild but beneath the surface they struggled hard and continuously to get a degree of independence and to check their husband's vices.

There was very little social pressure on the men in the slum. In actual fact Tíg was the only woman who had involved her mother-in-law in her struggle against her husband's infidelity and failure to support her and the child. In all other cases the women struggled individually. Friends and female kin might help them when things went really bad; but other women were in no position to put pressure on the men in question.

Men's control of women's behaviour was not accepted among the women themselves. Sămphaw said, "He can do it. He can go everywhere. But I am not allowed," and this was a typical attitude among the women. Nor did Pùu accept her father's criticism of her *feen*. "It had nothing to do with my father, it didn't concern him."

The women did not want to be golden flowers, as Sămphaw put it; they thought they had the right to make up their own minds about their relationships with others.

Gender Conflicts

Some women, like Sămphaw, talked about admirers, even women who like her were grandmothers. But they usually also said that they sent the admirer away, either telling him that they themselves were too old, or that he should think of his wife and children first.

Nor did the women think that men's control was necessary to keep them chaste; chastity itself was not that much valued among the women. Some, like Nŭu, had had several boy-friends before they married, others had had love affairs which also involved a sexual relationship. This was hidden from parents and the new boy-friend, if possible; but the young women themselves did not feel it to be humiliating. A mother to a girl who was jilted by her boy-friend, and who did not expect a high bride-price in any case, because she was poor and powerless, simply said, "Never mind. She will soon find another *feen*."

There was thus great disparity between men's and women's norms for decent behaviour. Men took it for granted that their consumption and their sexual relationships were their own business and that they ought to control women's relationships. Women, on the other hand, thought that men ought to support their families, that there ought to be some kind of equality, and that men ought not to be *hùang* but ought to accept women's own control of their relationships.

The differing norms, led to many conflicts between the sexes in the slum, especially where men had minor wives and squandered their incomes. The conflicts between the sexes must be seen as signs of changing roles for men and women within the family and the changing importance of the family itself in the slum.

In anthropological literature very little is mentioned about conflicts between the sexes. My women's stories from up-country may of course be idealized, since they were rather young when they left the villages and most people tend to idealize their childhood. But if their stories can be believed kin would step into conflicts and try to stop indecent behaviour at an early stage. For instance, Nŭu's grandmother asked her father to move out of the house when he drank too much and did not behave properly towards the children, Sămphaw's mother would ask the husband of her daughter to leave his minor wife (although without result) and so on. The social pressure for decent behaviour seems greater up-country.

The tendency to individualism in the slum not only means that men act more in their own private and less in the family's interest, it means too that social control is diminished. This is the case with the control of men's behaviour but to a degree with the control of women's too. It is mostly the individual man who tries to control wife and daughters.

Thus in the narratives the gossip among the men is of some importance for the attempt to control both Sămphaw and Pùu. The son and the friends of the husband tell him where she is. But he cannot build on any consensus or loss of status for the women in question as major mechanisms for making the women comply with his wishes; nor can he involve relatives with authority or outside institutions. In the last instance he has to fall back on giving money and gifts, and not least the threat of, or actual, physical violence.

Similarly, the women support one another, but cannot rely on other women to attempt to impress other ways of behaviour on the men. Pùu gets help from her mother, Tíg helps with communication when Pùu has run away, Tíg gets help from both Pùu and Sŏmcìd when she tries to get her husband to behave himself, and Sămphaw can escape to Lee's house, and is warned by her when her husband is prepared to hurt her physically. But this help and support is given when things have already developed fairly drastically and the women are unable to act in any way before the woman in question is in very real need. Thus both men's and women's pressure on one another are individualized and their success depends mainly on their individual power and talents.

Both men and women had networks of friends and family in the slum. For women these networks were a very important resource. Women built up their networks and they participated actively in groups of both men and women. It was, for instance, often women who were leaders of the many loan games and it was a woman (Lee) who was the main organizer of a trip to *tham bun*. She rented the bus, travelled up-country and made arrangements with the temple and her family.[8]

Still the networks of the women were in no position to put pressure on the husbands or fathers as the formally elected village leaders were not. The situation of structural inequality and the changes in relative positions of men and women determined to a great extent the means men and women used. The main means used by men were, as in this family, the withholding of economic support and gifts, and in several cases physical violence. For the women the situation was different. They did not control money resources of any importance for the men's consumption. They did perform services for the men, but only very rarely did they dare deny men services like food and cleaning, although they did in some cases deny their husbands sexual relations.

Structural inequality means that men are mostly dependent on women for socio-psychological reasons. To be married and have children (together with joining the monkhood) imply maturity in the eyes of the greater society and the men need to feel themselves to be masters in their own homes as a reflection of their status and their humanity. The women's socio-psychological needs may be much the same but they are also heavily dependent on husbands in material terms.

Not surprisingly, then, in conflicts between the sexes the women try their best to utilize their only asset, their *feen*'s dependence on their acceptance, admiration and love. All three women knew their husbands' likely reactions and tried to take them into account or manipulate them.

This is least true in Sămphaw's narrative. Probably this relationship is of too long standing for such means to be useful any longer. But when things were really bad after the *tham bun* trip and the fighting had ebbed she did not speak to her husband for months. This was the case in other families too. In one family the wife was extremely angry because her husband had many, always new, minor wives and did not react in any way to her complaints. The spouses did not talk to each other and had not done so for years except in really important situations (such as deciding what to do when threatened with eviction).

Both Tíg and Pùu utilize their knowledge of their husbands' reactions. When Tíg suspects the husband of having a minor wife she not only watches his reactions at home closely, she acts on her suspicion and has it confirmed when he drops his spoon at a meal. She even fakes a letter and an appointment. In the end she goes straight to the problem and solves it to her satisfaction. Now they live in relative harmony.

Pùu likewise plays on her *feen*'s feelings. She is very shocked herself at his strong reactions to her fear and criticism. She is in fact very much at his mercy and feels that she cannot return home without him. Still she pretends she doesn't mind and in the end makes him accept her again.

Men's need for women's acceptance, admiration and love should not be undervalued. In two of these narratives the *feen* starts weeping in situations where he fears the conflict is so serious that his wife has really rejected him.

Women have room for manoeuvre both if they want to maintain the relationships with their *feen* and if they break it off, at least if they have other kin to rely on. Still, their position relative to the men's is changing for the worse, both in production, where they are assigned to a secondary labour market, and within the family, where the old basis of their relative power has crumbled. Their continuing struggle to maintain the families and for some degree of freedom and happiness is, seen against this background, really impressive.

13. Slum Culture and Gender

Theravada Buddhism and folk beliefs in the slum

People in the slum are clearly integrated into a Thai culture of tradition based on Theravada Buddhism. The history of colonialism demonstrates that it is always difficult to say anything about culture or tradition. The colonial powers, especially England with its indirect rule, but also France in Vietnam, for example, have always built on local culture or traditions. In Vietnam the anti-colonial movement was extremely critical of French interpretations of the content and meaning of traditional culture (Marr 1971). At the same time, the anti-colonial movement built on its own interpretations of traditional culture (see Nguyên Khac Viên 1971 for a description of the relationship between one school of thought in Confucianism and Marxism-Leninism; also Fitzgerald 1972 and Woodside 1976). The colonial powers and post-war ideologists in Western countries have attempted to interpret cultural traditions to their own advantage.

Conversely, it is an important factor that Theravada Buddhism itself is wide open to different interpretations. As Tambiah (1976) shows, Theravada Buddhism has been given different interpretations in the three Theravada Buddhist countries (Burma, Sri Lanka and Thailand) and in different periods. There is great variation, too, between present-day interpretations in Thailand, ranging from the government's state-bolstering Theravada Buddhism (Chaloentiarana 1979) through the almost existentialist version of Buddhadasa (Tambiah 1976 pp. 414 ff.) to Sivarakasa's social criticism (1980).

Yet in all its interpretations Theravada Buddhism seems to take the relationship between the state (the king), the *sangha* (order of monks) and the layman as a central theme. It is "something more than a religion if by religion is meant a system of *personal* salvation" (Ling 1973 p. 16).

Various interpretations of Theravada Buddhism have also combined with folk beliefs to form counter-cultures proper as a basis for social and millenarian movements (Skrobanek 1976).

The cultural traditions of Thailand, however, include much more than Theravada Buddhism; the life of the villages is characterized just as much by belief in a number of demons and spirits (Turton 1972). Tambiah (1970) has shown how the activities of the monks and the spirit worship of the peasants are part of an interaction fundamentally linked to the agricultural cycle. The interaction between

Theravada Buddhism, animism and spirit worship in the everyday life of the peasants reflects the tolerance of the Buddha himself towards these beliefs.

> Beliefs of this kind appear to have been tolerated by the Buddha, and it is this kind of imagery which is used in some of the discourses to the more unsophisticated of his hearers (Ling 1963 p. 80).

> The teaching of the Buddha . . . does not close the frontiers of thought where it touches animism and popular demonology; it allows it to remain open but controls it from the Buddhist side and for Buddhist purposes (Ling 1973 p. 93).[1]

The integration of the slum-dwellers into Thai tradition is expressed in their close relations with monks, soothsayers and temples; the traditional forms observed at weddings and funerals; the use of amulets and spirit-houses and belief in omens. People consider and describe themselves as Buddhists, and Buddhist elements appear naturally in everyday discourse, as for example when a Christian woman was called not Thai because she took no part in the social events people normally attended. "She isn't a real Thai. She isn't a Buddhist and doesn't follow our customs."

Or when a married woman bemoaned her lot and concluded,

> When I hear a monk chanting I think I am suffering because I wasn't a good person in my former life. But I can't always think like that. Sometimes I think that it's unfair that some people have to work so hard and still be poor while others get rich.

However, the integration into Thai tradition is, as the last quotation shows, full of inner contradictions. This can be illustrated by a trip to a provincial temple in which I took part.

The trip was arranged by the local slum-dwellers. During both the preparations and the actual trip there was plenty of local pop music and live singing amplified through loudspeakers. A large sum was collected for gifts to the monks and a ceremony was held in the temple.[2]

The slum-dwellers were very absorbed in the trip, which was a mixture of expressions of piety, prayers and excesses. There was gambling in the temple most of the night, and even small children turned out to be extraordinarily skilful at this. The square outside, as with many temples, was a market-place with, for example, a violent action film on show. And the temple trip was also an occasion for flirting or starting up new sexual relationships. "I slept with a new *feen* last night," said one of the women happily and proudly the next morning.

The temple was a holy place and there was great respect for the monks; but it was also a sanctuary in the other sense, somewhere you could feel at home, experience a sense of community and at the same time do some good and acquire merit. These are important elements in Theravada Buddhism. The translation of the word *bhikkhu* should be "one who shares" (not, as usually translated "monk"; our monks separate themselves from or renounce the world). Their duty, in contradistinction to the western view, is to counteract increasing individualism and to help to create a community spirit, impart wisdom and guidance and set an

Woman and the Family

example; communal activity is an important element in Theravada Buddhism.

The temples (both the one we were bound for and others on the way) function as sanctuaries in more than one sense. The communal forms that are established and the content that finds expression through them are quite problematic and require from the better educated Buddhists all the tolerance demonstrated by the Buddha. The slum-dwellers really bring their own, normally repressed, culture with them to the temple. They are happy to take part in these trips, but the content they give them is far from the well-ordered, harmonious relationship between state, *sangha* and laymen which is strictly speaking the Theravada ideal. It is a far cry from the state with its laws and rules to the illegal activities that go on in the temples, and harmony is in fact achieved only through the acceptance, so to speak, of the breaches of the rules of the state. "The Police never come in here, we can gamble here as much as we like," as one girl said.[3] The great emphasis on social intercourse and passing the time pleasantly and amusingly also pervades everyday life in the slums.

The way many of the houses are constructed signals this interest in others. Sīi's house is an example.[4] A sketch of its plan looks like this:

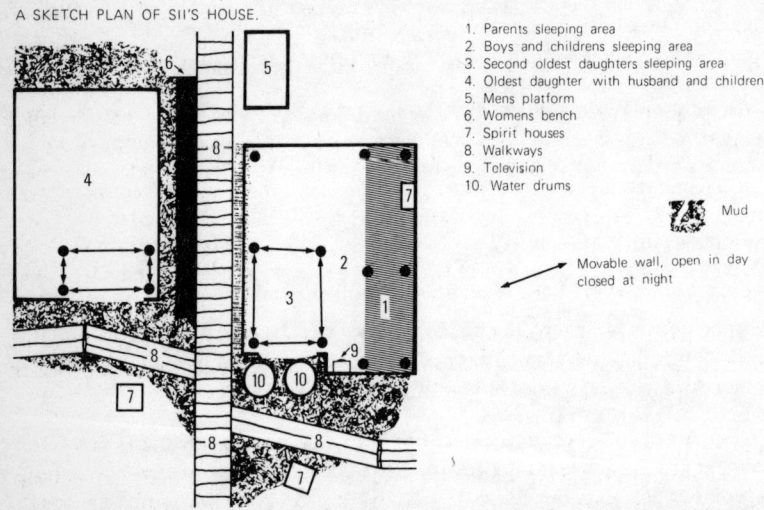

A SKETCH PLAN OF SII'S HOUSE.

1. Parents sleeping area
2. Boys and childrens sleeping area
3. Second oldest daughters sleeping area
4. Oldest daughter with husband and children
5. Mens platform
6. Womens bench
7. Spirit houses
8. Walkways
9. Television
10. Water drums

Mud

Movable wall, open in day closed at night

Much of the time in the slums is spent chatting to neighbours, friends and family. There is also a lot of gambling: by women mostly in the daylight hours, while the men (and a few of the middle-aged women) play in the evening and at night in the gambling-house.

There is also a good deal of drinking, mostly among the men; the women, either do not drink at all, or in some cases get really drunk like the men. Finally, most of the men have so-called minor wives, often with a child somewhere in the slum. A few of the women in my area were minor wives.

People's view of wealth is that it is an excellent thing, and they speak proudly about rich friends. One example was a woman who had telephoned Singapore, where her son-in-law had paid for the call. She was described as rich — but not rich in the sense that she constantly had money, or indeed a particularly high level of consumption. For a time she washed plastic to earn her living and pay off the interest on a loan.

Conversely, rich people are expected to be generous and lend money to the poor. Loans are by no means always paid back, but this does not bother the borrowers. Lending, like sub-contracting work or distributing other resources, is a way of building up a circle of friends or dependants, and esteem for a person is to a very great extent dependent on whether you are his or her friend. Sometimes men lend so much money out that they hardly have enough to keep their families, because of the prestige attached to helping others. Generosity is valued highly, as it is in Buddhist scriptures. Sharing with others is an ideal (which in practice also brings advantages for the giver).

People (realistically enough) rarely connect working with getting rich. Prestige is attached to *being* rich, especially if you are also generous; but there is no particular prestige attached to hard work. Men work to earn money; some do a lot of overtime and have extra jobs; others do not work more than they have to. Women are first and foremost expected to take care of the home and children, and if they do not do so they are looked down on by other women. But if work in the home like washing clothes and cooking is reasonably well done it carries no special prestige. The women seldom wash the walkways outside the houses, and if they do no one notices it particularly.

Very few people are proud of working hard. The female soothsayer Ùbon put it this way.

> I've had a hard life. Nobody's had as hard a life as me. I've worked since I was small, doing all sorts of things: I've made bricks and burnt charcoal; I've worked on building sites; I've even emptied privies. And where did that get me?

Those who can avoid hard work do so. Another woman said,

> It's much better to stay here in the slum. You can get something done here. Just think of the buses, they are terrible in this heat. An hour there and an hour back — I don't want to do that!

If work is not valued highly, time off work is when you look for as much fun, excitement and pleasure as possible. As far as people have time and opportunity they look for new experiences, talk, friendship and love. Conditions are tough, however, for pleasure, friendship and love, and there are of course many conflicts in the slum. In terms of the Thai culture with its great emphasis on non-aggression and friendship (Mulder 1978) there are many conflicts, and they are often about money. But considering the population density (about 700 per hectare) the level of conflict is not particularly high in European terms.

There are differences in status, and prestige is based on wealth (and generosity) and on the circles of friends people build up, usually among those who live in their immediate neighbourhood; but prestige is not built on hard work, either in the workplace or in the home, where peace and quiet, cleanliness and orderliness are not especially highly prized virtues.[5]

The slum-dwellers' relations with the surrounding society are full of contradictions. On the one hand they are bound by many ties to those in power, the state and its institutions, and they value these links; on the other they feel themselves to be despised outcasts. Theravada Buddhism is by no means a faith that encourages class hatred or class struggle. Trevor Ling (1973) sees the Buddha's teachings as an attempt to counteract the individualism, anomie and conflicts that came in the wake of early Indian urbanization (which undeniably took other forms than the type we know today) and the quest for harmony is a crucial element in Theravada Buddhism.

Nevertheless people in the slum feel strong antagonisms towards the surrounding society. Ambivalent feelings like these emerge in attitudes to state institutions. The police are loathed, and the slum is always buzzing with tales of bribery, torture during interrogation and police harassment. In practice the slum-dwellers have no legal protection, since, confronted with abuse of power, they cannot invoke their rights.

Stories about police harassment are not told openly but in small groups of very few people; when the police come on their frequent raids of the gambling-houses rumour usually runs before them and warns people; but policemen are treated with respect in their presence and sometimes people even have free and easy conversations with them.

Similarly, all the children in my area go to school, and both the children's and the adults' attitudes to school are ambivalent. On the one hand the children learn something and show respect for the teachers; on the other they often feel humiliated and express indignation about it or parody the teachers.

Antagonistic attitudes to established society play a very important role in people's behaviour, first and foremost in the form of a large number of illegal activities. Almost every single person in the slum does something that is against the law, and practically all activities outside working hours are illegal: gambling with cards or dice, production and drinking of bootleg whisky, loan games, money-lending, abortions, prostitution and of course picking pockets, burglary and heroin dealing. Activities like these are widespread. Among the 132 people I studied there were nine men who had been or were in prison (at least — there may have been some I did not hear about).

Over and above this there are all the other illegal activities given less attention by the police. Gambling is a borderline case: almost everyone takes part to some extent (men stake by far the largest amounts, and often drink hard at the same time); and the police, as mentioned above, carry out regular raids where they impose informal fines, as they are called. No great loss of prestige is connected with conflicts with the police. You are not immediately told that a husband, son or *feen* is in prison, just as a woman does not tell you at once that her husband has a minor wife; but it is simply one of the realities of life that almost everyone risks conflicts with the police, and people tell you all about it after a short acquaintance. Among the women the reactions to any illegalities the police might be interested in are first and foremost based on the danger and loss of income they expose the whole family to, not on any moral condemnation. Bon said, for example, "No, he doesn't gamble any more, he drinks," then, counting the empty bottles, "one bottle a day, I think. But that doesn't matter, it's cheap. And the police don't bother about it."

The attitudes of the slum-dwellers to the rest of society, to the rich and to state institutions are self-contradictory in all respects: there is withdrawal, indignation over injustice and aggression towards society, but also acceptance of where the power lies — an attitude balancing between fear and acknowledgement of the legitimacy of authority.

This also found expression in the organized opposition that met projected evictions of the slum-dwellers. (These had been announced, with a three-month deadline, in 1982, but had still not been implemented a year later). Schools and community centres in the slums had worked to get the people of the slums organized, and got every walkway to elect a village leader. Several committees were also formed, one of them with a former prime minister (Kriangsak, known for his activities in the heroin trade) as chairman. All legal political parties had contacts with one or more village leaders and the Slum Upgrading Office naturally had such contacts too (the leaders of the SUO are politically elected representatives, not civil servants).

People's accounts of their experiences during a previous series of evictions (in 1973/4) show that they thought they had been very badly treated. They had been forced to tear down their houses and had to sit waiting on their heaps of building material and possessions; a machine had spread mud over everything (filling-in operations?) and they had been brought before a court family by family. Students and the Catholic School had in the end managed to find a new place for them to move to, but they emphasized again and again that they should have organized. The normal Thai word used in the slum for organize, *chuâj kan* literally translated, means to help one another.

Slum culture or working-class culture?

Slum culture has its roots in the daily life of the slum areas with the insecurity caused by economic problems, housing problems and the lack of legal rights. It is probable that many other people in Bangkok experience similar but less extreme conditions and contradictions. In terms of housing and jobs the slum exhibits only differences of degree from many high-rise rehousing estates and some privately-owned houses.

The concept of slum culture has been chosen here rather than that of working-class culture because the latter is strongly associated with a limited section of the slum population (not with women, casual workers, the unemployed, small self-employed street vendors and the like) and because working-class culture is usually understood in terms of Western European, particularly British, workers' culture, built up around institutions like trade unions and political parties. In order to compare slum culture with working-class culture in this sense it is worth looking more closely at the English experience. This has been analysed in detail by Thompson (1964) and Roberts in *The Classic Slum* (1971) has given us a picture of the slum culture that was the basis of organization among workers in 1900–1920. His study focuses, like this one of Khlong Toey, on the everyday lives of ordinary people in the slum (see also Greenwood 1933, a novel from the Salford slums).

Here Roberts describes "the English proletarian caste system in all its late flower" (1971, p. 13). It is hard to tell whether people in the Salford slums were more or less poor than those in Khlong Toey: the English slum-dwellers had far more possessions, but their fear of ending in the workhouse seems to have been much greater than the Thais' fear of social degradation. The Salford slum was pervaded by a struggle for social prestige among the workers that was partly about men's work and incomes but also very much about respectability: scrubbed and shining steps outside the house, the right kind of clothes, and women's appearance. The little money English workers had therefore often went on ornaments for the mantelpiece or piano lessons for a daughter.

In the Salford slums there seems to have been a moral value attached to hard work (by both men and women), and to cleanliness, thrift and orderliness. It is hard to read Roberts' description without relating it to the Protestant work ethic.[6]

The eternal struggle to climb the ladder of social prestige (usually in vain) seems to have been closely connected with women's housework (cleaning, washing clothes) and their behaviour, and Roberts' description of the breakdown of the caste system around the end of the First World War shows that this happened at about the same time as women achieved considerably more social freedom (and began wearing far more relaxed clothing).[7]

In E. P. Thompson's analysis of the creation of a working-class culture from the end of the 1700s to the end of the 1800s, two important features stand out besides the material conditions built into (presumably all) capitalist production: the role of the declassed craftsmen as the most active, forceful and innovative group; and the influence of the French Revolution and the ideas of political democracy it inspired (see also Hobsbawm 1977).

In Thailand the situation is quite different. The role of the craftsmen in old Thailand (before the unequal treaty with Great Britain in 1855) was very different from that of the British craftsmen. There was fine craftsmanship, especially among metalworkers, jewellers and goldsmiths (Thorbek 1977). But these craftsmen were (hereditary) slaves, their social status low, and their skills unsuited to modern production. In the years just before the treaty a thriving ship-building industry was established (Bowring 1977), and here as elsewhere the workers developed qualifications that are presumably more relevant today; but, then as now, qualifications were something acquired at work, and acceptance of them depended not so much on simply having them as having them acknowledged by superiors. Pride in craftsmanship and the threat of becoming *declassé* were thus not an issue. There was nothing in Thailand corresponding to craftsmen's guilds.

Political culture is also very different. In South-East Asia the most important breaks with the culture of the past have taken place in connection with national struggles and struggles for socialism in various senses of the word (for example in Burma, China, Cambodia, Vietnam and Sri Lanka). Social and political struggles in South-East Asia and China have had an influence on the political culture of Thailand. The importance of the Kuomintang for the developments of concepts like democracy in the 1920s has been emphasized by Mokarapang (1972). The struggle of the Free Thais against Japan contributed to the founding of the first trade unions around 1945 (Thorbek 1981). A movement within the *sangha* or order of monks led by Phra Phimontham strove to establish international contacts, especially with

Burma (which led to his repeated imprisonment from the early 1960s on, because Burma was a socialist country). In 1956 students and monks were greatly inspired by Buddhists in China, where the compatibility of Buddhism and socialism was emphasized; and the influence of the Communist parties, especially the Maoist ones of China and Cambodia, was strong. In the city, however, the greatest influence of all probably came from the student revolution (as the people from the slum called the student demonstrations and the subsequent introduction of the parliamentary system in 1973–6).

Despite the very great cultural, social and political differences among these movements there is in all of them a conflict between respect for individualism and a yearning for happiness and well-being on the one hand, and on the other an emphasis on discipline in daily life and the responsibility of the state for the welfare of the population. The Thais are an individualistic people. Their social structure has been described as loose,[8] and complaints about their unwillingness to work go back to the late 1920s. At that time it was the representatives of the upper classes who emphasized the right of the peasants to enjoy life and not work too hard; it was the leader of the modernizing left-wing group who wanted more state intervention and harder work from the peasants (Pridi Phanomyoung in Landon 1939). In the post-war period the various left-wing movements (especially the Communist guerrillas) have also emphasized work and discipline. Concepts of democracy also played an important role for many of the movements mentioned, especially for the students.

Social structure and political culture are thus very different from those found in the West, and this makes it rather unlikely that a working-class culture of the western type, a union and party culture, will emerge. Besides this there are material considerations. The creation by skilled workers and craftsmen of a working-class culture, with its visions, critical stance and institutions, was an impressive achievement and has left a profound mark on most of present-day Europe. But for a long time the unions were an institution for the fortunate few. They also contributed to the caste system of the English working class and helped to keep women out of reasonably-paid work (see Hartmann 1976 on conflicts between men and women on the British labour market).

In his analysis of the Salford slums Roberts stresses the fact that the unions and the broader workers' culture centred on the Labour Party did not take on mass proportions until about 1920,[9] and he attributes this to the changes that took place in production, partly in the wake of an economic boom, partly because the First World War and technological changes necessitated the more systematic introduction of new groups (women and unskilled workers) into production.

But in Bangkok, as in so many other Third World countries, such a development is improbable. By the turn of the millenium half of the world's population will live in big cities (UN 1980) and it is highly unlikely that production will expand to such an extent that there will be work for all the people in the cities.

Work and the organization of participation in production are obviously important for the slum-dwellers, but it is not the unions that play the most important role. Much building work, coolie-work, and some of the work in the docks, is organized in terms of patron–client (*thâw kèe–hǔa nâa*) relationships adapted to modern conditions. Rabibhadana (1980) has described the system as used in building work in another slum area, and shows that it is a reciprocal relationship, as a *hŭa nâa* will often feel obliged to lend money to his workers when they are in need. This was also the case to some extent among the *hŭa nâa* I knew, but the system does leave much room for exploitation. This type of informal organization of work is visible and familiar, and important resources are distributed through the system. The union, which functions among a minority of the workers in the slum, operates more or less in the same way.

It seems unlikely, then, that a new culture in the slums will take the same form as the traditional English workers' culture that developed into a mass phenomenon in the inter-war period in Europe. This is because the material conditions make it unlikely that an industrial expansion will take place creating work for people in the cities. It is also because of Thailand's very different history, where there were no parallels to the groups which were of special importance for the creation of the British working class, and the region's political culture, in which the concept revolution was understood in different ways, mostly in connection with socialism. Finally, the everyday folk culture plays a role.

Thompson emphasizes the fact that Methodists succeeded in organizing the workers in periods when the workers' own organization was not making progress. In this respect his work can be seen as a critique or modification of Weber's thesis. Nevertheless many puritan features such as strict work discipline, the instilling of norms for a disciplined leisure life, thrift, a sense of order, industriousness and an acceptance of strict status differentiation in society, seem to have been characteristic not only of the people in the Salford slums, but also of those in most of Britain and Western Europe. These norms appear to be antithetical to the emphasis on the enjoyment of life rather than achievement, on fate, *kharma* and luck,[10] that were typical of the Thai slum-dwellers attitudes.[11]

Slum culture — counter-culture

By a counter-culture I understand not only a culture among the repressed, a sub-culture, but a culture with an opposition to established society and with the seeds of an alternative view of society.[12] In its full development a counter-culture must create its own social institutions, system of organization and a social movement; but systems of organization or social movements like these must be based on the consciousness and culture that already exist.

In the everyday life of the slum ambivalent attitudes are expressed towards the institutions of the surrounding society, and to a lesser extent towards Theravada Buddhism, which is, in its popular version, a very mild, tolerant religion, one that does not to any significant extent discipline daily life or interfere in the household interests of laymen.

Besides, some traditional concepts are in the process of transformation. In the patron-client relationship the poor, the receivers of help, are gaining self-confidence. People often regard a loan as a right, and have little or no feeling of humility when they ask for one or fail to pay it back. The relationship is also changing from the point of view of the patrons, who either concentrate more directly on accumulation and refuse to enter into the relationship at all; or, increasingly, they feel a sense of solidarity with the receivers. The same tendency appears in attitudes to evictions, where it is emphasized again and again that people are poor and have a *right* to stay where they are.

Generosity is an important virtue in Buddhist thought. The humility of the one part and complacency of the other which can be associated with generosity are disappearing, because the poor see the generosity of the rich and the distribution of wealth as their right.

One of the concepts recently introduced in Thai history that has spread into the slum context is democracy. This is true at the political level, but it is also true in everyday life, for example within the family. "At home father and mother decide everything. These days there ought to be democracy."

The concepts of democracy, organization, mutual aid and social responsibility thus have varying degrees of currency in the daily life of the slum, which when all is said and done is deeply marked by poverty, competition for jobs and general insecurity.

Leading figures in the slums, involved with schools, community centres and organizations set up to combat evictions expressed similar ideas. In the nearby Rama IV slum area the slum-dwellers had arrived at a model for the future use of the area (and a basis for negotiations in the face of evictions) by planning a cooperative that would own the land and distribute it to people. Those who were given land along the main road, where it was possible to open shops, were to pay part of their profits to the cooperative, which could use the money for projects, or direct help to those who were worst off. In this slum decisions were made at communal meetings.

In Khlong Toey there are several social institutions, the best known being that of Miss Prateep, who has established a school, a kindergarten, a creche, and organizations to combat slum clearance plans. Here people are organized in a system with elected village leaders in the individual walkways. The culture that is being built up around ideas of democracy, social responsibility and collective effort must be considered as a counter-culture, partly in opposition to, and partly integrated into the surrounding society.

Fear of the slums — of crime and of the emergence of social movements — is great among the Bangkok middle classes. The authorities are afraid of organized Communism, the left-wing fears the emergence of terrorist groups that can function as the tools of the forces of reaction. I discovered no such organizations during my study; but the fear is well-founded in so far as there are many good reasons for the slum-dwellers to organize or form social movements, and there is a culture in the slum that provides the necessary foundations.

There has been some discussion of the question whether rapid urbanization leads to the rise of social movements in slum areas. Fox Piven and Cloward (1979) have emphasized, drawing on American experiences, that urbanization entails the destruction of the social relations in which people are involved and thus of the social controls inherent in day-to-day routines. If such routines are not re-established, for example if people find themselves unemployed in the big cities, there is a strong impulse towards the creation of social movements. However, people rarely offer concerted resistance even when they are badly off economically, politically and socially: there is no simple relationship between material conditions and consciousness, and a simple base-superstructure model is inadequate (see Baron 1985 for a summary of English views).

We all live in a culture that legitimizes and guides our behaviour and understanding of the world. Fox Piven and Cloward (1979) discuss the conditions necessary before there can be a break with the culturally formed legitimacy of existing structures and conditions (see also Thorbek 1984a for a discussion). Loyd (1979) stresses the same aspects in terms of the cognitive structure of the slum-dwellers, and argues that the slums are "slums of hope".

Recent history demonstrates that urbanization creates the material conditions for the emergence of social movements; but this does not necessarily mean that social movements *will* develop; and if they do, the directions they take are unpredictable. In the West urbanization formed a background for Nazism and Fascism in the inter-war period; but also for strong social movements in the big cities of the USA in the late 1960s and in Britain today. In the Third World urban areas have been the cradles of reactionary terrorist organizations centred on the drug trade (McCoy 1973); of the Iranian revolution (Christensen 1980); but also of the Nicaraguan Sandinistas (Black 1981) and to a lesser extent of the Allende movement in Chile and the carnation revolution in Portugal.

The seeds of the counter-culture in Bangkok, as I encountered them in my area, seem to form a basis for movements where social responsibility, collective effort and democracy, and an emphasis on well-being and the enjoyment of life provide pointers for the future.

The gender struggle in the slum

Conflicts between the sexes are an important aspect of daily life in the slum. These conflicts are mostly about family matters, the functions, composition and internal relations of families. The women fight for a distribution of family incomes that allows for the real needs of children and adults, and against the excesses of the men: gambling, sprees in town and especially the minor wives. They also struggle for openness in the family: for sociable relations with others and the right of their own relatives to live with or near them. Finally, they fight for a certain scope of action: relative equality between the sexes and the opportunity to come and go freely and gain new experiences.

Among feminist researchers, Hartmann in particular has stressed the significance of the gender struggle. She defines patriarchy as follows.

> We can usefully define patriarchy as a set of social relations between men which have a material base, and which, though hierarchical, establish or create interdependence and solidarity among men that enable them to dominate women. Though patriarchy is hierarchical and men of different classes, races or ethnic groups have different places in the patriarchy, they are also united in their shared relationship of dominance over their women; they are dependent on each other to maintain that domination (1981 pp. 14, 15).

What is new and significant about this definition of patriarchy is that it gives equal weight to the domination of women in the family and in production rather than one-sidedly deriving it either from the forms of the family (and socialization) or from capitalism or other modes of production. Also, its emphasis on the gender struggle, on men's active organization in order to maintain the status quo or preserve dominance, is an aspect that makes it possible to develop a dynamic theory of patriarchy (where previous theories of patriarchy have tended to see the repression of women as a historical constant).

However, Hartmann's emphasis on the importance of men's organization and cooperation in the sphere of work to create or maintain privileges has led her to give a low priority in her own work to the struggles that also take place over the forms and relations of the family; and it is precisely this aspect that is evident in the Bangkok slum, where women's interest and efforts are greatest in matters of the family and its forms. The other problem in Hartmann's work on Marxism and feminism is that it is primarily men's struggle for their privileges that is given salience. Although men attain more power than women, as in the slum area studied here, it is evident from history that women also fight for their interests. But women's struggles are normally waged through non-formal organizations or networks and are therefore less visible. Men's *informal* organization to maintain their privileges presumably also — as in the slum — has crucial importance in the gender struggle. Hartmann's definition of patriarchy should therefore, to provide guidance in empirical studies, contain both an aspect dealing with gender struggles in family matters, and an aspect concerning women's active struggle for their interests, whether in formal organizations or informally, through family members, friends and neighbours.

The gender struggle in the slum culture studied is a prominent factor and is sometimes directly visible; its prominence in the slum must partly be understood in terms of the changes in social gender relations that are taking place with urbanization; but the gender struggle is also noticeable because women in Thailand are in a better position, relatively speaking, than in many other countries. This can at first sight seem paradoxical; but when we recall that women's traditional comparatively good position means that there is no strict sexual segregation in everyday life; that women are not significantly worse educated than men; that from the earliest age they have become used to working in the fields as well as in trade and in the home; and that in the villages they have an important mediating role and often administrate the family income; then it is less surprising if they react directly and visibly when in the cities they come up against men's arbitrary use of incomes, attempts to limit their scope of action, or a rejection of the natural way of living near one's mother, sisters or aunts.

Gender struggles also take place in much more patriarchal societies than Thailand; but in such countries women seem more passive and helpless. They have fewer people from whom they can seek direct support, because families are patrilocal and exogamous in relation to the village; and because there is a segregation of the genders that inhibits social relations with women outside the family (in Northern India, for example with their mothers and sisters). The results of the gender struggle in large areas of India, Bangladesh and in some Muslim

Woman and the Family

groups are an increasing control of women's behaviour in the form of demands for stricter observance of *purdah*. Another sign of the increasing control of women is the spread of the dowry system at the expense of the bride-price system, and the rise in amounts given as dowries.[12]

It may be assumed that the gender struggle is exacerbated by the rising level of conflict following urbanization in the form of harder competition, increased class struggle and ethnic conflict. In the Bangkok slum women's struggles for their interests have led to conditions that are better than in countries with predominantly patrilocal settlement patterns: there are few single women, but there are several women who have married a second time; couples are relatively stable and most have lived together for a number of years, although men often have minor wives; in most families the man gives a regular amount to the housekeeping; women can move around freely — to schools, workplaces and in the slum; it is quite common for young couples to settle down near the woman's parents or mother; and women take part in networks dealing with the affairs of the slum along with the men, and wield considerable influence.

The local settlement pattern achieved by women is perhaps what has the greatest strategic importance in the gender struggle. It allows everyday cooperation in the unpaid work women share and in finding work; and it is of great importance in the event of disputes with a father or husband.

Slum culture and changes in the family

In the slum, the meaning of the family has changed. I have argued that women's interests in such transformations are to keep a family with husband and children together, and to make sure that the family stays physically close to the woman's own kin, especially her mother and sisters. Men on the other hand are less interested in the composition of the family, although they prefer a nuclear family or closeness to their own kin. This is because for the men the family has lost its former material importance. It has not done so for the women, who need other women's help with housework and child care, if they have paid jobs, or with work producing and selling things from the house.

It is often assumed that urbanization leads to the formation of nuclear families; this is empirically doubtful. In many Third World cities women constitute a relatively large proportion of the population. The sex ratio in migrations to big cities varies: usually there is an excess of women among migrants in Latin America and the Caribbean, and of men in parts of Africa and in those parts of Asia where the repression of women is strongest (US Department of Commerce, Census Bureau 1980; UNCHRS 1985).

Many women are single: it is estimated that single women constitute about 30% of all women in the world, but there are far more in the big cities. In Latin America women in the big cities are typically single; many are the breadwinners in the family, they are young (under 45) and very poor; they work mainly in the so-called informal sector or as servants (Lycette and Jaramillo 1984). It is difficult to imagine these women living without the help of other women or girls. The studies that exist indicate that women in big cities build up or maintain contacts with female kin. In the West such female-centred networks are widespread (Yanagisko 1977; for Copenhagen, Thomsen *et al*. 1985); it has also been demonstrated that they exist in several rural areas with neolocal or matrilocal settlement patterns: in Indonesia (Geertz 1961; Tanner 1974); and in Malaysia (Stivens 1981 and Rudi 1983).

At least as interesting are the modified female-centred networks with kin in cities in areas with patrilocal settlement among the Chinese in Singapore (Wong *et al*. 1979) and northern India (Vatuk 1971). According to the Indian study, however, it seems to be a condition of frequent contacts between mothers and married daughters that the patrilinear extended family is geographically scattered. Women's networks have also been shown to exist in Harlem (New York), where many men are unemployed.

Although female-centred networks vary greatly, it seems to be characteristic of slum-dwellers that women try to build up or maintain close contacts with other women in the family. Nor is it especially difficult to see why women have or develop such a need for contacts in the context of urbanization. The separation of income-earning work from work for the family that follows in the wake of urbanization and industrial production makes matters to do with the birth, growing-up and care of children problematical for women. From the point of view of society and production that is a matter that can easily be left to the instinct of the workers for self-preservation (Marx 1965), and state intervention and support for the care of children are usually minimal if they exist at all.

As for the men, they may be happy to play with the children; there may be the pride and socio-psychological satisfaction of being masters in their own homes and seeing themselves reflected in other people, especially their wives; but materially speaking, the family is much less important than in agrarian communities, where it often controls the productive resources (land). In practice, therefore, women must often rely on themselves or one another as far as the absolutely necessary work of caring for growing children is concerned. In big cities everywhere women need help and support with children, and in most cases with housework. For women with paid work help with childcare is absolutely essential.

Urbanization and industrial production, then, create a need among women to build up or maintain networks with other women. Yet there are great differences in women's opportunities to create family structures where these relations are strong, and female-centred networks are associated with a wide range of family types: those characterized by the absence of men, with great material need for the women; those where men contribute to the maintenance of the family although they have a rather peripheral status and the role of the mother is valued highly in the local community (matrifocal families); and those where women, as in Bangkok, keep up relations both with husbands and female kin.

These differences depend not only on material conditions but also on the everyday gender struggle, and this is again influenced by the culture and traditions that have to be remoulded to suit the new material conditions. The cultural factors are of great importance here because they help to define who women should co-operate with, their scope of action and the value given to their activities.

In *The Making of the Modern Family* (1975 pp. 282, 283) Shorter, analysing developments in the West, emphasizes women's interests in freedom in earlier periods and their opportunities of becoming free through wage labour. It seems to me that Shorter in this work overlooks the fact that in these earlier contexts there were not only controls and limitations, but also a number of other aspects: valuable modes of association among women and communal activities (work and pleasure). He also lays too much stress in his analysis on freedom in terms of sexuality, and to a great extent ignores the burdens the combination of motherhood and wage work imposed on women in the West, as on those in the Third World today.

Shorter also argues that women in the cities are particularly interested in creating the closed family that isolates itself from kin and neighbours. In Khlong Toey this is not the case. If anyone insists on stopping chat, social relations and cooperation with neighbours and kin, it is the men. The women rather seek out the company and cooperation of others.

In the light of the globally widespread female-centred networks a hypothesis that women are particularly interested in isolation from the outside world seems dubious. Theoretically speaking, the contacts women establish with other women in the family, the neighbourhood or the workplace are also an important aspect of the gender struggle and it is doubtful that women would voluntarily isolate themselves from this support. Germaine Greer, for example, (1984) views women's communal bonds, even in the patrilocal and patriarchal family, as so valuable that their advantages outweigh the tight limitations on women's scope created by this type of family.

Women create slum culture

The gender struggle in Khlong Toey creates conditions for women that give them scope for a number of activities in, and sometimes outside, the slum. Women form friendships and networks in the slum, and are active in the creation of new gender relations and of slum culture in the wider sense. The women influence the slum culture by active participation in day-to-day work, in social structures built up by the people in the slum area; their awareness of conditions in the slum is parallel to that of the men.

Besides kin-based networks there are several fairly loosely structured groupings in the slum, and women take part in the formation of these along with men. They organize weddings and funerals, but they are also active in networks unconnected with family and kin. I have mentioned a temple trip; other trips of this type were organized in the slum. A middle-aged couple and their close friends, another couple, took the initiative and made the practical arrangements for the trip I took part in. The wife went to the temple in the country (in the village where her family lived) and made arrangements with the monks and her family. She also hired the bus and took care of the ticket sales, while man and wife together advertised the trip and collected all the money for gifts to the temple. The other married couple helped with these tasks, and the wife and her daughters made the money-tree, which was an important symbolic gift. On the bus trip itself some minor problems arose, as a couple of the men got very drunk and behaved badly. It was the wife who reasoned with them; and when the bus broke down on the way home it was again the wife who led us to a temple where we could wait until it was repaired. Women are generally, as in this case, active and influential in mixed groups in the slum.

This is also noticeable with the loose groupings who play the loan game. The game can be seen as a way of saving money, but with a strong element of gambling. The principle is that one or two leaders gather a group that meets regularly, for example every ten days, and pays an amount into a pool. The pool then goes the rounds of the players — first to the leaders, who do not pay interest. Then it is lent out, so that whoever wants it on a given day writes on a slip of paper the percentage of interest he or she is willing to pay. The person who promises the highest interest gets the pool. At the next gathering each person again pays to the pool, and those who have promised interest pay it, but only to those who have not yet drawn the pool. So the longer you can wait before drawing the pool, the less interest you will normally pay to fewer people (or rather hands, as a player can have several hands).

Rozenthal (1970) thinks that there is a strong element of exploitation in the game; but in the slum people deny that it is usually the same people who draw the pool last in different games. Although it is prohibited, the loan game is played all over Thailand, and in wide areas of Asia.

It is the job of the leaders to gather players and assess their ability to pay their debts. If a player does not pay, the leader will pay the pool, but not with interest (this was in my area — the rules vary from place to place). It is also the task of the leader to keep the accounts. As this is quite complicated, it demands literacy and numeracy. Both men and women play, often in two or three games at a time, but it is usually women who lead the game (see also Sevilla 1976).

Other groups are formed in the slum for gambling purposes. These are also mixed, but in these cases women play less than men and are less influential. Other groups again are formed for various types of legal or illegal business: the production and sale of food, money-lending, activities that are more a mixture of work and amusement like the lotteries women organize when they have found something particularly good at the market or produced something themselves as the prize.

The many loose and often overlapping groups are important as channels of information. Everyone knows who to ask about getting an abortion; if you want to travel, there are often people in the network who have family you can stay the night with; the networks spread information about the threat of eviction or activities to oppose it, political information and not least assessment of various people's creditworthiness and reliability. Women are active in these loose groups and have influence and responsibilities in sexually mixed networks. Some of them, like the loan games, are dominated by women.

The culture of the slum defines men and women's relations and behaviour, but women are active in creating this culture. Among women, the typical view of the relationship between husband and wife is that it should be monogamous and lifelong. As one of the women said, "I don't care for the idea of several wives or several husbands. I don't want to be one of many, little or big. I want to be one husband and one wife."

However, there is not the same burden of guilt connected with irregularities in women's sexual relations as there is in protestant countries. On the contrary, women express attitudes that are both pragmatic and subtle. A woman who finds a regular lover is accepted; prostitutes are assessed according to their situation and motives ("a woman looking for food", "a bad woman", "a woman out for a good time" are various expressions for prostitutes that exist beside the older terms — "the beautiful women in the big city", "a golden flower"). Minor wives are hated, but not so much that it was impossible for at least one woman to have lived for a year with one, with their babies of the same age. Minor wives who pose no threat to the main relationship are treated with indulgence and in some cases with sympathy and friendship. Women often show a more moral attitude to other women's lives and gambling. But it is not a matter of condemnation on principle; rather a flexible and practically motivated rejection of these vices.

Women's participation in the formation of groups that are critical of the surrounding society is no different from men's. They take part in meetings and activities along with the men, their knowledge of what is going on is as good as the men's, and there are many women among the village leaders. They are as active as men in the formation of the social structures of the slum culture, in opposing established society, and in many cases exhibit a high degree of solidarity with their men during conflicts with the police and authorities. They are also active in the creation of norms and expected standards of behaviour between the genders, in this case both conflicting and co-operating with men in the area.

Women as leaders

Women are active in the everyday life of the slum and in the creation of a counter-culture. Gramsci (1971) has connected the formation of a working-class culture in the Western European tradition with the rise of new groups of intellectuals associated with the class in opposition. He distinguishes between traditional intellectuals and organic intellectuals. The organic intellectuals of the working class are primarily organizers in unions and political parties; the traditional intellectuals are those, educated by the bourgeoisie, who are won over or go over to the side of the workers.[13]

If we take up the question of intellectuals in connection with the formation of a counter-culture in the slum, Gramsci's traditional intellectuals here correspond to students and public employees who work with the slum problems, while the organic intellectuals must correspond to people who are native to the slums and work there organizing help or opposition. Both types of intellectuals exist, and the active role of women in the slum corresponds to that of women among the organic intellectuals.

A good example is Miss Prateep, who, as mentioned above, runs a school, a fund, a kindergarten and a creche, and tries to organize people's opposition to evictions in the slum area I studied.

She is in her early thirties and was born and brought up in the slum, where her mother, now an old woman, still lives. She paid for her own schooling from the age of 10, and when she began to study at a teachers' training college she started a one-baht school on the open space under her parents' house. She managed to get fellow-students from the college involved in the work, and the school grew to become an institution also respected by society outside the slum.

The leading figure in the Rama IV slum is also a woman, a doctor who lives and runs a clinic in the area, as well as working with the above-mentioned organization against evictions. Several other examples of women like this who are active in organization and helping the slum-dwellers could be mentioned, for example one of the most active employees of the Slum Upgrading Office who helps with the organization of the residents in the slum area.

Common to these organic intellectuals is an emphasis on social responsibility, collective values and organization. They stress the slum-dwellers' own fight against evictions, their rights to the land, and democracy in organization (in the Rama IV slum in the form of joint decision-making meetings, and in Khlong Toey in the form of elected village leaders); and they are strongly influenced by the traditional Thai concepts of the sanctity of life, generosity and compassion for the poor.

The traditional intellectuals — students who were very active among the slum-dwellers during the period of parliamentary rule (1973–6), some of whom still work in the slums — lay great weight on democracy and solidarity across the boundaries of the individual slum areas.

The concrete problems that occupy women who work and function as organizers in the two slums mentioned are not specifically women's problems. In one (Muslim) slum a women's house was established; but it is more typical that the problems that are dealt with in practical projects are ones where women and men have a common interest, but which in practice lighten the burden of women's work — problems to do with health, child care, schools, sanitation in the slums, supplies of reasonably clean water — that is, general problems of day-to-day care.

The women's struggle and slum culture

In the slum the women's struggle takes place in and around the families, and here the women work to extend the nuclear family by bringing in their (mostly female) kin; but they also have a wider interest in an opening-up of the family to friends in the neighbourhood, and they take active part, with or without the men, in the looser networks of the slum. They are similarly involved in attempts to organize for the improvement of conditions and against evictions; and here, as in the looser networks, they are often leading figures (or organic intellectuals).

Slum cultures can be a basis for women's action, both in terms of the gender struggle and of broader forms of opposition. Rosaldo (1974) makes a theoretical distinction between the private and the public spheres, and emphasizes women's powerlessness in the public sphere. As a critic of Rosaldo's concepts (Keohane *et al.* 1982) has pointed out, this distinction is a problem in itself, and should be explained and examined, not taken for granted. But Rosaldo's hypothesis has also been criticized for being empirically problematical, for being based on a misjudgment of the social power that women actually have in many pre-capitalist societies (Leacock 1979).

In urban, industrialized societies, too, the concept of the private as opposed to the public is problematical. The distinction here is between a public or political sphere where everyone in principle is equal, and a private sphere where the family is the primary social institution; but whether the economic sphere is private or public is a current bone of contention. In the course of its growth the bourgeoisie carved out the economic sphere as its private area (Habermas 1962, pp. 24, ff.). But in the capitalist society of the last century workers' and poor people's movements have fought a constant battle to make the economic sphere public. For the capitalists production belongs in the private sphere; but for the workers it is hard to accept that the time they have sold belongs to someone else; that their lives throughout such a large proportion of their waking hours are someone else's property (Thorbek 1984b, pp. 146 ff.).

For men there is a contradiction between the political sphere where they are supposed to have power and influence, and the economic one, where they have none. For women there is, over and above this contradiction, another one between the private and economic spheres. The private sphere is supposed to cater for their needs and the reconstitution of their labour power, but in actual fact it is parallel to the economic one, inasmuch as their work here is great and their influence limited. Women's political power in the Third World is, like men's, usually limited because very few states have a democratic form of government. Their power in the economic sphere is also limited, often to a still greater extent than men's, because women function in this context as second-class labour power. Women's power and influence have therefore, as in Rosaldo's work, been linked with the home and family; and in the slum area studied it was in this context the gender struggle found its strongest expression.

However, the question is whether slum conditions give women a basis for exercising social power that extends beyond the family, without (as yet?) being real political power. In the Bangkok slum women's family struggles lead them out into the slum networks and the problem areas that have to do with day-to-day work for their children and families: living conditions, safety, water, waste disposal, health and so on.

There are similar examples from many big cities, both in the West and in the Third World, of women's active involvement in the daily life of the slums and their struggle for better conditions. In Nairobi women and their networks (not the direct kin networks) are of great importance for their opposition to police interference in their beer sales, and they are similarly active in broader tenants' organizations (Nelson 1979, on the Mathare Valley). In Nicaragua the slum residents were an important social base for the Sandinistas, and it is hardly a coincidence that precisely in Nicaragua women's issues and women's involvement were crucial for the revolutionary movement (Black 1981; Stolz Chinchilla 1983). In the West women in the slums were of great importance for the creation of welfare movements: in the USA in the 1960s (Fox Piven and Cloward 1979; Evans 1980); and in Barcelona (1910–1918) women were also important figures in the conflicts; they organized independently to support the struggle of the men, but also had their own demands as regards reproduction (Kaplan 1982).

In these social movements and day-to-day struggles women have usually seen their involvement as directed towards established society, not as a special organization of women concerned with issues in the gender struggle. As in the slums, there was no consciousness of sister solidarity: conflicts with the men were worked out in private, in the home. As far as content is concerned, women have in all these cases taken daily reproduction as their point of departure (with the possible exception of the Nairobi case).

It can be argued that urbanization, with its breaking-up of the existing social relations and the dubious or problematical involvement of people in new social relations and new forms of everyday social control, creates a material basis for counter-cultures and social movements. During this process the structure of the family is altered, and with it women's conditions and opportunities. Changes in the structure of the family can take many directions: the dissolution of families, the creation of nuclear families, the preservation of extended families, the formation of female-centred families, etc. The material changes that go with urbanization — the separation of the work of production and reproduction — make for generally worsened conditions for women; but women are themselves active in the creation of a new culture in the slum areas of the city, as they are active in the struggle over family structure.

In the gender struggle exacerbated by the new situation women fight for contacts, intimacy and the exchange of help with other women in their own families or in the neighbourhood. In slum areas where women achieve relative strength they become an important social force working for the improvement of the quality of life and the day-to-day work of reproduction — the creation of new people.

The transformation of material conditions, the break-up of old social relations and creation of new ones, provide a base for social movements and make transformations in the family and the gender struggle familiar features of everyday life; but these material changes in themselves do not determine whether counter-cultures or social movements emerge or the directions they take. Nor do changes in the material basis of the family in themselves give any indication of the family changes and other results that the gender struggle will involve. There is no simple relationship between changes in material conditions and the new forms that people will create, between base and superstructure.

Everywhere, however, changes in material conditions bring the gender issue into relief as a problem of urbanization. Children and the work of reproduction become problematical. In the most difficult situations even the day-to-day of reproduction is almost impossible to deal with, and in any circumstances it becomes a new problem in the sense that it is cut off from production. Often the problem is seen as women's responsibility, although deeper down it must be regarded as a problem for both men and women. But since women are seen as having the day-to-day responsibility for this kind of work in all modern urban societies problems of reproduction are often treated as gender-specific problems.

The gender dimension seems to be of crucial importance in slum cultures everywhere. Wherever women's interests in reproduction for one reason or another are not recognized in social movements; wherever their active presence, networks and groupings are not accepted, reactionary movements which exploit latent gender contradictions can be mobilized. Empirically, such mobilizations are found in connection with urbanization and the growth of slums both in the West and in the

Woman and the Family

Third World. The gender dimension played an important role for the National Socialist and Fascist movements in inter-war Europe (Macchiotti 1976; Mason 1976); it is a major issue for the New Right in the USA today (for various views on this see Elshtain 1984; Eisenstein 1981). In the Third World it seems to be crucial in the Iranian revolution and the Khomeini regime (London Iranian Women's Liberation Group 1981; and in Chile, where only the relatively uninfluential MIR attempted to mobilize women in the slums, women from the middle class appear to have formed an important mobilization basis for the fight against Allende (Stolz Chinchilla 1983).

Social movements of national importance with a social base in the slums among workers and peasants are hardly conceivable outside an alliance with other classes; Gramsci also pointed out the necessity of a combination of organic and traditional intellectuals. Such alliances have been characteristic of the extensive social movements we have seen in the last thirty years: the major forms have been: a party élite allied with peasants (China, Vietnam, Cambodia); students or other bourgeois intellectuals (i.e. traditional intellectuals) in alliance with other population groups (Thailand 1973, Cuba, Nicaragua); and in one case a party élite and the workers (Allende's Chile).

The importance of the gender dimension in the slum areas (and possibly in wider urban areas); the difficulties connected with reproduction, survival and bringing up children; and the potential or actual influence and social power of women in slum areas make women's problems and women's active participation in the formation of counter-cultures and social movements a crucial political issue for both feminists and socialists.

Appendix

Questionnaire administered in each house to an active mother (middle-aged) and adult daughters.

1. **Who lives in the house?**
   name, gender, age
   work, incomes, school, kindergarten
   family and kin-relations in the house
2. **Age at migration, travels back and forth**
3. **Place of origin:**
   work/school of person
   work of parents
   reasons for migration
   company and contacts at migration
4. **In Bangkok:**
   place of living at arrival
   movements in Bangkok
   living with whom at different places
   work for incomes in Bangkok
5. **Present situation:**
   work for incomes
   family and kin-relatives nearby
6. **Relations up-country:**
   contacts, visits in home-village
   ownership of land up-country
   access to land up-country (parents', relatives')
7. **Husband(s):**
   other/former husband than this one?
   children living elsewhere?
8. **Birth-control:**
   means, unwanted pregnancies, abortions
9. **Present or former trade union membership**
10. **Own and family's plans when evicted**

Notes

Chapter 1

1. Figures for migration are often contradictory. The figures here indicate trends. See Sternstein for a discussion of the problems in the Greater Bangkok Metropolitan Area, 1971.
2. The rice premium, in principle, amounts to the difference between world and home market prices. The quotas are licences for export distributed by government. Thus government can create a buyers' market and, with imperfect competition, set the Thai market price through the premium.
3. Chiengkul gives contradictory information on the degree of monopoly in the tapioca trade: "In tapioca . . . six transnational corporations control 99 per cent of the export share." (p. 62) and later (p. 82) he states that 15 big exporters control 66 per cent of the export volume. Both sources are stated in the Thai language. Probably the most important factor for the growers is, however, the local monopoly.

Chapter 2

1. Lichtfield's plan was made in 1960. Only in the 1970s was the sinking of Bangkok registered, and the possible effects of building canals on the sinking land is difficult to evaluate.

Chapter 3

1. F. W. Riggs (1968), in an analysis of labour market laws, has shown that they function to enable the bureaucracy to extort bribes from employers. Legislation that prohibits almost all forms of leisure activities in the slum (and elsewhere) must inevitably lead to an attrition of civil rights.
2. A collaborative survey by the NHA, the port officials and the police, took place while I was living in the slum.
3. N. Mulder (1978), lays great emphasis on conflict avoidance and friendly/polite social relations which conceal personal feelings as a characteristic feature of Thai's social character.
4. In the novel *Letters from Thailand* (Botan, 1977) the Chinese immigrant protagonist is described in terms of the virtues that Weber (1965) argued were characteristic of capital accumulation: industry, thrift, ambition. The Thai main character was characterized as having a strong social conscience.

Chapter 7

1. The Thai word is used here because it denotes both boyfriend and husband; there is no English equivalent.
2. Thitsa (1980) sees the superstitions and taboos relating to women (eg. menstruation, bodily secretions, clothing etc) as expressions of men's sexual insecurity.
3. This factor is an additional to the causes of prostitution cited by Pongpoichit (1982): poverty in rural areas (North East & East); recent fetishization/commercialization of sex; US bases in the North East; beauty competitions in the North; and, women's social networks (this latter in contrast to Cíab's story).

Chapter 8

1. Peasants indirectly subsumed under capital still have access to land; their surplus, and often part of necessary production, are extracted by trade, moneylenders, etc. This form of agriculture is usually marked by low productivity, with heavy objective constraints on developing productivity.
2. The Women's Study Group (1978) argued that, in the final analysis, Lacan's (1968) interpretation of Freud argues from biological factors, despite his claims to the contrary. Freud's analysis, based on the structure of the nuclear family in Europe in the late 19th early 20th century, can hardly be valid for societies in which both family structure and inter-familial relations differ (see Foreman 1978).
3. Pinchbeck thinks that women's position improved (in mid-20th century) mainly because their work for income diminished and living standards rose.
4. This distinction between the private and public spheres differs from that frequently employed in anthropology: the work-producers (employers) being seen as belonging to the private spheres; but production of objects and values cannot be considered as belonging to the public sphere. The real public sphere in capitalist societies is the political one, related to the state and government (see Habermas 1969).
5. The concept of domestication is sometimes applied to denote a deliberate policy of denying women access to income-earning activities (see Roger's 1980). In many societies domestication has confined women specifically to the home.
6. There is an on-going, long debate on the function of women's work for the family and the extension of housework for capital accumulation (see Hartmann, 1981, pp. 5-9). The possible functions of women's work for the latter has, however, been ignored by capitalist enterprises.
7. The diminishing material importance of the family and household under capitalism may be an important element to explain some family relationships in slums. Where there is extreme poverty the cost of maintaining a family may outweigh the advantages which, in any case, are minimal in families under extreme economic pressure. This probably accounts for the near to disappearance of men from slum families in the big cities of the USA and Latin America. In Bangkok, however, economic conditions were not too bad, and families were surprisingly stable.

De Beauvoir (1970) and Foreman (1978) argue that the capitalist mode of production with the alienating aspect of the workplace, creates or reinforces the need for men to have an environment that fulfils their need for control and for recognition of their humanity.

Chapter 9

1. In Potter's house the daughters washed their brothers' clothes. Young girls in the slum refused to do this.
2. Ellen Johnson's (1980) research in a middle-class area pointed out the striking absence of the use of force on children.
3. Chodorow (1974) points out the connection between the isolation of the mother and dependence of the daughter and the possibility and existence of a "healthy" interdependence between them among peoples where the dyad is not isolated and each has the opportunity to form relationships in other contexts.

Voices from the City

Chapter 11

1. In two cases the extended family incomes were administered by the nuclear family.
2. Men indulged in several of these activities and also drank a good deal — but alcohol was cheap. Men with minor wives did not spend money on them.
3. Sons-in-law do not inherit directly from parents-in-law, but will have a strong say in the management of wives inheritance; one son-in-law will probably try to buy out some of his wife's siblings' inheritance.

Chapter 13

1. This is perhaps easier to understand when it is recalled that for Buddhists *wisdom* is all-important and there are many paths to wisdom. For Christians on the other hand, *faith* is all-important, and it therefore important to define what should be believed *in* and distinguish good from evil. (For an excellent illustration of this in fictional form, see Eco 1984).
2. People in the slum think that they can acquire spiritual merit by giving gifts and food to the monks. This is considered to be beneficial to them in this life or the next, and is in accordance with Thai popular beliefs (Mulder 1978).
3. Strictly speaking the distribution of amulets and prophesying that took place in the temple were also examples of the brutish wisdom Gautama Buddha warned against. Thai pop music, created mostly by young men, but also a few young girls in costumes that were anything but conventional, is also considered by the middle class to be an obvious affront to their concepts of good behaviour and in particular to the piety that a trip like this is supposed to encourage.
4. Not all houses are built like this. For example the houses used for gambling are strictly separated from the common walkway, and so are a few other houses. But openness towards neighbours is typical.
5. Nevertheless the Thais like cleanliness, bathing and changing clothes often, despite the great effort involved in fetching water. The floors of the houses (which also do duty as tables and chairs) are always scrubbed clean. But cleanliness is seen as a pleasant convenience, not as a moral value.
6. Max Weber (1965) thought that the puritan protestant ethic explained why capital accumulation was established or succeeded better in some areas and population groups than in others, and saw it as the ethos of the capitalists.
7. The Thais are a very status-conscious people and there have traditionally been subtle social gradations (see Elliot on the *sakhdina* system and Rabibhadana 1968). But these status differences do *not* build on a moral sanctioning of work, thrift and orderliness.
8. In this context loose social structure is understood, not as a lack of organizational principles in village society and the family, but as a flexible, non-rigid system.
9. See also Hobsbawm (1968, Figs 50, 51).
10. *Kharma* means fate, in the sense of a deserved fate, where the present situation is the outcome of the person's conduct in this or a former life. The slum-dwellers interpreted their situation rather as the result of luck.

Notes

11. This culture could also easily pose a problem for the creation of a counter-culture in the slum. It is hardly a coincidence that most critical and social movements in Thailand have stressed the need for a certain amount of discipline.

12. One surprising feature is that the dowry system is spreading, and the amounts are increasing among the educated middle classes in the cities: in Sri Lanka (personal communication); Burma (Spiro 1977; Mi Mi Khaing 1984); Bangladesh (personal communication 1985); India (Sharma 1980; Srinivas 1984; Kishwar and Vanita (ed.) 1984; Prahaso Rao and Nandini Rao 1984).

The (Asian) dowry is supposed to be received by the bride or the young couple, but in practice it goes to the groom's family (Sharma 1980; Tambiah, in Goody 1973.) The bride-price may be given to the bride's family (in Thailand) or to the young couple (Burma, Spiro 1977).

13. The traditional intellectuals of the Thai bourgeoisie — the monks — take no part in this counter-culture in the slum.

Bibliography

Angel, S. (1982), 'Slum Reconstruction', Seminar paper, Asian Institute of Technology, Bangkok.
AMPO (Japan-Asia Quarterly Review) (1977), *Free Trade Zones and Industrialization of Asia*, Special issue, Tokyo.
Baross, P. (1982), 'The Articulation of Land-supply for Popular Settlements in Third World Cities', Seminar paper, Asian Institute of Technology, Bangkok.
Beauvoir, S. de (1970), *The Second Sex*, New York.
Becker Schmidt, R. *et al.* (1981), 'Familienarbeit im proletarischen Lebenszusammenhang: Was es heisst, Hausfrau zu sein', in *Gesellschaft, Beiträge zur Marxschen Theorie*, no. 14, Frankfurt.
Boonyabanghaa, S. (1982), 'Causes and Effects of Slum Eviction in Bangkok', Seminar paper, AIT, Bangkok.
Boserup, E. (1970), *Women's Role in Economic Development*, London.
Botan (1977), *Letters from Thailand*, Bangkok.
Bowring, Sir J. (1977), *The Kingdom and People of Siam*, vols. I, II, London.
Braverman, H.C. (1974), *Labour and Monopoly Capital*, New York.
Bruun, V. (1982), 'Workers and Labour unions in Thailand', in AMPO, vol. 14, no. 2, Tokyo.
Castells, M. *et al.* (1982), *Storbyens krise*, Kbh.
Chaloentiarana, Thak (1979), *The Politics of Despotic Paternalism*, Bangkok.
Chamratrithirong, A. *et al.* (1979), *Recent Migrants in Bangkok Metropolis*, Bangkok.
Chiengkul, W. (1982), *The Effects of Capitalist Penetration in the Transformation of the Agrarian Structure in the Central Region in Thailand*, The Hague.
Chodorow, N. (1974), 'Family Structure and Feminine Personality', in Rosaldo *et al.*
Davies M. (ed.) (1983), *Third World, Second Sex*, London.
Department of Labour (1978), *Year Book of Labour Statistics*, Bangkok.
DeVoy, R.S. *et al.* (1982), 'Land Banking for Low-Income Housing in Thailand', Seminar paper, Asian Institute of Technology, Bangkok.
Donner, W. (1978), *Five Faces of Thailand*, Hamburg.
Dube, L. (1980), *Studies on Women in Southeast Asia*, UNESCO, mimeo, Bangkok.
Durand-Lasserve, A. (1980), *Speculation in Urban Land*, mimeo, Bangkok.
Durand-Lasserve, A. (1982), 'The Urban Land Issue and the Balance of Power between Public and Private Sectors', Seminar paper, Asian Institute of Technology, Bangkok.

Elliot, D. (1978), *Thailand*, London.
Elson, D. *et al.* (1980), *The Latest Phase of the Internationalization of Capital and its Implications for Women*, mimeo, Sussex.
Elson, D. *et al.* (1981a), 'The Subordination of Women and the Internationalization of Factory Production', in Young *et al.*
Elson, D. (1981b), 'Some Social and Cultural Implications of FIZ Industrialization for Women Workers', Seminar paper, mimeo, Sussex.
Etienne, M. and Leacock, E. (1980), *Women and Colonization*, New York.
Eisenstein, Z.R. (ed.) (1979), *Capitalist Patriarchy and the Case for Socialist Feminism*, New York.
Far Eastern Economic Review, Dec. 1978, Dec. 1983.
Foreman, Ann (1978), *Femininity as Alienation*, London.
Freud, S. (1943), *A General Introduction to Psychoanalysis*, New York.
Geertz, H. (1961), *The Javanese Family: A Study of Kinship and Socialization*, New York.
Goody, J.R. and Tambiah S.J. (1973), *Bridewealth and Dowry*, Cambridge.
Goody, J.R. (1976), *Production and Reproduction*, Cambridge.
Gordon, D.M. (1982), 'Den Kapitalistiske udvikling og de amerikanske byers historie', in Castells *et al.*
Government of Thailand, *The Fourth National Economic and Social Development Plan (1977-1981)*, Bangkok.
Green, S.S. (1980), *Silicon Valley's Women Workers*, Hawaii.
Greer, G. (1984), *Sex and Destiny*, London.
Gupta G.R. (1974), *Marriage, Religion and Society*, New Delhi.
Haas M.R. (1978), in *Far Eastern Economic Review*, Dec. 1978.
Habermas J. (1969), *Strukturwandel der Öffentlichkeit*, Berlin.
Hancock M.A. (1981), *Electronics, the International Industry*, Honolulu.
Harris O. (1981), 'Households as Natural Units', in Young *el al.*
Hartmann B. *et al.* (1982), *A Quiet Violence*, London.
Hartman H. (1976), 'Capitalism, Patriarchy and Job Segregation by Sex', in *Signs*, vol. 1, no. 3.
Hartman H. *et al.* (1981), *The Unhappy Marriage of Marxism and Feminism*, Great Britain.
Hawes G.A. in *Far Eastern Economic Review*, Dec. 1983.
Heizer N. (1981), 'Towards a Framework of Analysis', in Young *et al.*
Ho Kwan Ping in *Far Eastern Economic Review*, Dec. 1978.
Ingram J.C. (1971), *Economic Change in Thailand 1850-1970*, New York.
Investor, vol. 13, no. 11, Bangkok.
Javillon G.V. (1979), 'The Filipino Family', in Sing Das *et al.*
Johnson E. (1980) *Not too High and not too Low*, mimeo, Bangkok.
Khoman, T. (1975), *The Magnitude of the Squatter Population of Bangkok 1974*, Bangkok.
Kumar Agrawal, P. (1975), *Mini-Squatters*, AIT, Bangkok.
Kuo E.C.Y. *et al.* (1979), *The Contemporary Family in Singapore*, Singapore.
Lacan, J. (1968), 'The Function of Language in Psychoanalyses', in Wilden.
Levi-Strauss, C. (1969), *The Elementary Structures of Kinship*, London.

Lichtfield et al. *Greater Bangkok Plan 2533*, Bangkok.
Lim Y.C. (1978), *Women Workers in Multinational Corporations in Developing Countries*, mimeo, Michigan.
Mabry, B.D. (1979), *The Development of Labour Institutions in Thailand*, New York.
Mackintosh, M. (1981), 'Gender and Economics' in Young *et al.*
Maher, V. (1981), 'Work, Consumption and Authority within the Household: A Moroccan Case', in Young *et al.*
Marx, K. (1965), *Capital*, vols. I, II, III, Moscow.
Mi Mi Khaing (1984), *The World of Burmese Women*, London.
Mies M. (1982), *The Lace Makers of Narsapur*, London.
Molander, C. (1978), *Kvinna i Vietnam*, Uppsala.
Morell, S. and D. (1972), *Six Slums in Bangkok*, Bangkok.
Moser, C. and Young, K. (1981), 'Women of the Working Poor' in Young *et al.*
Mulder, N. (1978), *Everyday Life in Thailand*, Bangkok.
Myrdal, G. (1968), *Asian Drama*, New York.
National Housing Authority (1980), *Present Standards and Prices on the Housing Market in Bangkok*, Bangkok.
Pakkesem, Phisit *et al.* (1978), *Impact of Green Revolution and Urban Industrial Growth*, Bangkok.
Pallegoix, Mgr. (1854) *Description du Royaume Thai ou Siam*, Paris.
Phipatseritham, Khirkhiat (1979), *Trends in Land Tenure and Security in Thailand*, Bangkok.
Piker, S. (1975), 'The Post-Peasant Village in Central Plain Thai Society', in Skinner *et al.*
Pinchbeck, J. (1981), *Women Workers*, London.
Piven, F.F. and Cloward, R.C. (1979), *Poor Peoples Movements*, New York.
Pongpichit, P. (1982), *From Peasant Girls to Bangkok Masseuses*, Geneva.
Potter, J.M. (1977), *Thai Peasant Social Structure*, New York.
Potter, S.H. (1977), *Family Life in Northern Thai Village*, New York.
Rabibhadana, A. (1969), *The Organization of Thai Society in the Early Bangkok-period 1787–1873*, Data paper no. 74, Cornell University, New York.
Rabibhadana, A. (1980), *The Rise and Fall of a Bangkok Slum*, Bangkok.
Rabibhadana, A. *et al.* (1981/2), *Preliminary Report of the Evaluation of Slum-upgrading Activities of the NHA*, Bangkok.
Raviwongse, V. (1978), *The Role of Young Women in the Development Process*, Bangkok.
Reich, M. *et al.* (1973), *Labour Market Segmentation*, New York.
Reiter, R.R. *et al.* (1975), *Towards an Anthropology of Women*, New York.
Riggs, F.W. (1966), *Thailand, the Modernization of a Bureaucratic Polity*, Honolulu.
Roberts, B. (1978), *Cities of Peasants*, London.
Rogers, B. (1980), *The Domestication of Women*, London.
Romm, J. (1970), *Urbanization in Thailand*, Bangkok.
Rosaldo, M.Z. *et al.* (1974), *Woman, Culture and Society*, California.
Roy S. (1979), *Status of Muslim Women in North India*, New Delhi.
Rozenthal, A.A. (1970), *Finance and Development in Thailand*, New York.
Rubin, G. (1975), 'The Traffic in Women' in Reiter *et al.*

Bibliography

Sarkar, N.K. (1974), *Industrial Structure of Greater Bangkok*, Bangkok.
Seidenfaden, E. (1967), *The Thai Peoples*, Book I, Bangkok.
Sevilla, R.C. (1976), *Share Economics*, AIT, Bangkok.
Shieh-Yu, W. (1979), *Estimating the Low Income Housing Stock in Bangkok*, AIT, Bangkok.
Sinh Das M. *et al.* (1979), *The Family in Asia*, London.
Sinha, G.P. (n.d.), *Women Construction Workers*, New Delhi.
Skinner, G.W. (1958), *Leadership and Power in the Chinese Community in Thailand*, New York.
Skinner, G.W. (ed.) (1975), *Change and Persistence in Thai Society*, Great Britain.
Skrobanek, W. (1976), *Buddhistische Politik im Thailand*, Wiesbaden.
Slum Upgrading office, NHA, (1980), *Slum Improvement Program*, Bangkok.
Spiro, M.E. (1977), *Kinship and Marriage in Burma*.
Stack, C.B. (1974), 'Sex Roles and Survival Strategies in an Urban Black Community' in Rosaldo.
Sternstein, L. (1971), *Greater Bangkok Metropolitan Area*, Bangkok.
Stivens, M. (1981), 'Women, Kinship and Capitalist Development' in Young *et al.*
Tambiah, S.J. (1976), *World Conqueror and World Renouncer*, Cambridge.
Tanner, N. (1974), 'Matri-focality in Indonesia and Africa and among Black Americans' in Rosaldo.
Thitsa, K. (1980), *Providence and Prostitution*, London.
Thorbek, S. (1973), *Thailand 1850–1950*, Copenhagen.
Thorbek, S. (1977), 'Fra Despoti til Diktatur' in *Marxistisk Antropologi*, Copenhagen.
Thorbek, S. (1982), 'Ny international arbejdsdeling ændrer u-landskvinders rolle' in *Information*, 22 September 1982, Copenhagen.
Thompson, V. (1957), *Thailand, The New Siam*, New York.
Tilly, L.A. (1978), *Women's Work and Family*, New York.
Turton, A. (1972), 'Matrilineal Descent Groups and Spirit Cults of the Thai Yuan in Northern Thailand' in *Journal of Siam Society*, Bangkok.
UNIDOS Working Papers (1980) *Women in the Redeployment of Manufacturing Industry to Developing Countries*, no. 18.
UNIDOS Working Papers (1980) *Export processing Zones in Developing Countries*, no. 19.
US Department of Commerce, Census Bureau (1980), *Illustrative Statistics on Women in selected Developing Countries*, US.
Van der Heide, J.H. (1906), 'The Economical Development of Siam', in *Journal of Siam Society*, Bangkok.
Vatuk, S.J. (1971), 'Trends in North Indian Urban Kinship, the "Matrilateral Asymmetry" Hypothesis', in *South-Western Journal of Anthropology*, vol. 27.
Weber, M. (1965), *The Protestant Ethic and the Spirit of Capitalism*, London.
Whitehead, A. (1981), '"I'm hungry Mum"', in Young *et al.*
Vichit Vadekan, V. *et al.* (1968), *Urbanization in the Bangkok Central Region*, Bangkok.
Wilden, A. (1968), *The Language of Self*, London.
Women's Study group (1978), *Women take Issue*, London.
Wong A.K. *et al.* (1979), 'The Urban Kinship Network in Singapore' in Kuo *et al.*

World Bank Report (1980), *Thailand*, Report no. 3044-TN.
Yanagisko, S.J. (1977), 'Women-Centered Kin Networks in Urban Bilateral Kinship' in *American Ethnologist*, vol. 4, no. 2.
Young, K. *et al.* (1981a), *Of Marriage and the Market*, London.
Young, K. *et al.* (1981b), *Women and the Informal Sector*, Sussex.
Young Yoon, S. (1979), *The Half-way House*, mimeo, Bangkok.